SNMP MIB Handbook

SNMP MIB Handbook

Essential Guide to
MIB Development, Use, and Diagnosis

Larry Walsh
SNMP Consultant and Trainer

 Wyndham Press

SNMP MIB Handbook
By Larry Walsh

ISBN: 978-0-9814922-0-9

Many examples of object syntax taken from standard MIBs are contained in this book. In several examples, the DESCRIPTION fields were abbreviated to fit the page. These DESCRIPTION fields can be accessed in their entirety by the reader in the referenced RFCs, which can be found at www.ietf.org.

Published by:
  Wyndham Press
  PO Box 898
  Stanwood, WA 98292
  www.wyndhampress.com
  info@wyndhampress.com

Printed in the United States of America.
10 9 8 7 6 5 4 3 2

Acknowledgments

Thank you GJ for your help designing the cover—your ideas and perseverance to make it *just right* have been invaluable. And thank you for your encouragement.

I met Mohit Tendolkar ten years ago. I was fairly new to SNMP, and he was already a seasoned SNMP practitioner—over time he has developed agents, MIBs, managers, agent toolkits, been involved in SMPTE MIB standardization efforts, and much more. His quality MIBs and superior knowledge of SNMP have been very helpful to me. Thanks to Mohit for his thorough review of this entire manuscript, and his many improvements.

John Fehl was an experienced SNMP network engineer before we met in one of my training presentations. His interaction during the class was valuable, and our time after class discussing how he used SNMP enlightening. Thanks to John for his careful review and for his many helpful suggestions.

There are many individuals that have contributed to this book directly or indirectly, and to whom I am grateful. Thanks to clients who asked great questions, took the time to explain how they use SNMP, gave me the opportunity to work with them, and to the several individuals who encouraged me to write this book.

Screen captures showing uses of Castlerock's SNMPc Manager software appear in a number of chapters. Thanks for their permission, and for their customer service support on many occasions: www.castlerock.com

Screen captures of Frank Fock's Agent++ validation compiler appear with his permission: www.agentpp.com. Thanks to Frank for this free service—and for the SNMP tools he has developed and offers on his web site.

The Simple Web validation compiler http://wwwsnmp.cs.utwente.nl/ietf/mibs/validate address is correct as shown) is discussed , along with a screen capture. Thank you to Dr. Aiko Pras for permission to use this, for providing this useful tool, and for the many tutorials offered on www.simpleweb.org/tutorials.

Screen captures of the libsmi tools web site (a comprehensive tool set which includes a validating compiler) also appear. Thanks to Frank Strauß and Dr. Jürgen Schönwälder for providing and maintaining this excellent tool set, and for their permission to use information in this book: www.ibr.cs.tu-bs.de/projects/libsm

Thank you to Gerard for permission to use screen captures of the MIB Depot web site, a popular and valuable tool for researching needed MIBs: www.mibdepot.com

Table of Contents

Table of Contents

Appendixes

Part 1

Introduction to SNMP and MIBs

Simple Network Management Protocol

SNMP—Simple Network Management Protocol is a tool for management of devices connected to a computer network that includes managers (software) communicating with agents (software) installed on the managed devices. Managers are tasked with collecting information such as *status*, and in some cases exercising *control* over devices. Agents are responsible for responding to manager requests, as well as sending unsolicited *traps* to mangers that report on important device events. *SNMP* refers to the totality of this scheme as well as to the protocol itself.

Management Information Base

A MIB—Management Information Base is a file containing strict syntax (called the Structure of Management Information—SMI), which is a hierarchical (tree-structured) virtual data base description of objects to be managed. It serves as a contract of information that enable agents and managers to communicate. MIBs are defined as the first step in providing SNMP support—agents are then coded based on MIB content. Managers load (compile) MIBs into their data base, and this shared knowledge is the basis of useful manager-agent communication.

Many SNMP topics are worth writing about, but MIBs are at the core of SNMP functionality. MIBs define data objects to be managed and trap objects (events) to be sent. The values of MIB objects are the topics of communication between SNMP managers and SNMP agents.

Chapter 1 *Why a Book on MIBs* describes goals, intended audiences, an overview of organization and content, and discusses notation.

Chapter 2 *SNMP Tutorial* is included to ensure that terminology used in the book is well understood.

Chapter 3 *Getting the Most Out of SNMP* is an overview of key ingredients to successful SNMP product development and network management integration.

Why a Book on MIBs?

When I first started working with SNMP in 1997, I was faced with quickly coming up to speed in areas of MIB design and agent software development. I was fortunate to have a client that purchased a very good agent development kit, and the software effort came together nicely.

But figuring out how to design really good MIBs was a bit of a puzzle. The differences between the two syntax standards, SMIv1 MIB syntax and SMIv2 MIB syntax, were (to me) subtle, a little vague, and confusing. Deciding what to monitor and how to organize data was another problem. I thought I understood traps pretty well, but it wasn't until I later worked closely with SNMP management software that key issues came to light.

So I did what engineers facing tight schedules sometimes do—I adapted syntax, organization, and style from existing MIBs. Most of my early MIBs used SMIv1 syntax (rather than the improved SMIv2 syntax) because there were so many more SMIv1 examples.

My consulting activities expanded to include all aspects of SNMP: MIB and agent development, manager configuration, and training. Training led to the formalization of six training modules—this book contains information from four of those:

- *SNMP Foundations*
- *Managing SNMP Networks*—and using MIBs to best advantage
- *Understanding MIBs*—MIB syntax, designing MIBs, diagnosing MIB problems
- *SNMP Agent Development*

This is what this book is about, and contains *practical advice* as well as *technical information*.

There are two groups designing MIBs. The first group designs *standard MIBs* as defined in IETF (*Internet Engineering Task Force)* RFC (*Request for Comments)* documents. Prior to publication, these MIBs undergo a rigorous review process, and as a consequence are usually quite good.

The second group designs *enterprise MIBs*. An *enterprise* is any organization that is not a standards group. Most of these are hardware or software manufacturers that design MIBs and agents to support their products. Many enterprises craft good MIBs that will pass validating compiler testing with few, if any, errors; Cisco is an example of such a vendor.

However, some enterprise MIBs have problems. MIBs that have not been well reviewed and properly validated may not successfully compile into all managers. Network engineers will on occasion encounter such issues, and how to diagnose MIBs is an important skill set addressed in this book.

Target Audiences

Target audiences include two overall groups—*SNMP developers* and *network engineers*.

SNMP developers include:
- MIB authors
- Agent software developers
- Personnel involved with SNMP standardization efforts
- Those establishing SNMP policies at corporate levels—how products will implement SNMP, or how SNMP will be used to manage networks within the corporation
- Developers of management software suites
- Engineers writing plug-ins for manager tools, or developing management applets for support of specific SNMP-capable products
- Developers of utility products such as agent SDKs, MIB compilers, MIB browsers

The term *network engineers* is used to describe end-user consumers for SNMP. This includes folks from a wide range of professional disciplines—for example:
- Personnel from IT departments whose job it is to keep servers, routers, switches, and workstations running and secure
- Microwave engineers maintaining cellular telephone networks
- Utility company engineers monitoring electrical power distribution
- Television broadcast engineers
- Military personnel managing surveillance platforms
- And many other job titles, including that of *network engineer*

Book Goals

The SNMP MIB Handbook is intended as an *instructional manual* and as a *reference handbook*. It is designed to be read from cover to cover, as well as to resolve specific issues.

Learning any new discipline takes time, even for simple technologies. SNMP is built from simple concepts (although there are a few SNMP topics that are somewhat complex). Book discussions move from the simple and build to discuss more complex topics.

Book content is based on the author's work experience, and extensive interaction with SNMP practitioner clients. When presenting training, we encounter a challenging variety of questions from participants. As a result, training materials are continually edited to explain topics more thoroughly or in different ways. These refinements are reflected in this book.

Book content describes real-world situations, discusses practical matters, presents standards, but is *not* just a paraphrasing of SNMP standards documents (RFCs).

Book Organization

The book is organized into six major *parts*, with each part containing several related *chapters*.

Part 1 is an overview of the book, including a comprehensive *SNMP Tutorial*, and a chapter on *Getting the Most Out of SNMP*.

Part 2 discusses *Preliminary Topics*. MIBs are constructed from objects, and all objects have names and numeric identifiers, which are discussed in Chapter 4. Chapter 5 describes valuable SNMP-centric software tools, and provides useful hints for managing MIBs.

The seven chapters in Part 3 discuss the SMIv1 and SMIv2 versions of *MIB Syntax*. This includes *Structure, Header Information, Nodes, Data Base Types, Derived Types, Trap Objects,* and *Conformance Objects*.

Part 4 includes four chapters on *Complex MIBs*. Topics are *Indexed Tables, Index Data Types, Row-Create Tables,* and *Elements of Advanced Complexity*.

Part 5, *Advanced Trap Topics*, has four chapters—*Manager Trap Filter Configuration, Trap Models, Trap Syntax Issues,* and *Agent Semantics*.

Part 6 discusses *MIB Organization* in four chapters—*Standard MIBs, Types of Enterprise MIBs, Data Organization and Uses,* and *MIB Design Process* for developers.

Finally, appendixes provide additional information—a consolidated reference list, a glossary of terms, discussion of ASN.1 (Abstract Syntax Notation) as used by SNMP, a MIB diagnosis checklist, two compete MIB examples, and an explanation for the multiple uses of the term *enterprise*.

Examples

Reading MIBs is as important as *reading about MIBs*, and so a variety of example MIB syntax has been included throughout the book.

Many of these examples are taken from *standard MIBs*. In addition to reinforcing syntax concepts, the reader will become aware of the rich variety of standard MIBs available for use in managing networks—this is important to network engineers, as well as to developers who may recognize existing MIBs as useful for managing their products. Developers will also benefit from review of existing MIBs by incorporating clever design concepts into their own product MIBs.

Enterprise MIB examples for a mythical organization, *Vronx,* are adapted from actual *enterprise MIBs* (non-standard MIBs developed by product vendors). *Adapted* means that the example is an amalgam from several enterprises, none of which are named. This allows the presentation of more concise examples.

Chateau Systems enterprise MIB examples are taken from the author's training seminar series, and the complete MIB files are included in the appendixes, as well as on-line.

Many illustrations and tables appear as needed to clarify concepts.

Screen captures of SNMP tool usage appear. These diagrams help introduce readers to SNMP reality better than just abstract diagrams.

Design discussions and examples are provided, and all of these reflect what has been done and seen in existing MIBs. Readers experienced in SNMP may take exception with some of these—but please take them for what they are, examples that may or may not apply in specific design circumstances, but which might be a starting point for more elegant efforts.

MIB syntax examples are shown in a unique font, sometimes embedded as elements of syntax in the text, but more often in boxed syntax examples.

```
cdStaticConfig OBJECT-IDENTITY
    STATUS current
    DESCRIPTION
        "CD Static Configuration Node"
    ::= { chateauCDProdConfig 1 }
```

Embedded Notation

Many chapters have embedded notes of various kinds to clarify information.

MIB Diagnosis Hints
 • Intended for network engineers encountering problems loading MIBs into managers, and as descriptions of problems developers should avoid

SNMP Jargon
 • Terminology definitions
 • The *glossary* in Appendix B provides a summary

SNMP Tidbits
 • Additional information that will be useful to the reader, but which is somewhat orthogonal to the main topic
 • Boxed syntax examples are often followed by a brief tutorial that further discusses the MIB the example was taken from

MIB Naming Rules
 • An *overlay topic*. All MIB objects have textual names, and rules regarding those names

Communication From a Network Engineer
 • A few stories from the field regarding SNMP encounters

Exercises

Exercises are provided at the end of most chapters. Some exercises are quiz questions, and others involve hands-on activities. All are intended to reinforce concepts—mental involvement on the part of the reader is an important part of learning.

Answers to quiz questions appear in Appendix F.

Chapter 2

SNMP Tutorial

The *SNMP MIB Handbook* is suitable for current practitioners, as well as those new to the technology. This chapter establishes a common base of concepts and terminology before moving on to discuss SNMP and MIBs in more detail.

SNMP (Simple Network Management Protocol) describes the language that is spoken over a network between SNMP software entities (managers and agents), along with some rules—the concepts of SNMP are each fairly simple:

- Which software entities initiate which messages (managers or agents)
- The topics of their conversations (data object values and traps defined in MIBs)
- The vocabulary of the messages (message types and structure)
- And how to keep communications secure (administrative structure—configuration and message content issues)

SNMP Management

SNMP facilitates management of networked devices from central locations. Designed originally for network appliances such as routers and switches, its application has grown to encompass the management of diverse types of hardware and software.

SNMP is used to manage television broadcast studios, automated fare collection systems, airborne military platforms, space agency mission control networks, energy distribution systems, telephone company facilities, emergency radio networks, university and business networks, and much more.

In the infancy of computer networks, there was no common way to configure, diagnose, or monitor network elements. Each equipment vendor employed a proprietary scheme, and the job of network engineers was a nightmare. What was needed was a simple management tool that could generically monitor network elements—this was the goal of SNMP designers, and they were eminently successful. Simple concepts (messages, data definitions, agents, managers) are pieced together to create sophisticated network management solutions.

However, attempting to deploy SNMP without inherent understanding will result in frustration and disappointment. A major goal of this book to remove any mystique surrounding SNMP, and to make users comfortable as well as competent with the technology.

Before moving on to discussing details of standards, a few examples of the types of data managed by SNMP should be useful to the novice.

Examples of Managed Data

General *examples*

> Enumerated status values (online(1), offline(2))
> Data trended over time (microwave radio received signal levels)
> Trend reports over longer periods (monthly platform up-time statistics)
> Rates (CPU utilization)
> Fault data (parity error counters)
> Capacity gauges (printer marker level)
> Fault status (upstream signal loss detected)
> Location (GPS coordinates)
> Read-write data for control and configuration (set interface to off-line)

Example data object enumerated values from the standard Printer MIB

> prtCoverStatus {
>   other(1),
>   coverOpen(2),
>   coverClosed(4),
>   interlockOpen(5) }

Example data objects from the Host Resources MIB (data objects in an indexed table describing host storage devices)

> hrStorageType
> hrStorageDescr
> hrStorageAllocationUnits
> hrStorageSize
> hrStorageUsed

SNMP Manager-Agent Architecture

SNMP architecture is composed of three major elements:

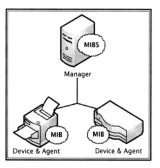

- *Managers* (software) are responsible for communicating with (and managing) networked devices that implement SNMP agents.

- *Agents* (also software) typically reside in devices such as servers, workstations, switches, routers, microwave radios, and printers, and provide information to managers. Agents respond to manager requests for data object values and also send unsolicited traps (or notifications) to managers.

  Agents can also reside outside of the managed devices, and communicate with managers on behalf of those devices.

- *MIB* (Management Information Base) describes data objects and trap objects to be managed by an agent within a device. MIBs are files containing parsable syntax, and shared knowledge of specific MIBs is the basis of meaningful communications between managers and agents.

  MIBs of interest must be *loaded* (or *compiled*) into managers.

  Agents, on the other hand, are coded to know about specific MIBs and do not need run-time copies.

Client-Server Model

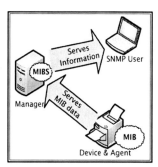

In the SNMP model, managers are viewed as clients, and agents as servers. Agents *serve* data and traps to managers.

Client-server models are relative. Manager software (e.g. Castlerock's SNMPc product) runs on a server platform, and workstations connected to that server are clients receiving management data from SNMPc.

However from the viewpoint of managers and agents, the agents are the servers.

Master Agent–Subagent Model

In a managed device, an agent may be *monolithic* or may conform to the *master agent–subagent* model.

Monolithic means that all agent functionality is contained in a single software executable. This is common in heavily embedded agents, where code space and CPU cycles are critical resources.

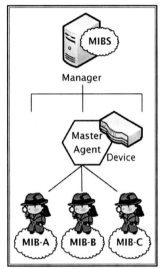

However, a managed device may contain a master agent and many subagents—each a separate executable. The master agent is responsible for communications with the manager platform (decoding messages, verifying security parameters, encoding messages), as well as local management of its subagents.

Subagents and master agents communicate using agent SDK vendor proprietary protocols, or may use the relatively new SNMP standard AgentX protocol. When a subagent executable starts up, it registers the MIB object space it manages with the master agent. When the master agent receives a manager request for the value of a MIB data object, it passes the request to the responsible subagent for processing.

Often a subagent's MIB space is mapped to one specific MIB, but more complicated mappings are common (e.g., one subagent managing multiple MIBs, or one large MIB managed by multiple subagents).

Manager-Agent Mutual Access

Managers and agents must be suitably configured in order to communicate successfully using SNMP.

> **SNMP Jargon.** An SNMP *community* is a group of managers and agents that will share MIB information. A *community string* is a configurable textual value that identifies such a group. This value is included in SN-MPv1 and SNMPv2c messages and is used to validate that the message originated from a member of the group. Defining community string values is part of the configuration process for managers and agents.

Typical manager configuration requirements:
- IP address of a device hosting the SNMP agent of interest
- Message protocol to be used (SNMPv1, SNMPv2c, or SNMPv3)
- For SNMPv1 messages and SNMPv2c messages
    o read-only community string
    o read-write community string
    o *trap* community string (although some managers will accept all traps from agents regardless of the community string value sent with the trap)
- For SNMPv3 messages, there are additional configuration requirements beyond the scope of this tutorial

Typical agent configuration requirements:
- Message protocol to be used (this may not be an option for a given agent)
- For SNMPv1 and SNMPv2c messages
    o read-only access community string
    o read-write access community string
    o *trap* community string
- A list of manager IP addresses to which *traps* (or *notifications*) will be sent
    o The size of this list is implementation dependent.
- Optional (for SNMPv1 and SNMPv2c)—an *Access Control List* containing IP addresses of managers allowed read-only or read-write access to this agent
    o The size of this list is implementation dependent
- For SNMPv3 messaging, there are additional configuration tasks

SNMP Network Management Architectures

SNMP is quite flexible in supporting organizational needs and goals, and is used for centralized management, for distributed management, and in hybrid networks. Each of these is briefly described.

Centralized Management of Distributed Networks

SNMP diagrams often illustrate one manager networked to (and managing) a large number of local, remote, and very remote devices. And indeed, the protocol supports this, and such configurations are quite common.

For example, one cellular telephone company uses a single manager to monitor their nation-wide network of hundreds of microwave radios, many of which are in very remote locations.

Distributed Management of Networks

SNMP also supports the connection of many managers, or manager-type tools with limited capability, to a network of managed devices. This model may be manifested in a number of ways.

There may be multiple hierarchical managers, each geographically distributed and located near the managed networks (perhaps divisional facilities, or multiple campuses). Each of these may report to a single, central manager that consolidates information (or some subset of the total information monitored).

In some networks an agent on a monitored device may be responding to requests from, and sending traps to, multiple managers (where each manager has a unique focus or mission).

Hybrid Management of Networks

A diagram of a simple hybrid network is shown on the next page.

An organization's network may be a hybrid of centralized and distributed management. For example, centralized management is responsible for *baseline monitoring*—ensuring that network connections are intact, that servers are up and not overloaded, etc. IT department managers are very interested in seeing monthly reports of network and device up-time.

> **SNMP Tidbit.** *Baseline monitoring* involves recording parameters of interest while the monitored system goes through its various use cases. These measurements are the expected behavior, or *baseline*. The management tool is configured to monitor these same parameters, and to a) trigger notifications if significant excursions from baseline occur, and b) to generate longer-term trend reports. This allows the organization to set up Quality of Service and SLA (service level agreements), which are used for billing, enhancing facility productivity, and planning network expansions.

With baseline taking care of routers, switches, workstation status, etc., other manager tools monitor the status and performance of an organization's mission specifics. For example:
- Data base software metrics
- Video titles cached for television transmission
- Microwave radio received power levels
- Utility power distribution metrics
- Status of very specialized equipment or software

Responsibility for distributed management tools may also be distributed throughout the organization.

- Engineering may be monitoring the status of prototype hardware and beta software.
- A technician might purchase an inexpensive SNMP-focused tool to acquire metrics for subsystems that person is responsible for.
- Quality Assurance might use SNMP to test printers prior to shipment to customers.
- Emergency power backup may be provided by equipment that is monitored by Facilities using SNMP.

Example Hybrid Network

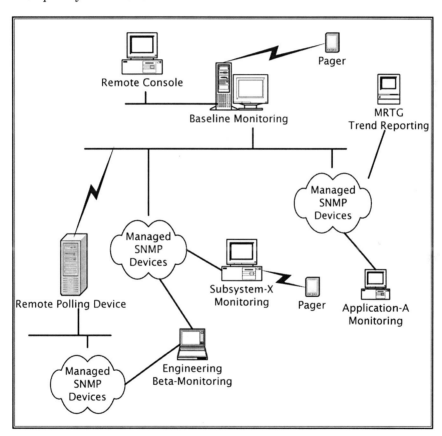

SNMP Standards and Versions

SNMP standards are described in Request for Comments (RFC) documents published by the Internet Engineering Task Force (IETF.)

Standards topics (for SNMP) are loosely categorized into:
- *Message protocols* between managers and agents (which includes security issues)
- *MIB syntax standards.* This book discusses details of MIB syntax (and quite a bit more).
- *Standard MIB definitions.* RFCs frequently contain definitions of standard MIBs which can be *stripped* out of their definitional RFCs, and saved to MIB files for compilation into managers.
  - For example, RFC-3805 *Printer MIB v2* contains the actual standard Printer MIB, an associated MIB, as well as extensive discussions of the MIB objects. The standard Printer MIB is supported by agents developed by many different printer manufacturers.

Request for Comments (RFCs)

RFC (*Request for Comments)* documents deserve a little more discussion. RFCs document IETF standards (SNMP and many other networking topics), and are assigned formal *status* values { *proposed, draft, full standard, experimental, historic, informational* }.

Early in their life, RFCs really are a request for comments from members of standards committees—but once the standard is established, further comments are no longer solicited. All SNMP standards are published as RFCs, but not all RFCs represent current standards.

RFCs undergo revisions—for example *proposed* or *draft* RFCs are replaced with new RFCs with new number assignments as they move to *full standard.* If *full standard* RFCs are revised, they are republished with new number assignments.

SNMP RFCs *may* also contain embedded MIBs. Determining the most current RFCs and extracting MIBs from RFCs are important skills that are discussed in Chapter 5.

A sampling of RFC topics for SNMP:
- RFC-1067—A Simple Network Management Protocol
- RFC-1089—SNMP over Ethernet
- RFC-1187—Bulk Table Retrieval with the SNMP
- RFC-1418—SNMP Over AppleTalk

Message Protocols

Three SNMP message protocols for manager-agent communication are defined. SNMP messages are quite *simple*.

SNMPv1 Messages

SNMPv1 was the first protocol introduced, and it is still widely used. It implements messages:

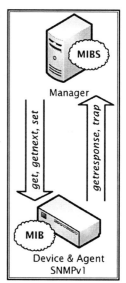

- From manager to agent—*get, getnext, set*

  get messages request values for MIB data objects. A single *get* message can request values for multiple MIB data objects.

  getnext messages are similar—but relate to data object ordering in MIBs (called lexicographical ordering). Managers return values for the *next* ordered MIB object. This facilitates discovering (enumerating) all of the information available from an agent. Successive *getnext* operations are performed until the agent returns an *end-of-MIB* error. This is called MIB-walking.

  set messages allow a manager to direct an agent to modify values of read-write objects. Values for one or more data objects can be *set* in one message.

- From agent to manager—*getresponse, v1trap*

  getresponse messages contain requested data values in response to *get* and *getnext* messages.

  trap messages are unsolicited alerts sent to managers. Synonyms for traps are notifications, and events.

Message security for SNMPv1 is based on a textual *community string* value (e.g. "VronxPrivate") that is transmitted with each message. The community string acts as a password. If the manager includes the correct password in a request to an agent, the agent will send a response. Messages from agents to managers are similarly checked for correct community strings.

Different community strings can be configured separately for read-only and read-write access modes, as well as for *traps*.

Community strings are sent with messages in the clear (not encrypted), and thus the security provided is quite weak.

SNMPv2c Messages

SNMPv2 nearly always refers to *SNMPv2c*. There were a number of efforts to develop a version 2 of the protocol, primarily to enhance security. Version designations include SNMPv2c, SNMPv2sec, SNMPv2u, SNMPv2p, SNMPv2*—you will find references to these in the literature, and elements of these proposals contributed to SNMPv3.

Only SNMPv2c has any significant commercial product support. It contains a number of improvements, but does not improve security. Its IETF status is EXPERIMENTAL, is not an IETF approved standard, but is an important topic.

SNMPv2c provides expanded messaging operations: *getbulk, inform, report,* and a new *v2trap* operation (also called *notification,* and with the same functionality as the SNMPv1 *trap*). It also introduces the ability to transmit values for a new SMIv2 data type, Counter64.

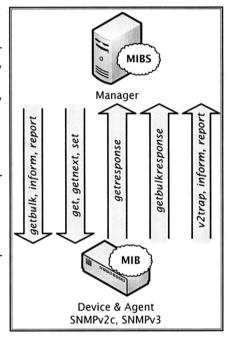

New SNMPv2c messages:

- New messages from manager to agent—*getbulk, inform, report*

  getbulk is an optimization of the *get* and *getnext* messages. *get* and *getnext* can request multiple values, but a particular agent implementation may have insufficient buffer space to return the requested number of values. So the agent returns an error code and no data values. *getbulk* solves this problem—an agent will return what it can, along with information that allows the manager to request the remaining values.

  inform is intended as an improvement to trap messages. *inform* messages contain the same information as traps, and managers return a similar message to acknowledge that it was received.

report messages are defined in SNMPv2c, but were not used until SNMPv3. They contain responses that report communication errors or that facilitate message synchronization between SNMPv3 entities.

• New messages from agent to manager—*getbulkresponse, inform, report, v2trap*

getbulkresponse messages return values for a *getbulk* request, along with encodings that identify objects whose values were not returned.

v2trap messages have the same functionality as *v1trap's,* but are encoded differently.

SNMPv2c messages include expanded error reporting codes in response to *get* and *get-next* requests that the agent could not properly process. A single error code reported by an SNMPv1 agent maps into several SNMPv2c refined error definitions.

> **SNMP Tidbit.** RFC-3584 *Coexistence between Version 1, Version2, and Version 3 of the Internet-standard Network Management Framework* contains a table of *Error Status Mappings* between SNMPv1 and SNMPv2c.

Closely related to SNMPv2c enhanced error codes is the concept of SNMPv2c *exceptions.* If an SNMPv1 agent received a *get* or *getnext* request for multiple objects, any difficulty in returning values for any of the objects resulted in the return of no object values, along with a general error code.

If an SNMPv2c agent receives a *get* or *getnext* request for multiple objects, all possible values will be returned. Any object values that cannot be returned will be flagged with an exception code (such as noSuchObject or noSuchInstance). Exceptions are separate from the SNMPv2c expanded error code definitions, and are encoded differently in the return message.

SNMPv2c utilizes the same community string security as SNMPv1, and so, is not considered very secure.

SNMPv3 Messages

SNMPv3 is the most recent standard, and is a major improvement in the security of the protocol. *SNMPv3* uses the same message types (PDUs) as defined by *SNMPv2c*—however, the overall message structure is quite different than for SNMPv1 and SNMPv2c.

Enhancements include a *User-Based Security Model* (USM) and a *View-Based Access Control Model* (VACM). A full discussion of SNMPv3 is beyond the scope of this book—a brief overview follows.

User Authentication

User authentication verifies the identity of the SNMP entity (manager or agent) sending the request. Managers and agents share knowledge of *valid users*, along with a unique *shared secret key* for each user. When an entity sends an SNMPv3 message, the secret key for a particular user is used to create a hash of the message, and this hashed value is inserted into the message. If the receiving entity can re-create this hash using the *shared secret key*, then the message is *authenticated* as from a valid user.

Traps are also sent on behalf of valid users, and agents can be configured to exercise more detailed control over transmission of *traps* to managers.

Message timeless checks are also part of the User-Based Security Model (USM) and ensure that messages are not delayed or replayed.

Message payload *variable bindings* are the pairing of a data object identifier (or handle) with its value { OID, dataValue }, and can be optionally encrypted based on a second shared user key. Variable binding message syntax for SNMPv3 is identical to SNMPv2c.

View-Based Access Control Model

Agents can be configured to control *who* can access *which* MIB objects under agent management. For example, User = *Operations Supervisor* can access critical read-write control data, while User = *Plant Maintenance* can access only specific read-only status data.

Summary of Message Capabilities

SNMP protocol differences encompass message definitions themselves and associated security of messages.

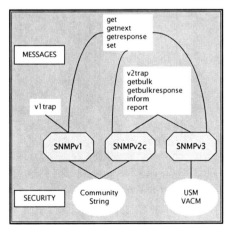

All versions include operations for *get, getnext, getresponse,* and *set.*

SNMPv1 *v1trap* and SNMPv2c *v2trap* messages reflect the different syntax of SMIv1 TRAP-TYPE objects and SMIv2 NOTIFICATION-TYPE objects. The format of *v2trap* messages is also more consistent with other SNMPv1 and SNMPv2c messages (*v1traps* are not). However their functionality is the same. In fact, SMIv2 NOTIFICATION-TYPE traps can be transported by *v1traps* and SMIv1 TRAP-TYPE traps can be transported by *v2traps.*

Message operations defined by the SNMPv2c and SNMPv3 standards are identical, and *v2trap*, *getbulk*, and *getbulkresponse* are always implemented. Some (but not all) SNMPv2c implementations include the *inform* operation to provide *trapResponse* capability. Only SNMPv3 implements the *report* message, to communicate protocol errors and to synchronize agent-manager communications.

SNMPv1 and SNMPv2c share community string security, with separate community strings typically configurable for read-only, read-write, and *trap* operations.

SNMPv3 implements a very secure protocol, using the *User-Based Security Model* (USM) and the *View-Based Access Control Model* (VACM).

Message Transport

SNMP was designed as a connection-less protocol, in keeping with its intent to be *simple*. The most common transport environment is IP, and uses dedicated UDP ports 161 and 162. Managers send *get*, *set*, and other requests to agent port 161, and agents send *traps* to manager port 162.

Both of these ports are normally configurable, but must be consistent for agents and managers.

> **SNMP Tidbit**. SNMP over TCP has been proposed by RFC-3430 *Simple Network Management Protocol Over Transmission Control Protocol Transport Mapping*. Status is EXPERIMENTAL. There are a few such implementations in manager and agent products, but this feature is not widely available.

Specifications also exist for SNMP over:
*   AppleTalk networks
*   Novell networks (SNMP over IPX)
*   OSI networks using the CMIP network management protocol use SNMP on the OSI stack

MIB Syntax Standards

MIBs are files written in a syntax (defining structure, content, and naming rules) describing product information to be managed. Objects of interest to managers are *data* and *traps*. MIBs have been compared to data base schema, and at first this can be a good way to think of them. If this comparison is useful to you, then hang onto it.

> **SNMP Tidbit**. A schema defines data and data base organization. MIBs define data and trap objects, but say nothing about how data is organized

within the agent. In fact the agent may not maintain a formal set of data values at all—if a manager issues a *get* request for the value of a data object, the agent may find the value in a hardware register, acquire it from a software API, or need to perform a calculation to produce it.

MIBs are foundational to SNMP. The data and traps defined in MIB files are the topic of communications between SNMP management software and SNMP agent software residing in managed devices.

The syntax or language that MIBs are written in is formally called the SMI (Structure of Management Information), and has two formal revisions. SMIv1 was the original version, and SMIv2 is an enhanced version as well as the currently recommended version.

> **SNMP Jargon.** *SMI* has some closely related usage. Some MIBs are named with some variant of *SMI*, which usually refers to a MIB that defines a high-level organization under which product MIBs are organized. An example of this is the CISCO-SMI.my MIB.

> An *SMICng* validation compiler also exists, which is discussed along with other MIB compilers in Chapter 5.

> **SNMP Jargon.** A *MIB module* is a named, self-contained collection of syntax for defining and describing SNMP *objects*. It is delineated by BEGIN and END statements, and can import definitions from external MIB modules.

SMIv1 MIB Syntax

SMIv1 is the earliest version and was introduced at the same time as SNMPv1. Sometimes SMIv1 MIB syntax is referred to as SNMPv1 MIB syntax. To minimize confusion, this book always refers to them as SMIv1 MIBs. SMIv1 MIBs are very functional and quite common.

SMIv2 MIB Syntax

SMIv2 was introduced at the same time as SNMPv2c. Sometimes SMIv2 MIB syntax is referred to as SNMPv2 MIB syntax. To minimize confusion, this book always refers to them as SMIv2 MIBs.

SMIv2 enhancements include the following (later chapters provide details):
- Better self-documenting object syntax
- More consistent syntax for trap objects (called *notifications* in SMIv2)
- Richer base data types

- Formalized syntax for derived data types (called *textual conventions* in SMIv2)
- Statements which organize data and trap objects into conformance groups which are then specified as mandatory or optional for agent support

SMIv2–SMIv1 Syntax Conversions

SMIv1 MIBs can usually be translated into SMIv2 MIBs. Minor syntax differences may require tweaking.

An SMIv2 MIB can usually be translated into an SMIv1 MIB. Important exceptions are listed here, and coming chapters discuss details:
- A Counter64 type object cannot be translated from SMIv2 to SMIv1.
- An improperly coded SMIv2 NOTIFICATION-TYPE cannot be translated into an SMIv1 TRAP-TYPE with the same object identifier (OID).
- Some subtle object naming and enumerated value naming issues present problems.

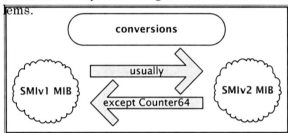

MIB Syntax and SNMP Message Protocol Versions

Data defined by SMIv2 MIB objects can be transmitted between managers and agents by any of the three messaging protocols—SNMPv1, SNMPv2c, or SNMPv3. The only exception to this is Counter64 object data which cannot be transported by SNMPv1 messages.

Message Transport for SMIv1 and SMIv2 MIB object values

Transport Message	SMIv1 MIB Objects	SMIv2 MIB Objects
SNMPv1	yes	except Counter64
SNMPv2c	yes	yes
SNMPv3	yes	yes

Traps defined in an SMIv2 MIB using the new NOTIFICATION-TYPE syntax can also be transmitted from agents to managers using SNMPv1, SNMPv2c, or SNMPv3 messages.

Preferred MIB Syntax

It should be no surprise that the *preferred MIB syntax is SMIv2*. SMIv2 MIBs are easier to read and comprehend, and include many refinements that encourage good embedded documentation.

IETF standard MIBs *must* be written in SMIv2, although there are older (and still current) MIBs that remain in SMIv1 syntax.

Unless a developer has a really good reason, *enterprise MIBs should be coded in SMIv2*. Care must be taken to ensure that they can be converted to SMIv1. SMIv1 MIBs may still be needed for older or low-end management tools, and some vendors (such as Cisco) deliver all MIBs in both the SMIv2 and SMIv1 formats.

> **SNMP Tidbit.** Although SMIv1 MIBs are sometimes called SNMPv1
> MIBs, and SMIv2 MIBs are sometimes called SNMPv2 MIBs, there is
> no new SMIv3 MIB syntax standard associated with SNMPv3.

MIB Syntax Examples

To remove any mystique about MIBs, it may be useful to take a preliminary peak at some sample syntax. Syntax examples of a data object and of a trap object are shown below. Some of the syntax may still be a bit puzzling, but the example should be useful.

Example of MIB data object syntax (SMIv2)

```
cdChStTemperature OBJECT-TYPE        -- Object name
    SYNTAX          Integer32        -- Data type (signed 32-bit integer)
    UNITS           "Celsius"
    MAX-ACCESS      read-only         -- maximum manager access allowed
    STATUS          current           -- vs. obsolete or deprecated
    DESCRIPTION                       -- information for the user
        "CD Player internal chassis temperature"
    := { cdChassisStatus  4 }         -- part of object identifier formation
```

Example of MIB notification (trap) object syntax (SMIv2)

```
cdChassisTempAlarmEv   NOTIFICATION-TYPE          -- Notification name
    OBJECTS      -- values of these data objects are sent with this trap
        { cdDynCfgUserAlias,
        cdStCfgModel,
        cdChStTemperature,
        cdEvSeverity,
        cdEvDescription }
    STATUS current
    DESCRIPTION                  -- Agent semantics descriptions for the user
        "Sent when cdChStTemperature > cdChassisTempAlarmThresh.
        Will not be resent until cdChStTemperature drops below
        cdChassisTempAlarmThresh minus 10%.
        Trap can be disabled by setting cdChassisTempEvTrapEn =
        the value trapDisable."
    ::= { cdEventList 10 }                  -- trap OID specification
```

Object Identifiers—OIDs

Closely associated with MIB objects is the concept of *object identifiers,* or *OIDs*. Each MIB object definition has a unique OID, which is a dotted listed of integers.

Example—In the Host Resources MIB, the name and OID for a data object are:

```
hrDiskStorageCapacity

        is identified by

1.3.6.1.2.1.25.3.6.1.4
```

When managers and agents communicate, they refer to MIB data objects using OIDs. An OID sent with a corresponding value { OID, value } is referred to as *variable binding.* Software developers might view the OID as the *handle* for the data value.

MIB trap objects also have OIDs. When a trap is sent from an agent to a manager, the manager recognizes the trap based on its OID.

Example—In the Chateau Systems CD player MIB, the name and the OID for one of the trap objects are:

---

cdChassisTempAlarmEv

1.3.6.1.4.1.10910.2.2.3.1.1.10.0.10

OIDs in MIBs also have other uses, such as identifying nodes in a hierarchical MIB structure, and defining globally unique enumerations.

For all of this to work reliably, OIDs need to be universally unique. And they are—this is discussed in Chapter 4.

Data Object Instance Values

Data object OIDs can also be appended by *instance values*—additional dotted decimal digits that extend the OID for a specific *instance* of an object defined by the OID.

MIBs support scalar data objects as well as indexed tables of objects (Chapter 13).
- Instance values of scalars (objects defined in non-indexed tables) are always '.0'
- Instance values of objects defined in indexed tables are equal to the index value itself

Example—for the Host Resources MIB example given above:

---

hrDiskStorageCapacity
> is defined in an indexed table. There is one table row for
> each disk on the system. To specify the value for the disk of
> interest, the index (e.g., **5**) is appended to the OID.

hrDiskStorageCapacity.**5**

1.3.6.1.2.1.25.3.6.1.4.5

---

get messages must always specify an instance value. For example:

> *get* { communityStringValue, OID.instance }

For *getnext* messages, instance values are optional. For example:

> *getnext* { communityStringValue, OID }
> *getnext* { communityStringValue, OID.instance }

OIDs and instances are discussed further in Chapter 4.

Enterprise MIBs and Standard MIBs

Depending on the origin (organization and author) of MIBs, they can be categorized as either:
* Enterprise MIBs
* Standard MIBs

Enterprise MIBs are authored by non-standards-committee organizations (e.g., Cisco, Hewlett-Packard, Chateau Systems, University of Nebraska). All such organizations must apply for a unique *enterprise identifier* issued by the Internet Assigned Numbers Authority (IANA). Enterprise MIBs are then organized under these unique IDs.

Standard MIBs are authored by persons (usually) associated with the IETF. For example, a standard Printer MIB exists, and printer manufacturers commonly implement an agent (or subagent) to support this MIB in addition to their own enterprise MIBs.

Standard IETF MIB examples include:
* mib-2
* Host Resources MIB
* X.25
* Modems
* DS1, DS3
* Bridges
* ATM
* Token Ring
* Fibre Channel Fabric Element MIB
* Ping, Traceroute, Lookup MIBs
* Print Job Monitoring MIB
* ICMPv6 MIB
* Mail Monitoring MIB

Other vendor consortiums and standards bodies also author MIBs—for example, the FibreChannel Alliance, CCITT (telephone company MIBs), DVB (Digital Video Broadcasting), IEEE, and others.

Exercises

1. What are the three major elements of SNMP architecture?

2. Name the three SNMP message protocol standards.

3. Name the two SNMP MIB syntax standards.

    a. List some of the improvements of the most recent standard.
    b. Does the newer standard obsolete the first?

4. What is the most commonly used message transport protocol used by SNMP?

5. MIB syntax defines a variety of objects. Information associated with two types of objects is transported by SNMP messages. What are those object types?

6. Can data and trap objects defined in SMIv2 MIBs be transported in:

    a. SNMPv1 messages?
    b. SNMPv2c messages?
    c. SNMPv3 messages?
    d. Any restrictions?

7. Managers and agents communicate using data and trap *handles*. What is the SNMP terminology for these *handles*?

8. How do standard MIBs and enterprise MIBs differ? Which MIB syntax can be used for each type?

9. Use your browser to access the IETF web site:

    www.ietf.org

    Click on the link to *RFC Pages*

    Bookmark this in your *favorites*—you will need it for future exercises,

    a. Click on the link to RFC Index. This is a summary of all published RFCs along with their current status.

    b. After the Index File loads (it may take a while), search for 1759.

    c. You will see an entry for the *Printer MIB*—RFC-1759 and that it has been obsoleted by RFC-3805.

d. Search for 3805, and find the RFC *Printer MIB v2*. Note that its status is PROPOSED STANDARD, but is in fact the preferred standard for support by agents.

e. Click back to the RFC pages link, and in the box adjacent to *RFC Number* enter 3805, and click *GO*. This will take you to the RFC that defines the standard Printer MIB.

f. You are now viewing header information for the RFC. Take some time to browse. When you are ready, search for BEGIN. This will take you to the first line of one of two MIBs embedded in this RFC. This first MIB contains textual convention definitions used by data object definitions in the second MIB. The first line will look like:

IANA-PRINTER-MIB DEFINITIONS ::= BEGIN

g. Search again for BEGIN, and you will find the first line of the second MIB, which contains data and trap objects. The first line will look like:

Printer-MIB DEFINITIONS ::= BEGIN

h. Spend some time scrolling down through the MIB text. If you scroll far enough, you will find the last line in the MIB

END

Congratulations! You have just reviewed your first RFC, and had a peak at your first MIB syntax.

Chapter 3

Getting the Most Out of SNMP

The simplicity of SNMP is the main reason for its initial and continued success—simple MIB objects define information that is transported by a simple message set. Yet it still requires users to have a good grasp of its concepts and to direct its proper use.

Since you bought this book, and may have read other SNMP books, you are well on your way to getting the most out of SNMP. This short chapter contains some guidelines.

SNMP—Scalable and Flexible

SNMP is deployed in many types and sizes of networks to monitor a wide variety of devices.

Scalable and flexible:
- Monitor a single device, small networks, medium networks, or very large networks
- Single managers or multiple managers
- Local and remote network management
- Centralized, distributed, or hybrid management of networks
- Monitor simple data values (such as temperature) or complex network metrics (e.g., identifying devices on a remote link that are the busiest senders and busiest receivers of network traffic at specific OSI levels)
- Open source tools, inexpensive tools, affordable tools, and high-end solutions
- Simple security or very secure SNMP communication
- Trap-centric networks (managers wait for agents to signal problems), or proactive polling of device status values
- Monitor MIB data object values or abstract values calculated from that data (arithmetic and logical relationships)
- Monitoring only, or remote configuration and control of network devices

Good Tools

There is an old adage:

"If your only tool is a hammer, then everything looks like a nail."

Some who express disappointment with SNMP may have learned the technology solely through the use of an unremarkable tool, and have not yet had an opportunity to explore or understand all that SNMP offers.

Others have used good tools, but without sufficient time or technical background to fully exercise them, and only skim the surface of possibilities.

Tool categories include:
- Graphical MIB editors
- MIB validating compilers
- MIB browsers
- Comprehensive managers
- Focused management tools
- Command-line tools to perform basic SNMP message operations
- Tools to strip MIBs from RFCs
- Agent SDKs
- Agent protocol validation suites

Many excellent SNMP tools are available, both open source and commercially—we are fans of both. Many of the commercially available tools are reasonably priced.

Investment in proper tools will save engineering time, both for developers and for those managing networks. Tool selection mistakes can result in negative leverage (i.e., investment in mastering and configuring the tool is greater than benefits realized). For example:
- Purchase of a complex tool that requires significant expertise to master, by a team with limited time and resources
- Use of an open source tool that requires extensive scripting and configuration to provide needed results—this cost can sometimes exceed that of a more turn-key commercial offering
- Some tools offer SNMP features but are not truly SNMP-centric
- Not understanding SNMP itself or the problem to be solved prior to selecting tools, is often an issue

Network Engineers

Organize team specialists—network engineer teams are encouraged to designate individuals to be expert in accomplishing specific SNMP tasks:
 * Manager network discovery, network map setup, and manager-side configuration of managed devices
 * Configuring SNMP agents residing on managed devices
 * Manager report configuration and generation
 * Configuring manager trap filters
 * MIB syntax and diagnosis specialist

Understand MIB syntax—this is not difficult. Most network engineers are competent with various programming and scripting languages. MIB syntax is different yet easily learned.

Select a good MIB browser—this makes reviewing MIBs for useful content much easier. Mid- to high-end managers include browsers, and many good stand-alone browsers are available.

Choose suitable manager tools—a wide variety of tools are available, some simple and some complex. Ensure that your tools scale to the networks to be managed and for the purposes intended. If possible, contact current users of tools being considered.

Understand your management goals before selecting tools.
 * High-end tools are available which support SNMP well, and have capabilities far beyond just SNMP management. Many of these vendors will contract to set up, configure, and otherwise support your network management effort.
 * Very capable commercial mid-range manager tools that meet many organizations' requirements should be considered.
 * Several open source managers are available, and may be suitable for your needs.
 * Inexpensive (as well as open source) tools are available to perform limited but useful functions—for example, generate trend reports for single data objects, or listen for specific traps. Most of these run on an individual's laptop or workstation and facilitate the *distributed network management* approach discussed in Chapter 2.

Developers

Become expert in SNMP—many developers have discovered (sometimes to their dismay) that their customers view them as the SNMP experts. Deployment of SNMP products will increase customer service calls; deployment of quality agents and MIBs will minimize these calls.

Acquire suitable tools:
- A good MIB browser is a great way for developers to review MIB organization and design.
- A mid-range manager facilitates agent testing, and helps the developer to understand how their SNMP products will actually be used.
- Many good agent SDKs are available.
  - Plan for SNMPv3—today's market expects the security that SNMPv3 offers. If not planned for first release, ensure the selected SDK provides an upgrade path.

Test, test, test:
- Testing agents for all possible manager requests, including improper requests (e.g., a *set* to a read-only object), is tedious but must be done.
- Test for proper generation of all agent traps (it can be difficult to create conditions that force all traps).
- Stress test agents with rapid manager requests, with the agent simultaneously sending continuous traps. Check CPU usage, for agent failures, and for memory leaks.
- Test agent behavior with multiple managers making simultaneous requests.
- Test suites for correct agent protocol operations are available.
  - Ask your SDK provider if they use such a suite to test their tool set.
  - Even if they do, your agent or subagent extensions will benefit from further formal testing.

Craft great MIBs—this is a primary topic for the entire book. The next section provides an overview.

Crafting Great MIBs

Great MIBs are first of all syntactically correct, and SMIv1 and SMIv2 syntax is never mixed.

All MIBs should be run through several validating MIB compilers prior to release. MIBs that have been properly validated will compile into managers with no problems.

Manager compilers are not designed to be *validating compilers*, and many are not rigorous in checking MIB syntax. They attempt to be MIB-friendly (and hence user-friendly) and make an effort to accept syntactically incorrect MIBs if they can make sense of them. There are no rules for such permissiveness, so a MIB may compile just fine using one tool but fail using another.

Permissiveness is not a criticism of managers—they are simply recognizing the fact that MIBs with syntax problems occur, are trying to make life easier for network engineers, and are attempting to reduce the number of customer service calls they receive concerning MIB problems.

New MIBs should be coded to the SMIv2 standard. Some vendors (Cisco is an example) ship MIBs in both SMIv1 and SMIv2 format, to accommodate the variety of tools that are used by customers. Great MIBs can be converted between SMIv2 and SMIv1 syntax with no errors and no OID definition differences.

Great MIBs define data objects that model their product thoroughly, that are useful for monitoring performance and faults, and that may allow remote configuration and control.

Traps must be designed with many considerations in mind, including:
* Definition of the trap objects themselves
* Defining what data object values will be sent with each trap
* Understanding how network engineers will configure manager trap filters
* Trap filters process traps for multiple purposes:
  ○ To be logged as per severity
  ○ To be logged into categories
  ○ To trigger appropriate actions
  ○ To allow multi-state traps (e.g., good/bad events) to auto-acknowledge each other

MIB syntax offers many opportunities to provide users with information about data objects and traps, and to discuss agent semantics. A well-written MIB contains sufficient descriptions for end users and should not require supplemental documentation.

The status of all objects must be clearly stated. SMIv1 and SMIv2 both provide for object STATUS values of obsolete and deprecated. It is imperative that OIDs not be re-used to define new or different objects. This simple rule allows agents (coded to MIB-revisionA) and managers (with MIB-revisionB compiled) to communicate coherently (although not necessarily about all possible data and objects).

Exercises

1. Stand up and stretch—the next chapters get into the details!

Part 2

Preliminary Topics

Preliminary topics include two chapters of need-to-know information before delving into MIB syntax.

Chapter 4 discusses *MIB Object Names and Identifiers*, which applies to a variety of MIB objects. Object identifiers (OIDs) are numeric *handles* for MIB objects, which also have textual names (and associated naming rules). It is important to understand object names and OIDs prior to tackling syntax.

Chapter 5 is about *Managing MIBs—Tools and Hints*. Understanding tools is also dependent on understanding object names and OIDs (Chapter 4).

These descriptions of OIDs, object names, and tools assume some prior knowledge of MIB syntax, which is presented in later chapters.

However, the syntax chapters assume familiarity with OIDs, object names, and tools.

If you are new to SNMP, you may want to review Chapters 4 and 5 now, and again after studying syntax.

Chapter 4

MIB Object Names and Identifiers

Before discussing MIB-related tools and MIB syntax it is important to understand the concepts of *object names*, *object identifiers* and *object instance values*.

MIB objects have textual names, as well as numeric object identifiers (OIDs).

OIDs are used as data and trap *handles* in SNMPv1/v2c/v3 messages, as well as to identify a few other MIB objects not sent in messages. Instance values extend an OID to identify specific instances (think *indexes*) of data objects.

Command-line tools and manager MIB browsing tools utilize OIDs and instance values.

Managers also use *OID enumerations* to select network map icons appropriate to the managed device (e.g., a printer icon for a printer device), and for other purposes.

A MIB *object identifier* is a dotted list of positive decimal integers.

> *Example.* The textual name and the equivalent OID of a data object from the standard mib-2 system table are:
>
> | |
> |---|
> | sysContact |
> | |
> | 1.3.6.1.2.1.1.1 |
> | |
> | where sysContact is a read-write data object of type DisplayString (text) |

Example. Textual name and equivalent OID of data object from the UC Davis enterprise UCD-SNMP-MIB

---

dskPercent

1.3.6.1.4.1.2021.9.1.9

where 2021 is the UC Davis Enterprise ID assigned by IANA

dskPercent is a read-only data object of type Integer32

Most elements of MIB syntax have OID assignments, and OIDs must be defined to be universally unique. Elements include:

- *Managed Objects*
  - Data objects
  - Trap objects

- *Node Definitions*—MIBs are organized as a hierarchy, with a root node of iso(.1) where .1 is the first element of all object identifiers. Other node objects are defined to create trees and branches. Although *node* is not official SNMP terminology, we use the term in this book. Nodes provide structure within a MIB—data and trap objects are organized under nodes. Nodes are defined by several different MIB objects.
  - Simple node definition syntax (OBJECT IDENTIFIER and OBJECT-IDENTITY)
  - *Table objects* and table *entry objects*, which are also part of indexed table syntax
  - MODULE-IDENTITY statements (SMIv2)

- *Conformance Objects* (SMIv2)—statements organizing data and trap objects into groups, and specifying those groups as mandatory or optional.

OID Size and Value Limits

Each dotted unsigned integer in an OID can have a maximum value of 4294967295.

The maximum length of an OID is 128 dotted integers. Also discussed are *instance values* (think *indexes*) for data objects, which are appended to an OID to identify a particular *instance* of a data object. For data objects, the maximum length of the OID.instance is still limited to 128 dotted integers.

When defining data object OIDs, assigning a value of zero (.0) for the last integer value is discouraged. A zero value confuses the OID with the instance value for scalars (which is zero).

For node object OIDs, a value of zero (.0) for the last integer value is normally reserved for a node appearing just above SMIv2 NOTIFICATION-TYPE (trap object) declarations. The reason for this rule will be explained when trap syntax is discussed, along with how to convert SMIv2 trap syntax to SMIv1 (Chapter 11).

MIB Object Naming Rules

Authors of standard MIBs (defined within RFCs) are required to make all object textual names universally unique, and this is enforced by the review process.

Authors of enterprise MIBs are encouraged to support uniqueness of textual object names within their own enterprise MIB space.

> **MIB Diagnosis Hint.** Most compilers will report problems if duplicate object names occur within one MIB. Some compilers may not do well if there are duplicate object names within a set of loaded enterprise MIBs— the compiler may not be vocal, but subtle errant manager behavior may be observed. Other compilers will be unhappy if there are duplicate object names within MIBs from different enterprises.
>
> If MIB developers use progressive naming of objects (described below), the chances of duplicate names are minimized.
>
> Network engineers encountering duplicate name problems are often able to edit MIBs to rename objects to be unique.

MIB object names begin with a letter (it should be lower case) and can consist of up to 64 letters and digits. Identifiers longer than 24 or 32 characters may encounter problems with some tools, and are discouraged. For example, object names displayed in a manager GUI may be truncated, resulting in multiple objects displayed with the same apparent name.

Names must not contain underscores.

SMIv1 syntax allows names with hyphens, but SMIv2 syntax does not. Including hyphens in SMIv1 object names is discouraged because it makes conversion to SMIv2 syntax difficult, and for a second reason.

> **SNMP Tidbit**. If an SMIv1 MIB is passed through an agent development kit compiler to generate code stubs (e.g., in the "C" programming language), names with hyphens will be misinterpreted as multiple arithmetic variables separated by minus signs.

> **MIB Diagnosis Hint.** Object names with underscores may be acceptable to a permissive compiler, but will not pass through stricter compilers. SMIv2 MIB object names with hyphens may also be treated permissively.

MIB style guidelines suggest that object names have progressive prefixes that are suggestive of the object's purpose and organization within the MIB. This helps to maintain name uniqueness.

Example of progressive object naming

The Unsigned32 object

cdEvCtlAgtPollFreq

is from an example MIB that models compact disc (CD) players, and is in a MIB branch that contains data objects for controlling trap behavior. It specifies an agent polling frequency—the periodicity in seconds that the agent checks the data for alarming conditions.

Sometimes this guideline is taken to excess, and produces object names that are confusing or too long, exceeding a manager's ability to display properly.

Recognizing OID Preambles

There are several standard OID preambles that allow network engineers to quickly identify what general category a particular MIB object belongs to. The names of these preambles are listed below, and are shown as typically displayed by an SNMP manager browser on the next page.

- Standard management MIBs (under mib-2, which is under the *mgmt* node)
- Standard experimental MIBs under the *experimental* node
- Enterprise MIBs under the *private* node
- Standard MIBs for SNMPv2 and SNMPv3 support. These are SMIv2 MIBs designed to support and help manage the SNMPv2c and SNMPv3 messaging protocols

Actual OID definitions are discussed in the sections following the browser illustration.

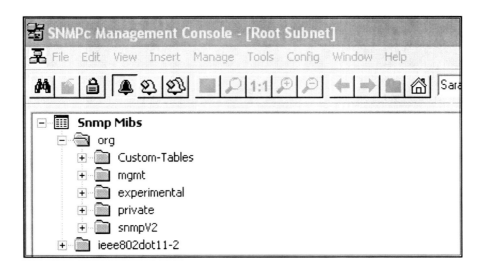

Standard Management MIBs

Standard MIBs are defined by the IETF within RFCs, and are organized under the following prefix (where each of the prefix elements is a node).

Common notation for expressing node progressions

> iso(1).org(3).dod(6).internet(1).mgmt(2).mib-2(1)
>
> *or simply*
>
> 1.3.6.1.2.1

Such sequences of nodes are often displayed graphically, as shown in the diagram to the right. iso(1) is called the root node of a MIB tree.

Multiple nodes following the mib-2 node are defined, and each of these is the top-most node of one standard MIB.

All non-node objects will have an OID that can be described by a sequence of integers, one per node, terminated by an integer value defining the object itself (e.g., a data object or trap object).

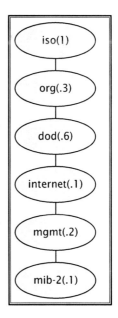

Example. Short list of standard MIBs organized under mib-2

MIB Name	MIB OID (top node definition)
Host Resource MIB	1.3.6.1.2.1.25
Entity MIB	1.3.6.1.2.1.47
Printer MIB	1.3.6.1.2.1.43
AgentX MIB	1.3.6.1.2.1.74

Experimental Management MIBs

Non-IETF organizations, such as IEEE, also produce standard MIBs. Some are organized under an *experimental MIB* branch. Although labeled *experimental*, some of these MIBs are in actual use by agents responsible for managing production equipment.

```
iso(1).org(3).dod(6).internet(1).experimental(3)

or simply

1.3.6.1.3
```

Example. Short list of standard MIBs under the experimental prefix

Node Name	MIB OID (top node definition)
ieeeBridgeSNMP	1.3.6.1.3.14
ibmpMIB	1.3.6.1.3.59
ifExtensions	1.3.6.1.3.6

SNMPv2 and SNMPv3 Support MIBs

A third category of standard MIBs includes *SNMPv2 and SNMPv3 support MIBs* defined under the prefix:

> iso(1).org(3).dod(6).internet(1).snmpV2(6)
>
> *or simply*
>
> 1.3.6.1.6

This is where the SNMPv2c *generic trap* equivalents and SNMPv3 configuration MIBs are organized.

> **SNMP Tidbit.** *Generic traps* were originally encoded in the SNMPv1 message layer as generic trap numbers 0 to 5, and were not assigned an OID. In SNMPv2, generic traps were assigned OIDs within a new SNMPv2 MIB. Generic trap numbers and their SNMPv2 equivalent OID definitions are:

Generic Trap SNMPv1 Encoding	Equivalent Trap OID SNMPv2c
Cold Start (0)	1.3.6.1.6.3.1.1.5.1
Warm Start (1)	1.3.6.1.6.3.1.1.5.2
Link Down (2)	1.3.6.1.6.3.1.1.5.3
Link Up (3)	1.3.6.1.6.3.1.1.5.4
Authentication Failure (4)	1.3.6.1.6.3.1.1.5.5
EGP Neighbor Loss (5)	1.3.6.1.6.3.1.1.5.6

> *coldStart* and *warmStart* traps are sent when an agent starts or restarts.
>
> *linkDown* and *linkUp* traps report the status of interfaces as per data defined in the mib-2 interface table.

authenticationFailure traps are triggered when an agent receives a *get* or *set* message with an invalid community string.

EGP—Exterior Gateway Protocol (now obsolete) *egpNeighborLoss* traps.

Appendix E, *Enterprise Definitions,* elaborates on the topic of generic traps.

SNMPv3 MIBs are also organized under the 1.3.6.1.6 node, and are used to configure SNMPv3 managers and agents to support advanced security features. (There are several SNMPv3 configuration MIBs.)

Enterprise MIBs

Enterprise MIBs are those authored by organizations other than standards groups. All enterprise MIBS are organized under:

---

iso(1).org(3).dod(6).internet(1).private(4).enterprises(1)

or simply

1.3.6.1.4.1

Individual enterprises are assigned a single digit (by the Internet Assigned Numbers Authority—IANA) that is appended to this prefix. All of an enterprise's MIBs are organized under this augmented prefix.

Examples of enterprise OIDs

Enterprise Name	Enterprise OID Prefix For All MIBs
Cisco	1.3.6.1.4.1.**9**
Hewlett-Packard	1.3.6.1.4.1.**11**
Chateau Systems	1.3.6.1.4.1.**10910**
Compu-Share	1.3.6.1.4.1.**26885**

Network engineers quickly learn to recognize the 1.3.6.1.4.1 prefix, and to know that the following digit defines the enterprise associated with a particular MIB object or trap.

This is the first step in finding needed MIBs for a manager when an agent reports a trap that is not correlated with a known MIB.

> *Example.* Resolving the origin of an unexpected trap

A manager receives a *trap* that does not correlate with any previously compiled MIB. The trap OID is displayed in the log as:

> 1.3.6.1.4.1.10910.2.2.3.1.1.10.0.20

Or, depending on the manager, the trap OID may be displayed as:

> iso(1).org(3).dod(6).internet(1).private(4).enterprise(1).10910.2.2.3.1.1.10.0.20

A network engineer can go to the IANA web page www.iana.org, browse links to *Enterprise Numbers,* and identify Chateau Systems Inc (=10910) as the enterprise that published the MIB defining this trap.

With the enterprise identified, it is usually fairly easy to acquire the needed MIB.

MIB-walking with repeated *getnext* requests will similarly display received data values with no MIB correlation.

Requesting an Enterprise ID Assignment

Developers should first access the IANA web site to see if their organization already has an assignment. SNMP project teams have been surprised to find that an assignment for their company already exists.

Some very large companies have multiple enterprise OID assignments for various divisions, or for very different business units under a corporate umbrella.

Assign a contact person within your organization, along with their email address. This information is published on the IANA web site.

> **SNMP Tidbit.** If a network engineer is trying to track down a vendor MIB, this may be a useful (although last resort) contact. Unfortunately, contact information is not always current.

Finally, contact IANA for your ID assignment.

IANA Contact Information

```
iana-pen@iana.org
www.iana.org
310-823-9358
```

Example Screen capture of IANA web page for enterprise numbers

```
PRIVATE ENTERPRISE NUMBERS

(last updated 2007-08-28)

SMI Network Management Private Enterprise Codes:

Prefix: iso.org.dod.internet.private.enterprise (1.3.6.1.4.1)

This file is http://www.iana.org/assignments/enterprise-numbers

Decimal
| Organization
| | Contact
| | | Email
| | | |
0
  Reserved
    Internet Assigned Numbers Authority
      iana&iana.org
1
  NxNetworks
    Michael Kellen
      OID.Admin&NxNetworks.com
2
  IBM
    Bob Moore
      remoore&us.ibm.com
```

Managing the Enterprise OID Space

Once an enterprise has an IANA assigned identifier, it becomes responsible for managing OID assignments under that prefix. For example, the University of Nebraska is responsible for assigning and managing all OIDs under their assigned prefix:

1.3.6.1.4.1.**9904**

There are three important OID-related enterprise management tasks:
- Organization of enterprise MIB branches (defined by nodes) under this prefix, for MIB development use
- Ensuring that all OIDs assigned within the organization are unique
- Ensuring that OIDs are not duplicated or reused in any future revised MIB definitions

As long as each enterprise carefully manages its OID space, each enterprise's unique prefix will guarantee all OIDs are universally unique. If this discipline is not maintained, serious problems will show up in managers.

When a MIB is *published* (i.e., made available for public use such as loading it into managers), the OIDs defined in the MIB are deemed *registered*. MIB registration is informal (there are no registration procedures), but developers must not modify definitions of registered objects.

> Communication from a *network engineer*
>
> "I had already defined all the trap filters for the traps defined in the old MIB, when I discovered that the new MIB had different trapVarBind names and values. The new MIB was not defined to be backward compatible. This means that 1) the current software is issuing traps based on old MIBs, but did not define all the traps, and 2) the new MIB defines new traps but uses different trapVarBind names, OIDs and values."

Important rules:
- If a data or trap object is no longer supported by the agent, use the object's STATUS clause to indicate it as obsolete. Do not remove the object from the MIB (which helps prevent future developers from redefining the OID's definition).
- If a data or trap object is supported in limited circumstances, change its STATUS to deprecated.
- Never reuse an OID for a different type of MIB object.
- Never redefine the type (or SYNTAX) of a data object.

Resolving OID Problems

Matching MIB and Agent Revision Levels

Ideally, revision levels of MIBs loaded in managers and of agents running in managed equipment should match. Revision level specifics can be found in release notes or on provider web sites. Sometimes an agent (or subagent) will communicate its revision level when it starts—for example, by printing to a console or in response to a *get* request (the latter requires definition as a MIB data object).

It can be difficult for a managed facility to achieve 100% deployed agent revision level consistency. There may be hundreds of microwave radios in remote locations that need software updates which are applied incrementally, but only one manager that needs a MIB update. Or a new shipment of radios with updated agent software arrives, and there are now mixed revision levels deployed in the network.

The *good news* is that if the MIB/agent provider has exercised care and not redefined any OIDs, out-of-revision manager MIBs and agents will run fairly well together.

- If the MIB in the manager is more current than the agents, it can *get* values for the subset of commonly known data objects.
- If the manager attempts to *get* data for a newer MIB object, the agent will respond with an error, but no real damage is done.
- If the agent is newer than the MIB compiled into the manager, the manager will never attempt to *get* values for newer data objects.
- If *getnext* requests are made to an agent, revisions discrepancies will be revealed—expected data will not be returned, or values will be returned with no OID correlation to the manager's MIB.
- An agent may send *traps* that are not known to the manager. These will be logged by the manager with an OID sequence that indicates a newer MIB is needed. Again no real damage is done—this may be the first clue that an updated MIB is available, and many managers will still allow trap filters to be constructed for this event.

Duplicate OID Definitions in Separate MIBs

It happens rarely, but if a vendor has supplied a set of MIBs with duplicated OID definitions, managers may behave strangely, and it may be difficult to diagnose the problem.

A network engineer's best recourse is to contact the vendor—it is dangerous to try to edit this problem away.

MIB Revision Contains an OID with Revised Definition

An OID that was previously a node is now a data object. Or the OID previously defining a data object is now a trap. More commonly, a data object has SYNTAX typed differently.

When loading a new MIB version over a previous version, managers attempt to maintain user configurations related to that MIB (e.g., *trap filters* and *trend reports*). Data object SYNTAX changes can result in strange manager behavior.

If you suspect this problem, first unload the older MIB and recompile, and then compile in the new MIB. This may work, but you will then have to reconfigure trap filters, trend reports, custom tables, and perhaps other details.

Data Object Instance Values

In addition to OIDs, data objects have *instance values.*

> **SNMP Jargon.** A *fully instanced object* is an object's OID with an instance value appended, as OID.instance

The instance value is zero (.0) for scalar objects (i.e., data not in an indexed table).

Example of instance value for a scalar data object

The CD player Firmware Revision object of type DisplayString

  cdStCfgFirmwareRev

  has the OID

  1.3.6.1.4.1.10910.2.2.3.1.1.1.1.10

The *fully instanced* object is

  cdStCfgFirmwareRev.0

  1.3.6.1.4.1.10910.2.2.3.1.1.1.1.10.0

The instance value for data objects in an indexed table is the index of the row containing the data.

Example using an Unsigned32 INDEX

The CD Player MIB contains a table indexed by CD slot number (an Unsigned32). One entry in this table is the MIB data object:

  cdChangerSlotStatus

  1.3.6.1.4.1.10910.2.2.3.1.1.3.2.2.1.2

Which is a read-only enumerated INTEGER with values

  { containsCD(1), empty(2) }

Example table showing the INDEX, the cdChangerSlotStatus OID.instance, and its value

cdChangerSlotNbr (Table INDEX = *instance* value)	cdChangerSlotStatus.*instance*	Example value of object.*instance*
1	1.3.6.1.4.1.10910.2.2.3.1.1.3.2.2.1.2.1	empty (2)
2	1.3.6.1.4.1.10910.2.2.3.1.1.3.2.2.1.2.2	containsCD (1)
3	1.3.6.1.4.1.10910.2.2.3.1.1.3.2.2.1.2.3	empty (2)

The example above uses an integer INDEX that adds a single decimal digit instance value to an OID. Chapter 14 discusses additional index data types that result in instance values expressed as multiple dotted decimal numbers.

Using Instances

get messages from managers to agents must include object instance values, and these same instance values will be contained in agent *getresponse* messages.

get (OID.instance)

get (OID1.instance1, OID1.instance2, OID3.instance7)

A *get* message, initiated from a manager GUI or from a console using command-line tools (Chapter 5), which does not specify an instance value, will fail. Agents will return an error message like *no such OID* or *no such instance*.

For *getnext* messages, supplying the instance value is optional. The agent accepts the OID or OID.instance supplied with the *getnext* request, and searches for the next sequential (lexicographically ordered) OID.instance value that exists, and returns that object value. The agent's *getresponse* message also contains the OID.instance of the returned value.

This is the basis of *MIB-walking.*
- Use *getnext* to ask for any OID or any OID.instance, or even to specify the OID of the top-most node in the MIB.
- If the value for any object that is lexicographically greater than the specified OID or OID.instance exists, the agent will supply its OID.instance along with the value.

- Ask again with a *getnext* specifying the OID.instance of the last returned value—and so on until the agent runs out of managed data and returns an *end-of-MIB* error.

SNMP Jargon. *Lexicographical ordering.* The official definition can be confusing. A good example suffices. The following OID.instance values are lexicographically ordered. This is the order in which an agent will return data for successive *getnext* requests.

> 1.3.6.1.4.1.10910.2.2.1.3.1.2.3
> 1.3.6.1.4.1.10910.2.2.1.3.1.2.4
> 1.3.6.1.4.1.10910.2.2.1.3.1.3.1

SNMP Tidbit. Some command-line tools (for *get, getnext, set* operations) require that OID values be specified with a preceding decimal point. And some of them are not very good about revealing what the problem is. *Example* of OID showing the preceding decimal point:

> .1.3.6.1.4.1.10910.2.2.1.3.1.3.1

Traps and Data Instances

Trap objects are defined by OIDs, but do not have instance values. Most *trap* definitions include data objects whose values will be sent with the *trap*. Such data values are sent with the trap as { OID.instance, value } bindings.

OIDs as Globally Unique Enumerations

Background information—MIB syntax provides for defining enumerated INTEGER values. Such definitions are local to the MIB in which they are defined.

Enumerated integers are common in software programming languages and are easily understood. An example is given below and on the next page, followed by a discussion (and examples) of using OIDs as globally unique definitions.

> *Example.* The Host Resources MIB defined in RFC-2790 contains an indexed table, hrDeviceTable, listing information about devices which exist on the host.
>
> hrDeviceTable contains an enumerated INTEGER data object, hrDeviceStatus, that can take values that are *locally* (within this MIB) unique.

```
hrDeviceStatus OBJECT-TYPE
    SYNTAX    INTEGER { unknown(1), running(2), warning(3),
                        testing(4), down(5) }
    MAX-ACCESS read-only
    STATUS    current
    DESCRIPTION "... omitted from this example..."
    ::= { hrDeviceEntry 5 }
```

MIBs *also* commonly use OIDs to enumerate values. Since OIDs are globally unique, OID enumerations are also *globally unique*. Globally unique OID enumerations are common and useful, and we review two examples below. (This usefulness is similar to the usefulness of unique MAC ethernet address enumerations.)

MIB-2 sysObjectID Example of OID Enumerations

Globally unique OID enumerations are used to identify *the vendor's authoritative identification of the network management subsystem contained in the entity.* This is the well-known sysObjectID object in the mib-2 *system* table, with SYNTAX OBJECT IDENTIFIER.

Example of *getnext* for sysObjectId value from a Microsoft platform agent, using SNMPc's MIB browser

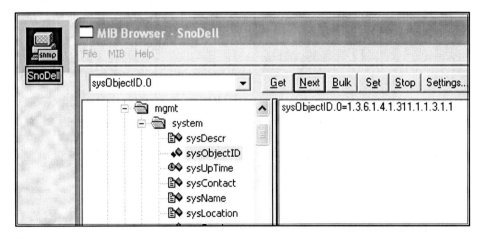

The response shown in the screen capture is:

OID value for sysObjectID.0 = (1.3.6.1.4.1.311.1.1.3.1.1)

which shows the *enterprise* to be = 311 = Microsoft, and the trailing digits of the OID identify the managed equipment as a Microsoft workstation.

Note that the response to the *getnext* request includes the instance value of '.0' for the scalar sysObjectID.

The OID value has an equivalent textual sequence that describes the entire path:

iso(1).org(3).dod(6).mgmt(1).private(4).enterprises(1).microsoft(311).
.software(1).systems(1).os(3).windowsNT(1).workstation(1)

This OID definition appears in the Microsoft MIB shown below (a complete but very short SMIv1 MIB); in the next chapters we discuss the syntax of these MIB elements in more detail.

```
MSFT-MIB DEFINITIONS ::= BEGIN
IMPORTS
    enterprises
      FROM RFC1155-SMI;

microsoft       OBJECT IDENTIFIER    ::= { enterprises 311 }
software        OBJECT IDENTIFIER    ::= { microsoft 1 }
systems         OBJECT IDENTIFIER    ::= { software 1 }
os              OBJECT IDENTIFIER    ::= { systems 3 }
windowsNT       OBJECT IDENTIFIER    ::= { os 1 }
windows         OBJECT IDENTIFIER    ::= { os 2 }
workstation     OBJECT IDENTIFIER    ::= { windowsNT 1 } -- sysObjectId value
server          OBJECT IDENTIFIER    ::= { windowsNT 2 }
dc              OBJECT IDENTIFIER    ::= { windowsNT 3 }


END
```

To complete this example, we show an SNMPc screen capture of the value for sysObjectID, in a table view (vs. the browser view previously shown). Note that the manager has interpreted the OID for us and displays the *name* of the managed device from the Microsoft MIB—workstation.

SystemInfo (SnoDell)

Descr	Hardware: x86 Family 6 Model	
ObjectID	workstation	
UpTime	0 days 03:25:24.43	
Contact	Larry Walsh	
Name	SNOHOMISH	
Location	Camano Island	
Services	76	

When a manager is polling for SNMP-compliant devices to construct a network map (called *Discovery*), it polls devices for their value of sysObjectID. The manager is configured with a file that correlates values for sysObjectID with *map icons* which it applies to its network map. Map icon graphics are often supplied by equipment providers as part of their SNMP package.

Thus, discovered workstations have workstation icons, routers look like routers, discovered printers look like printers, and so on.

Managers may also poll for other objects to fully determine the nature of the polled device—for example values for sysServices indicate the levels of networking services provided by a network device.

Some platforms may be running agents that have sysObjectID values hard-coded. For example, a Windows platform may be running a dedicated software application, but a query for sysObjectID may still identify it as a workstation. This is a consequence of using the Microsoft native SNMP master agent with a subagent extension coded to monitor the unique application.

Alternatively the Microsoft agent could have been replaced with a third-party agent SDK, allowing programmer control over the value of sysObjectID.

Host Resources MIB Example of OID Enumerations

The next example uses syntax that will be more formally discussed in coming chapters.

The example is taken from the standard MIB that models host resources. A data object is defined with SYNTAX (i.e., data type) OBJECT IDENTIFIER. That object takes enumerated OID values defined elsewhere in the MIB.

> *Example.* The syntax for hrDeviceType is shown below. SYNTAX AutonomousType specifies the object type as OID. This object has an OID assignment or identifier, but *also* contains data values typed as OID. Valid OID values are not enumerated within the SYNTAX clause (as they are for INTEGER enumerations), but hrDeviceType takes values defined elsewhere in this MIB.

```
hrDeviceType OBJECT-TYPE            -- name of this data object
    SYNTAX      AutonomousType      -- equivalent to OID data type
    MAX-ACCESS  read-only
    STATUS      current
    DESCRIPTION " ... omitted for this example... "
    ::= { hrDeviceEntry 2 }
```

Example continued from the same MIB. These are three of many enumerated OID values that object hrDeviceType can assume.

```
hrDeviceProcessor OBJECT-IDENTITY
    STATUS current
    DESCRIPTION
       "The device type identifier used for a CPU."
    ::= { hrDeviceTypes 3 }

 hrDeviceNetwork OBJECT-IDENTITY
    STATUS current
    DESCRIPTION
       "The device type identifier used for a network interface."
    ::= { hrDeviceTypes 4 }

 hrDevicePrinter OBJECT-IDENTITY
    STATUS current
    DESCRIPTION
       "The device type identifier used for a printer."
    ::= { hrDeviceTypes 5 }
```

The full OID for the enumerated value of hrDeviceProcessor is:

   1.3.6.1.2.1.25.3.1.3

which can be represented by the equivalent textual string:

   iso(1).org(.3).dod(.6).ineternet(.1).mgmt(.2).mib-2(.1).
   host(.25).hrDevice(.3).hrDeviceTypes(.1).hrDeviceProcessor(.3)

Integrated OID Tree Diagram

The next page shows a diagram of an integrated OID hierarchical tree summarizing much of this chapter's discussion.

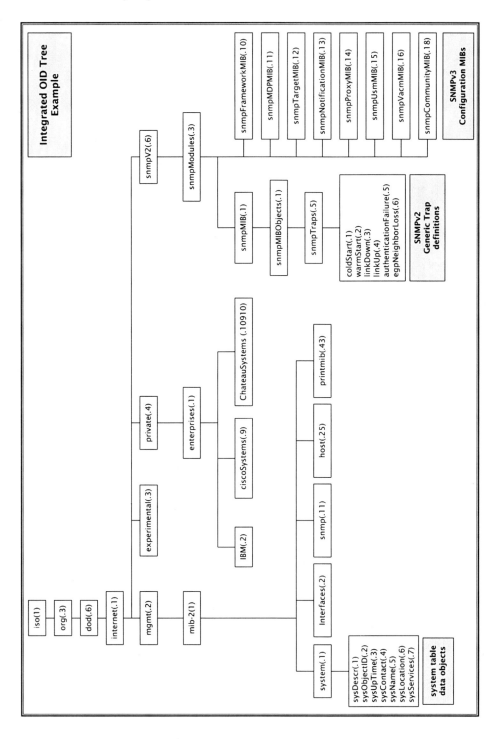

Exercises

1. Identify the following OID prefixes (i.e., what category of MIBs do they prefix).

   a. 1.3.6.1.2.1
   b. 1.3.6.1.3
   c. 1.3.6.1.6
   d. 1.3.6.1.4.1

2. Browse the IANA web site to see if your organization has an enterprise identifier.

3. What problems do you see with the following MIB object name (hint: there are three problems)?

   Csi_CdPlayerStatus.1

4. What is an object *instance* value, and how is it related to the object's OID?

5. Research the name of the enterprise that is responsible for the MIB defining the data object with the following OID:

   1.3.6.1.4.1.148.1.1.2.1.1.2

6. Name the six *generic traps*.

7. Your manager is reporting multiple *authentication failure traps* for a device on the network. What is happening?

8. You are using your manager's MIB browser to *get* sysDescr from the mib-2 system table. This is a well-known textual object with OID = 1.3.6.1.2.1.1

   The agent returns an error message of *unknown object identifier*. You double-check the OID you are sending the agent, and it is definitely correct.

   What is going wrong?

Chapter 5

Managing MIBs—Tools and Hints

Managing MIBs encompasses a variety of activities. This chapter describes useful tools as well as helpful hints.

- Creating new MIBs
- Validating MIB syntax
- Moving MIB files between Unix and Window platforms
- Finding MIBs needed for compilation into a manager
  - Determining the latest version of a standard MIB and getting a copy
  - Finding enterprise MIBs needed for managing products
  - Locating dependent MIBs (imported by other MIBs)
- Converting SMIv2 MIBs into SMIv1 syntax
- Browsing MIBs for structure and content to identify useful objects for managing devices and networks

Editing MIBs

Edit Tools

Your most useful tool is simply a *text editor*. These include vi, emacs, kedit, and others. Some managers will compile Rich Text Format (RTF) MIB files, and sometimes MIBs are delivered to customers coded in RTF.

But a true text editor is your best choice, with the most reliable results.

If you are repairing problem MIB syntax, use a text editor—unless it is already in RTF format.

When designing new MIBs, graphical MIB design tools are available that generate syntactically correct text file outputs; such tools combine the MIB design and editing processes, and are recommended. However developers should be comfortable with the details of syntax before moving on to abstract tools and methods.

Chapter 24 describes a multi-step MIB design process. If you follow this, the last step is to *edit* the MIB text file and then to *validate* it, which together seldom take more than a day's work to accomplish.

A simple method for editing a new MIB is to start with an existing syntactically correct MIB, and cut/paste objects into the new MIB (with appropriate renaming and reorganization). This assumes that the MIB has been completely designed prior to editing the actual file.

Operating System Conversion Tools

If you are working with MIB files in both the Unix and the Windows environments, you may need file conversion command-line tools.

> *Example*: You take delivery of a Unix platform with SNMP agent support. Often, MIBs supported by the agent are contained in a folder near the agent executable. These MIBs are *not needed* by the agent (a common misconception), but have been provided for compiling into the customer's manager. If your manager is Windows based, then the MIB text files may need conversion using command-line tools common on Unix platforms.
>
> Tool usage examples (with the command-line prompt "#" shown and many optional switches not shown):

```
# unix2dos inputFileName outputFileName

# dos2unix inputFileName outputFileName
```

MIB File Suffixes

Some SNMP compilers are fussy about the MIB file suffix (if it is not to their liking, they will not recognize it as a MIB file). Common suffixes are:

```
MibFileName.mib
MibFileName.my
MibFileName.mi1    -- Less common, to designate an SMIv1 MIB
MibFileName.mi2    -- Less common, to designate an SMIv2 MIB
```

Edit MIB file suffixes as needed to keep your compilers content.

MIB Names vs. MIB File Names

When working with MIBs, it is important to distinguish between *MIB names* and *MIB file names.*

When information is imported into a MIB from another MIB, the IMPORTS syntax will refer to the *MIB name* declared as part of MIB syntax. This name is defined in the first line of a MIB file:

```
CHATEAUSYSTEMS-REGISTRATIONS-MIB DEFINITIONS  ::= BEGIN

-- Double-dashes precede MIB comment lines
-- The name of this MIB is CHATEAUSYSTEMS-REGISTRATIONS-MIB
-- The body of the MIB appears between the BEGIN and END lines

END
```

When a MIB is dependent on another, it uses the IMPORTS statement to identify imported objects, along with the *MIB name* to import from.

```
IMPORTS

        chateauCDProduct    -- imports this MIB node definition

FROM CHATEAUSYSTEMS-REGISTRATIONS-MIB; -- from this MIB
```

MIBs are compiled into managers based on *file names*, and the *MIB file name* is usually different than its syntactic *MIB name*. In the above example, the *MIB name* is CHATEAUSYSTEMS-REGISTRATIONS-MIB, but the MIB file name might be:

ChateauRegMIB-v2.mib

You will also encounter MIB file names that bear no resemblance to the syntactic *MIB name*. For example, it may be related to a manufacturer's product part number, along with revision information. You may see file names like:

vronxPN898125-04A.mib

A single MIB file can contain one or more MIBs, each contained within a BEGIN . . . END pair. Each MIB within the file will have a different *MIB Name*.

When a MIB is compiled into an SNMP manager, the file containing the MIB (or MIBs) is first copied into a known manager directory (or folder). Using the manager user interface, a *MIB File Name* is then selected for compilation into the set of MIBs to be managed.

Example of SNMPc MIB compiler functionality

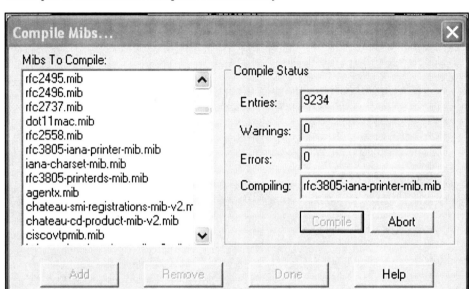

SNMP Tidbit. Although *MIB Names* and *MIB File Names* are separate designators, there are managers that require them to be the same. If all such MIBs are contained in the same directory, the compiler is able to resolve all IMPORTS issues by automatically loading needed IMPORTS MIBs. This will require the network engineer to change MIB file names to be the same as the MIB names.

MIB Compiler Purposes

A *C++ Compiler* has expected behavior. It checks for program syntactic correctness and generates binary code. All C++ compilers are expected to have identical syntax-checking capabilities.

Not so with MIB compilers, which differ in purpose and in style concerning syntactic correctness. There are many types of MIB compilers available. Some are *validation compilers* discussed below, and others are unique or proprietary.

Discuss the syntactic rigor of any compiler with its provider before trusting it to validate MIB syntax.

Manager compilers tend to be MIB-friendly and permissive about minor syntax issues. Some may be stricter. However *permissive,* is not necessarily a bad thing. Network engineers will appreciate a compiler that overlooks small issues and loads a MIB successfully. There are no rules defining degrees of permissiveness, and various manager compilers behave differently.

SNMP developers should *not* depend on manager compilers to validate their MIB syntax.

Agent development compilers are used to generate code stubs that are then hand-coded to return values for *get* requests, to process *set* commands, or to send *trap* messages. These compilers are usually more rigorous in checking MIB syntax, but it is still recommended that developers not depend solely on an agent software development kit compiler to validate MIBs.

Validation compilers are available whose primary purpose is to ensure correct MIB syntax. Network engineers can use these tools to diagnose problem MIBs. Developers should pass their MIBs through at least one, and preferably several, validation compilers prior to product release.

MIB Validation Compilers

The purpose of validation compilers is to check MIB files for SMIv1 or SMIv2 syntax correctness. Commonly used compilers are discussed below. Other good products are available.

When network engineers encounter MIB syntax errors, validation compilers can be very helpful in pinpointing problems. For the relatively rare case that a manager compiler is the problem (vs. the MIB), these tools help isolate that issue.

SNMP developers should always validate their MIBs using these or equivalent tools prior to proceeding with agent coding.

Simple Web Validation Compiler

Simple Web offers a free web-based validating MIB compiler. It allows the user to specify one of 6 severity levels—level 3 is suitable for many goals. Selecting level 6 will diagnose a MIB quite thoroughly—including more esoteric problems. (The web address below is correct.)

http://wwwsnmp.cs.utwente.nl/ietf/mibs/validate

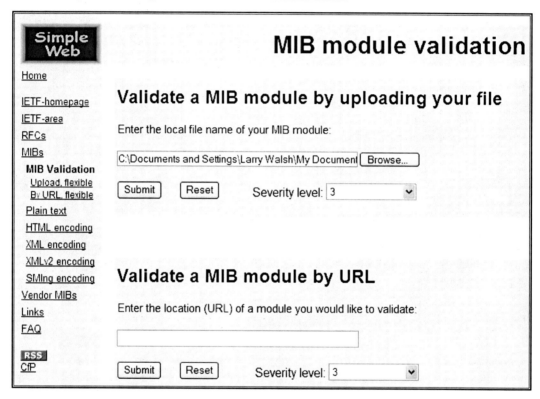

In addition to the MIB module validation site, there is a site containing tutorials for SNMP and related topics:

www.simpleweb.org/tutorials

Agent++ Validation Compiler

The *agent++* web site offers a free web-based validating compiler. MIB files can be submitted as text files or as zip files containing the MIB text files.

www.agentpp.com/mibtools/mibtools.html

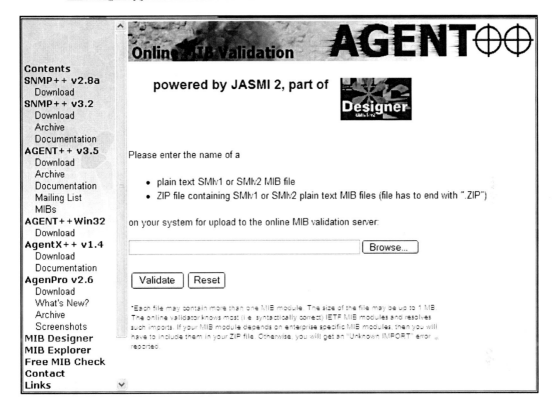

In addition to the validating compiler, several other tools are available:
- Agent development tools.
- MIB Designer—a tool to visually create, edit, and compare MIB modules. It can be used to create new SMIv2 MIBs or to edit existing SMIv1 or SMIv2 modules.
    - Includes a feature to lock released MIB objects, preventing incompatible changes as required by the SMI.
- MIB Explorer—a Java-based MIB browser that can be used to browse, configure, debug, monitor, and discover SNMP entities.

SMICng Validation Compiler

SMICng stands for *Structure of Management Information Compiler new generation.* There was an original SMIC compiler that is not discussed here. SMICng is a command-line compiler that runs under multiple operating systems.

It is a validating compiler, can also be used to convert SMIv2 MIBs to SMIv1 syntax, and is offered in two editions:

- On a CD included with the book *Understanding SNMP MIBs*, by David Perkins and Evan McGinnis, published by Prentice Hall.
  - The CD also contains a useful command-line tool, *mstrip,* that strips MIB files from RFC files.
- A professional version of *SMICng* is available from David Perkins' web site www.snmpinfo.com

libsmi Tools

The libsmi web site:

www.ibr.cs.tu-bs.de/projects/libsmi

has a number of excellent (and free) tools for the Unix environment, as well as web-based use. Good on-line documentation is provided.

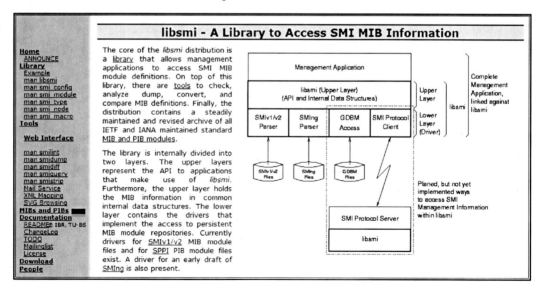

libsmi Unix tools include:
- *smilint*—MIB validation compiler
- *smidiff*—to compare the contents of two MIBs. Useful to quickly understand updates in a revised MIB
- *smidump*—to translate SMIv2 MIBs to SMIv1 syntax, and to other output formats (such as CORBA IDL). All options are shown on the next page
- *smiquery*—command-line tool to communicate with agents (*get*, *set*, etc.)
- *smistrip*—strips MIB files out of RFC files

libsmi Web Interface Tools

Select the libsmi Web Interface link to access three of these tools online:

www.ibr.cs.tu-bs.de/projects/libsmi/tools/

- *smilint*
- *smidump*
- *smistrip*

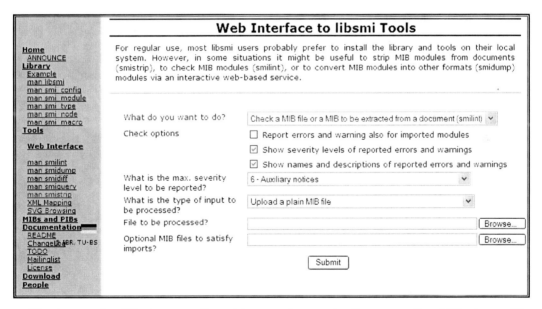

smilint is a good validating compiler with several very nice features—the ability to specify any of seven severity levels to check for, specification of any required IMPORTS MIB files, and MIBs that can be contained within an RFC or other document.

smistrip is also available from the web interface and strips MIBs from RFCs or other documents.

smidump processes MIBs and outputs a rich variety of information in various formats. Available options are listed in the libsmi screen capture below.

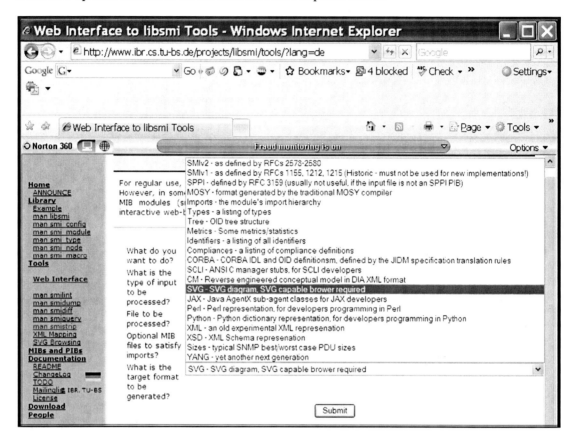

IETF MIB Doctors

IETF MIB Doctors web site. Both the *smilint* and the *SMICng* compilers are discussed further on this web site:

> www.ops.ietf.org/mib-review-tools.html

MOSY Compiler

MOSY is supplied with the ISO development environment. MOSY has a long history with SNMP, and variants are used by several commercial products (such as agent SDKs).

Validation Compiler Hints

Submission of a MIB to several validation compilers may (surprisingly) return slightly different results. Differences are minor, and not a cause for concern.

Some compilers allow you to specify a *severity level*. A maximum value will flag the compiler to check everything. Developers should validate MIBs with maximum severity specified.

One common issue in dealing with validation compilers is the need to also submit MIBs referenced in the IMPORTS statement. Normally the best way to supply the additional MIBs is to create (using a text editor) a single concatenated MIB file with all needed MIBs in IMPORTS order. Note that the *libsmi* web interface *smilint* compiler provides for specifying IMPORTS MIBs directly.

This raises a question. Which of the MIBs listed in an IMPORTS statement need to be supplied to the validating compiler? If you don't feed a compiler correctly, it will explain what is missing. But there are some general guidelines.
- Well-known SMIv1 or SMIv2 standard MIBs related to the syntax itself do not need to be provided. For example:
  - For SMIv1 MIBs—RFC1155-SMI, RFC-1212, RFC-1215, SNMPv2-TC-v1-MIB
  - For SMIv2 MIBs—SNMPv2-SMI, SNMPv2-TC, SNMPv2-CONF
- IMPORTS from other standard MIBs *may* require the MIB to be specifically loaded.
- Any IMPORTS from enterprise MIBs *will* require such MIBs to be supplied.

Finding Needed MIBs

Network engineers are frequently faced with tracking down MIBs needed by a manager to support products. Typical situations are described below.

Unknown traps are logged. A manager is receiving *traps* from a device, and they are being logged in the event log by OID, not by trap object name. This is a clear sign that a MIB is missing or that a newer revision is available.

MIB-walk returns data for unknown data objects. From a manager, select an agent platform of interest, and invoke MIB-walk (command-line tools for MIB-walk are also available). MIB-walking allows you to select a top node, and to perform automated *getnext* operations. The agent returns data for all of the supported MIB data objects.

This is a good way to investigate the extent of agent support, as well as to identify any MIBs that are missing from the manager.

Example. Use a manager or command-line tool to initiate a MIB-walk beginning at the top iso(1) node. The agent will return (in lexicographical order) data values for all MIBs and MIB objects under its management. Object names and values will be displayed by the manager. If an object OID is unknown by the manager (because a MIB is missing or is of a lower revision than the agent sending the data), then it displays the object OID received from the agent (vs. the name of the object), along with the value. Network engineers are quick to recognize that a MIB is missing, or needs to be updated.

Compiling new MIBs into a manager fails. The logged error tells you that a dependent MIB is missing.

Product agent supports RFC-based MIBs, but did not ship with copies of them. Vendors sometimes leave responsibility for acquiring standard MIBs to their customers. While many standard MIBs are pre-loaded into managers, some are not.

Some of a manager's MIBs pre-loads may not be current, and the network engineer needs to determine what is current, and then to get copies of those MIBs.

There are two examples provided for finding the most suitable version of standard MIBs.
- In this chapter, see the section *IETF Web Site MIB Search Scenario* for the most current version of the Entity MIB.
- Chapter 21, *Standard MIBs,* provides an extended example of tracking down the latest versions of the interface table MIB (section *Determining MIB Updates to the Interface Table*).

Required MIBs can be acquired from a variety of sources:
- Included product CDs
- From the agent platform file system (often in a directory near or adjacent to the agent binaries)
- Vendor web site
- IANA or IETF web sites
- MIB Depot web site
- Other MIB-support web sites

The following sections elaborate on some of these sources.

IANA Web Site for Enterprise Information

If a manager receives a trap with an OID that indicates a missing MIB, or a MIB-walk determines that a MIB is missing, the network engineer can easily inspect the object's OID to discover the enterprise ID. The name of the enterprise that authored the MIB can next be determined by accessing the IANA web site, browsing to Protocol Assignment Services, and then to Enterprise Numbers.

http://www.iana.org/assignments/enterprise-numbers

Knowing the enterprise, the engineer can search for the MIB on the MIB Depot web site. If that fails, the engineer can go directly to the vendor web site.

> **SNMP Tidbit.** The above process may not always work. Technology companies are frequently acquired by other enterprises, and the acquired organization will no longer be a source of MIBs—instead the acquiring company becomes the support point.
>
> In the same vein, an SNMP-compliant platform may have subagents that support MIBs from a variety of legacy enterprises.

IETF Web Sites for Standard MIBs

If you are looking for a standard MIB, most can be found embedded in RFCs available on the IETF web site. RFCs (Request for Comments) are standards specifications for many network disciplines, including SNMP.

http://www.ietf.org/rfc.html

On the Request for Comments window shown on the next page:
- Entering an *RFC number* will take you to the RFC document itself, which may also contain an embedded MIB.
- Clicking on *RFC Index* will display a document containing all RFCs in numeric order. Searching by keywords or RFC numbers will reveal RFCs and MIBs of interest, as well as their release status (e.g., EXPERIMENTAL).

An example is shown on the next page.

Request for Comments

The first choice below connects to the RFC repository maintained by the IETF Secretariat. The second choice connects directly to the RFC Editor's Web Page.

Be advised that there is a slight time period when the two directories will be out of sync. When in doubt, the RFC Editor Web Page is the authoritative source page. **Please Note:** The IETF repository retrieval is for those who know the specific RFC number desired. There is no index or search feature -- those capabilities are available at the RFC Editor Web page.

RFCs associated with an active IETF Working Group can also be accessed from the Working Group's web page via IETF Working Groups.

IETF repository retrieval:

RFC number: [   ] [go]

Alternatively, if you do not have Javascript enabled you can type the following in the location field of your browser:

http://www.ietf.org/rfc/rfcNNNN.txt

where NNNN is the RFC number prefixed with zeroes as necessary to make a four digit number.

RFC Index

Also useful for researching RFCs is the related RFC Editor web site.

http://www.RFC-editor.org/

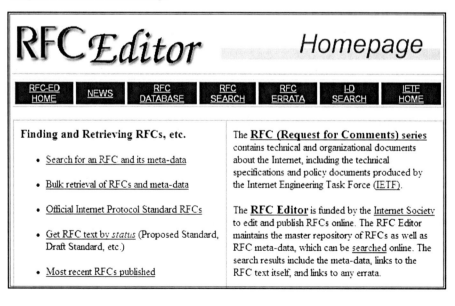

A third IETF web site is targeted to IETF MIB developers, and also contains useful tools and information.

http://tools.ietf.org/tools/

IETF Tools

IETF related tools hosted on tools.ietf.org.

 Search, show and print documents

Browse and search IETF documents
RFCs and drafts with hyperlink markup for easier reading and browsing, with a Google search interface.

Internet-drafts archive.
Find old and current drafts by full or partial name. If a complete draft name without version indication is used, the latest revision of the draft is provided.

Internet-drafts archive.
Find old and current drafts by full or partial name. If a complete draft name without version indication is used, the latest revision of the draft is provided.

PDF versions of IETF documents
A repository of RFCs, and old and current drafts in PDF format for easy printing. If no native PDF version of a document is available, a PDF conversion is provided.

 Prepare documents

Fix document spacing.
Fix up the spacing between sentences to use two spaces.

Check internet-drafts for submission nits
Use idnits to check that your draft has the desired formatting, boilerplate, references consistency and more.

Run a spelling-check on your internet-draft
Idspell uses an IETF-specific wordlist built from the last 2 years' published RFCs, surnames of recent I-D authors and some manually added words.

Draft Diff Tool
When looking at updated drafts, you want a diff with the previous draft which ignores changing page layout and moved page headers and footers. Get it here.

more author tools ...

IETF Web Site MIB Search Scenario

A subset of SNMP RFCs contain embedded standard MIB definitions.

RFCs also have a status:
- DRAFT STANDARD
- PROPOSED STANDARD
- STANDARD
- EXPERIMENTAL
- HISTORIC
- INFORMATIONAL

Search for the most current RFC with STANDARD status. However it is not uncommon to encounter agents supporting MIBs from RFCs that are PROPOSED, DRAFT, or even EXPERIMENTAL.

When searching for a MIB, you may know the RFC it is contained in, or you may know key words. Going to the RFC Index will enable you to correlate keywords to RFC number, and will enable you to find the most current RFC.

> *For Example:* Many Cisco products (and other vendor products) support the Entity MIB, which models product or chassis inventory. A chassis contains slots, which contain modules, which contain daughter boards and ports. A manager can *get* data from an agent managing the Entity MIB, which provides a nice inventory of product components.
>
> But first the latest Entity MIB revision must be loaded into the manager.
>
> Start by accessing the IETF RFC Index page, and then search for "Entity".
>
> http://www.ietf.org/iesg/1rfc_index.txt
>
> First find RFC-2037. Notice that RFC-2037 was obsoleted by RFC-2737, and it in turn was obsoleted by RFC-4133. All show the status PROPOSED STANDARD, but the latest update is RFC-4133, and contains the needed MIB.
>
> Here are the actual RFC Index entries:

```
2037 Entity MIB using SMIv2. K. McCloghrie, A. Bierman.
        October 1996.(Format: TXT=74362 bytes) (Obsoleted by
        RFC2737) (Status: PROPOSED STANDARD)

2737 Entity MIB (Version 2). K. McCloghrie, A. Bierman.
        December 1999.(Format: TXT=125141 bytes) (Obsoletes
        RFC2037) (Obsoleted by RFC4133(Status: PROPOSED
        STANDARD)

4133 Entity MIB (Version 3). A. Bierman, K. McCloghrie. August
        2005.(Format: TXT=136711 bytes) (Obsoletes RFC2737)
        (Status: PROPOSED STANDARD)
```

> Next use the *mstrip* tool or the *smistrip* tool (command-line or web-based) to extract the Entity MIB from the RFC. Both of these tools were discussed in previous sections.

Save RFC-4133 to a text file, RFC4133.txt, and then strip out the Entity MIB using command-line syntax (# is the CLI prompt):

```
# mstrip  RFC4122.txt > EntityMIB.mib
```

You're not quite done. The Entity MIB does not compile properly—it's missing a dependent MIB, as described by the MIB syntax:

```
IMPORTS SnmpAdminString
    FROM SNMP-FRAMEWORK-MIB;
```

So you go through the process again, and discover that the Framework MIB is contained in RFC-3411. Strip out the SNMP-FRAMEWORK-MIB, load it into the manager, and now the Entity MIB compiles successfully.

This is a fairly typical process.

SNMP Tidbit. MIB stripping tools used to extract MIB files from RFCs typically only extract the first MIB. If an RFC contains multiple MIB files (such as RFC-3805 *Printer MIB v2*), the RFC will need to be copied/pasted and manually edited to isolate the MIBs into two files. Then apply *mstrip* or *smistrip* to each of the files to extract all of the MIBs.

MIB Depot Web Site

The MIB Depot web site, www.mibdepot.com, is a MIB search engine that is an excellent place to find enterprise MIBs. It is well maintained, with over 10,000 enterprise MIBs submitted to date.

MIBs are listed by vendor, and you can submit searches based on MIB object names or Object Identifiers (OIDs)—this search capability is an important tool for managing MIBs.

The example MIBs listed in Appendixes G and H are also available from MIB Depot.

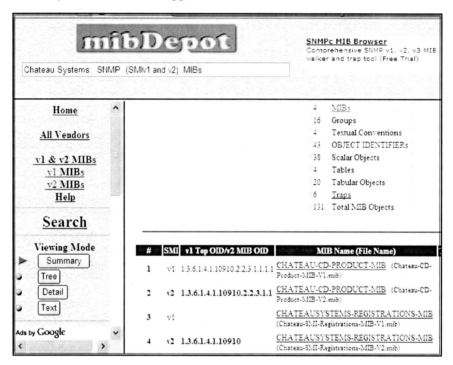

Cisco MIBs

Cisco's enterprise ID is '9', an indication of Cisco's early involvement with SNMP. RFC authors sometimes include Cisco employees. All of their MIBs are provided in SMIv2 and SMIv1 syntax, and can be found on the Cisco web site, as well as on MIB Depot.

Cisco also has web sites with SNMP tutorials, and others which facilitate researching Cisco MIBs. Cisco provides a good model for SNMP developers to emulate. A few Cisco web sites that may be useful are:

Tutorial with Cisco specifics:

www.cisco.com/univercd/cc/td/doc/product/webscale/css/css_740/admgd/snmp.htm

Select a product for a list of supporting MIBs:

www.cisco.com/public/sw-center/netmgmt/cmtk/mibs.shtml

Cisco Navigator Tool. Enter Cisco MIB object names or OIDs and returns useful information:

http://tools.cisco.com/Support/SNMP/do/BrowseOID.do?local=en

MIB Browsers

When network engineers take delivery of a product with new MIBs, they are very interested in identifying those objects that will be useful in managing the new product. The two main categories of interest are:
*   data objects
*   trap objects

The easiest way to investigate a MIB is to use a MIB browser product. MIB browsers are integral to SNMP managers. Simply load (compile) the MIB into the manager and browse its contents. MIB structure will be obvious. Good stand-alone browsers are also available.

Example using the SNMPc MIB browser, view the node structure of Chateau Systems MIBs that are loaded, and view the specific *properties* of the cdCtlPower data object.

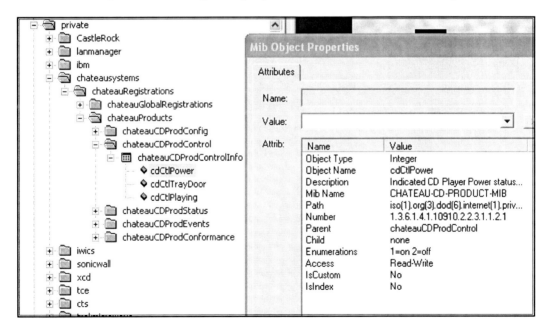

Displayed *properties* of the cdCtlPower data object include:
*   SYNTAX or data type is an enumerated integer with values { on(1), off(2) }
*   Access to the object is read-write

- The object name cdCtlPower
- MIB DESCRIPTION field contents
- The OID is displayed numerically as well as textually

MIB Diagrams

Understanding a MIB's structure and syntax by just reading the MIB text file can be difficult for the beginner. For more complex MIBs, this is difficult for everyone.

In the absence of a MIB browser, hand-drawn MIB diagrams can be useful.

Examples of MIB diagrams are shown in Appendixes G and H. Although these were drawn using Visio, sketching them by hand works just as well.

Command-line Message Tools

Unix and Linux implementations typically include SNMP command-line tools to accomplish manager messaging operations. These can be quite useful in setting up SNMP networks, as well as testing agents at the most basic level. The names and specific capabilities vary, but typical functionality includes:

- snmpGet
- snmpGetNext
- snmpGetBulk
- snmpSet
- snmpWaitForTrap (for a specific trap to be received)
- snmpSendTrap (less common)
- snmpMibWalk

Windows tools are also available.

- SNMPUTIL is a native set of tools that is distributed with the Win32 SDK.
- A comparable tool set (SNMPTOOL) is included on a CD distributed with the book *Windows NT SNMP*, by James D. Murray, published by O'Reilly.
  - ○ This is also a good reference for developers of subagents for the Windows native master agent. (Currently out of print, but available used— be sure the CD is included.)

Exercises

1. Name some common MIB file suffixes.

2. MIB syntax allows for importing definitions from other MIBS using the IM-PORTS (*definition*) FROM (*something*). What is *something*?

3. Validate the Entity MIB.

    a. Strip the Entity MIB from RFC-4133 as described previously.
    b. Submit it to the SimpleWeb validating compiler—select severity = 3.
    c. Resubmit it with severity = 6.
    d. Submit it to the agent++ web site.
    e. Submit it to the libsmi web site.
    f. Compare results.

4. Your manager has logged a trap with an OID as its identifier. This indicates a missing MIB.

    a. The logged OID is:
        1.3.6.1.4.1.9.10.27.2.0.1
    b. A quick inspection tells you that this is a Cisco (enterprise = 9) trap.
    c. Go to the MIB Depot web site, and search for this OID. The search will go more quickly if you select only Cisco MIBs to search.
    d. The missing MIB is identified as:
        CISCO-6400-CHASSIS-MIB
    e. Open the SMIv2 version of the MIB and view it as text. By selecting "all" and "copy", you can paste the MIB to a text file, and save it. Note that it IMPORTS a number of objects from other MIBs. One of interest is:
        IMPORTS
                ciscoExperiment
        FROM CISCO-SMI;
    f. Get a copy of the ciscoExperiment MIB also. You will need both for your manager.
    g. Concatenate the two MIB files together, and submit to any or all of the validating compilers.
        Specify severity = 3
        Specify severity = 6
    h. You will observe some minor errors. The MIB was last revised in 1998; those few errors are simply due to minor compiler refinements since then.

5. Browse the MIB Depot web site, and select an enterprise product MIB for validation testing. Check any needed IMPORTS, and append those MIB files to the top of the product MIB for submission to the validation compiler you decide to use. Validate at various severity levels.

6. Your MIB browser has determined that the sysObjectID value for a device on the network is (1.3.6.1.4.1.9.1.520). Determine what type of equipment this is.

Part 3

MIB Syntax

Chapter 6 discusses *MIB Structure* for SMIv1 syntax and for SMIv2 syntax. This is a brief chapter which serves as an outline for subsequent chapters, where MIB elements are discussed in detail.

Chapter 7 contains information about MIB object naming rules, BEGIN-END statements, IMPORTS of object definitions from other MIBs, and the syntax for MIB comments.

Chapter 8 discusses *Node Definitions* and the types of MIB objects that serve in this role.

Data Object Base Types are detailed in Chapter 9, followed by a discussion of *Data Object Derived Types* (or subtypes) in Chapter 10. SNMP derived types are formally referred to as *textual conventions*.

Chapter 11 describes *Trap Objects*, and compares the significantly different syntax used in SMIv1 and SMIv2 MIBs. (Part 5, *Advanced Trap Topics*, discusses traps beyond just syntax.)

Conformance Objects, which apply only to SMIv2 syntax, are described in Chapter 12.

One aspect of MIB syntax is deferred until Chapter 13, *Indexed Tables*.

Chapter 6

MIB Structure

There are two versions of MIB syntax. SMIv1 is the earlier version, and many MIBs are written to this specification. Suppliers of SMIv1 MIBs are not required to update them to the newer SMIv2 standard but are encouraged to do so if revisions are published.

SMIv2 was introduced later and encompasses many improvements. SMIv2 is a near-super-set of SMIv1 and codifies common design practices based on extensive SMIv1 experience. SMIv1 concepts flow naturally into SMIv2 syntax.

This brief chapter describes MIB elements for both versions and shows how elements are ordered within a MIB text file. Syntactic details are described in the following chapters.

The following diagram illustrates MIB object types, along with attributes (listed along the bottom) that apply to some or all object types.

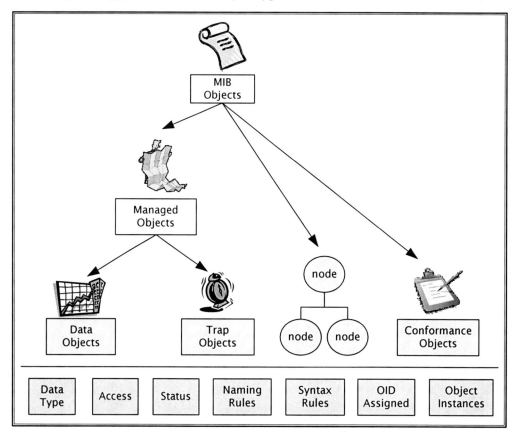

Data objects and trap objects are frequently referred to as *managed objects*.

Trap object syntax differs in SMIv1 and SMIv2.

Node objects appear in a variety of forms, some of which serve other purposes.

Conformance objects appear only in SMIv2 MIBs.

Following chapters discuss all of these objects in detail, including which attributes apply to each.

The following table provides a summary of object types and applicable attributes.

	Object	Data Type	Access	Status	Naming Rules	Syntax Rules	OID Assigned	Object Instances
Data	OBJECT-TYPE (SMIv1, SMIv2)	yes	yes	yes	yes	yes	yes	yes
Traps	TRAP-TYPE (SMIv1)				yes	yes	yes	
Traps	NOTIFICATION-TYPE (SMIv2)			yes	yes	yes	yes	
Nodes	MODULE-IDENTITY (SMIv2)				yes	yes	yes	
Nodes	OBJECT IDENTIFIER (SMIv1, SMIv2)				yes	yes	yes	
Nodes	OBJECT-IDENTITY (SMIv2)			yes	yes	yes	yes	
Nodes	Table and Entry Objects (SMIv1, SMIv2)		yes	yes	yes	yes	yes	
Conformance	OBJECT-GROUP (SMIv2)			yes	yes	yes	yes	
Conformance	NOTIFICATION-GROUP (SMIv2)			yes	yes	yes	yes	
Conformance	MODULE-COMPLIANCE (SMIv2)			yes	yes	yes	yes	
Conformance	AGENT-CAPABILITIES (SMIv2)			yes	yes	yes	yes	

From this table you can see that MIB syntax rules can be a bit tedious, and it is not unusual to encounter MIBs with subtle issues.

SMIv1 MIB Elements

MIB structure is not complex. The fundamental elements of *SMIv1 MIB syntax* are shown to the right. Some ordering of elements is required, and other ordering shown is typical. This is an outline, with a lot of details yet to come.

A MIB always begins with the:

> DEFINITIONS . . . BEGIN

statement, and ends with a line END. The DEFINITIONS statement also includes the specification of the MIB Name.

```
DEFINITIONS MY-MIB-NAME ::= BEGIN

IMPORTS syntax

Data sub-typing definitions
Node definitions

Scalar Data Objects

Table Object
Entry Object
Table SEQUENCE statement
Table Data Objects

TRAP-TYPE Objects

END
```

Multiple MIBs within a single text file are delineated by multiple BEGIN . . . END lines.

The IMPORTS statement follows BEGIN, and its purpose is to import definitions and objects from other MIBs.

Local data subtyping definitions (also called derived types or textual conventions) usually follow the IMPORTS.

Node definitions may appear next, or may appear further down, but typically appear before they are referenced by other MIB objects (*nodes, data, traps*).

In the above table, *scalar data objects* (i.e., data objects in non-indexed tables) are shown, followed by *indexed table* definitions. However, there are no specific ordering rules for nodes, scalar data, and indexed tables of data objects.

Indexed Table definitions require three statements, followed by the definitions of the data objects themselves. Data objects contained in indexed tables have syntax identical to scalar data objects. The statements needed to define an indexed table are:

> *Table object* which also defines a node
>
> *Entry object* which also defines a node and specifies the INDEX (or indexes) for the table
>
> SEQUENCE *statement* which lists all table data objects by *name* and *data type*

TRAP-TYPE object definitions are shown last. Although there is no rule that they appear last, they often do. Traps are normally sent with values of specified MIB data objects. For the benefit of one-pass compilers, trap definitions appear near the end so that referenced MIB data objects are defined first.

> **MIB Diagnosis Hint**. The majority of MIB compilers are two-pass. However, some tools are one-pass, which requires MIB objects to be defined prior to being referenced by other objects. Good design practice is to define objects in use order. A MIB not so ordered will compile fine using a two-pass compiler, but a one-pass compiler will complain about undefined objects. A network engineer can fix such problems by re-ordering MIB objects.

SMIv2 MIB Elements

Elements of *SMIv2 MIB syntax* are shown to the right.

Additions include:

The MODULE-IDENTITY statement provides MIB documentation and revision information, and also serves as a node definition. It is often the lexicographically superior (top-most) node in the MIB.

TEXTUAL-CONVENTION statements formalize syntax for definitions of derived data types.

The NOTIFICATION-TYPE statement replaces SMIv1 TRAP-TYPE syntax, but provides the same functionality. With care (to be explained later), both compile into objects with identical OIDs and purpose.

The inclusion of conformance objects is new. Data objects are organized into *groups*, trap objects are also grouped, and then named *groups* are declared as mandatory or optional.

```
DEFINITIONS MY-MIB-NAME ::= BEGIN

IMPORTS syntax

MODULE-IDENTITY statement

TEXTUAL-CONVENTION definitions
Node definitions

Scalar Data Objects

Table Object
Entry Object
Table SEQUENCE statement
Table Data Objects

NOTIFICATION-TYPE Objects

OBJECT-GROUP lists
NOTIFICATION-GROUP lists
MODULE-COMPLIANCE grouping lists

END
```

MIB syntactic elements for SMIv2 and SMIv1 are shown below side by side.

SMIv2 MIB Syntax

```
DEFINITIONS MY-MIB-NAME ::= BEGIN

IMPORTS syntax

MODULE-IDENTITY statement

TEXTUAL-CONVENTION definitions
Node definitions

Scalar Data Objects

Table Object
Entry Object
Table SEQUENCE statement
Table Data Objects

NOTIFICATION-TYPE Objects

OBJECT-GROUP lists
NOTIFICATION-GROUP lists
MODULE-COMPLIANCE grouping lists

END
```

SMIv1 MIB Syntax

```
DEFINITIONS MY-MIB-NAME ::= BEGIN

IMPORTS syntax


Data sub-typing definitions
Node definitions

Scalar Data Objects

Table Object
Entry Object
Table SEQUENCE statement
Table Data Objects

TRAP-TYPE Objects




END
```

Most (but not all) MIB statements result in an OID definition.

The few that do not are:

```
DEFINITIONS NAME-OF-MIB ::= BEGIN

IMPORTS

TEXTUAL-CONVENTION and SMIv1 Subtyping statements

Table SEQUENCE statement

END
```

SMIv2 Improvements

SMIv2 MIBs are more pleasing to read than SMIv1 MIBs, provide richer data types and subtypes, and contain improved documentation elements.

The MODULE-IDENTITY statement is new, defines a node OID, and encourages better MIB file documentation by providing text fields for LAST-UPDATED, ORGANIZATION, CONTACT-INFO, DESCRIPTION, and REVISION information.

NOTIFICATION-TYPE syntax replaces TRAP-TYPE syntax. SMIv1 trap syntax was not consistent with other MIB syntax. The new syntax provides the same functionality, but is easier to read and understand.

Improvements include a DESCRIPTION field for several objects where there was none in SMIv1.

SMIv2 has richer base data types, including BITS and Counter64.

Although derived data (subtypes based on base types) can be defined in SMIv1, SMIv2 formalizes the TEXTUAL-CONVENTION syntax and introduces some standard textual conventions such as DisplayString and TruthValue.

New conformance statements categorize data and trap objects into groups that specify mandatory or optional agent support. For example, some Printer MIB data objects are mandatory for all implementations, and others are optional (based on the printer technology being modeled or on the importance of the object).

MIB Syntax RFC References

SMIv1 is defined in the following RFCs that can be found on the IETF web site:
- RFC-1155—Structure and identification of Management Information for TCP/IP-based Internets
- RFC-1212—Concise MIB Definitions
- RFC-1215—Convention for Defining Traps for Use with The SNMP

SMIv2 is defined in these RFCs:
- RFC-2578—Structure of Management Information Version 2 (SMIv2)
- RFC-2579—Textual Conventions for SMIv2
- RFC-2580—Conformance Statements for SMIv2

Exercises

1. You need to extract (strip) a needed standard MIB from an RFC. You retrieve the RFC from the IETF web site. It is usually wise to first check for multiple embedded MIBs within the RFC. What is a quick way to do this?

2. What is one general but important improvement of SMIv2 over SMIv1?

3. The example on the opposite page is a very short MIB that loads with no errors into several manager tools. Yet it has problems in syntax, style, and semantic definitions.

   If you have previous SNMP experience, see how many problems you can spot.

   After you have read the next several chapters, try again to find the problems.

```
CSI-MIB DEFINITIONS ::= BEGIN

IMPORTS
      MODULE-IDENTITY, OBJECT-TYPE, NOTIFICATION-TYPE,
      Counter32, TimeTicks, Unsigned32, mib-2
      FROM SNMPv2-SMI

SnmpAdminString
      FROM SNMP-FRAMEWORK-MIB

MODULE-COMPLIANCE, OBJECT-GROUP, NOTIFICATION-GROUP
      FROM SNMPv2-CONF;

csiMib MODULE-IDENTITY
      LAST-UPDATED "200712040000Z"
      ORGANIZATION "CSI"
      CONTACT-INFO "details of contact info omitted"
      DESCRIPTION "CSI Support MIB"
::= { iso(1) org(3) dod(6) internet(1) private (4) enterprises(1) chateausystems (10910) }

csiMibObjects OBJECT IDENTIFIER ::= { csiMib 1 }

-- Traps

csiTraps OBJECT IDENTIFIER ::= { csiMibObjects 1 }
csiDescr OBJECT IDENTIFIER ::= { csiMibObjects 2 }

generalTrap NOTIFICATION-TYPE
      OBJECTS { trapDescription }
      STATUS current
      DESCRIPTION  "Trap describing CSI events"
::= { csiTraps 1 }

trapDescription OBJECT-TYPE
      SYNTAX SnmpAdminString (SIZE(0..128))
      ACCESS read-write
      STATUS current
      DESCRIPTION "Textual description of trap"
::= {csiDescr 1}

END
```

Chapter 7

MIB Header, IMPORTS, Comments

This chapter describes what might (informally) be called a MIB's *boilerplate* (but necessary) elements.

BEGIN-END and MIB Name Declaration

Multiple MIBs can be defined within a single text file, and are delineated by multiple:

> DEFINITIONS . . . BEGIN-END

pairs.

Remember that *MIB Names* are unique from *MIB File Names*.

MIB names have some rules:
- Must be globally unique
- Must start with an upper case letter
- *Most MIB names are all upper case*
- Can contain hyphens (but not the last letter)
- *Most do contain hyphens*
- Compilers may complain if the name is longer than 32 characters

```
DEFINITIONS MY-MIB-NAME ::= BEGIN

IMPORTS syntax

MODULE-IDENTITY statement

TEXTUAL-CONVENTION definitions
Node definitions

Scalar Data Objects

Table Object
Entry Object
Table SEQUENCE statement
Table Data Objects

NOTIFICATION-TYPE Objects

OBJECT-GROUP lists
NOTIFICATION-GROUP lists
MODULE-COMPLIANCE grouping lists

END
```

IMPORTS Statement

A MIB can have at most one IMPORTS statement, which is used to import information from other MIBs.

The FROM clause refers to the *MIB name* (not the *file name*) of the MIB that it is importing from.

Types of imported information include:
- Syntax keyword definitions
- Base data type keywords
- Node OID definitions that allow this MIB to build under nodes defined in other MIBs
- Table *entry object* OID definitions, which allow this MIB to extend tables defined in separate MIBs
- Textual convention definitions (sub-types defined in other MIBs)
- OIDs of data objects defined in other MIBs
  - For example, a MIB might import sysDescr from the standard mib-2 *system* table, and include that data object in trap definitions (the value of sysDescr would be sent with these traps).

```
DEFINITIONS MY-MIB-NAME ::= BEGIN

IMPORTS syntax

MODULE-IDENTITY statement

TEXTUAL-CONVENTION definitions
Node definitions

Scalar Data Objects

Table Object
Entry Object
Table SEQUENCE statement
Table Data Objects

NOTIFICATION-TYPE Objects

OBJECT-GROUP lists
NOTIFICATION-GROUP lists
MODULE-COMPLIANCE grouping lists

END
```

Example of SMIv2 MIB IMPORTS

```
IMPORTS
      MODULE-IDENTITY, OBJECT-IDENTITY, NOTIFICATION-TYPE,
      OBJECT-TYPE, Unsigned32, Integer32, Counter32
          FROM SNMPv2-SMI
      OBJECT-GROUP, NOTIFICATION-GROUP, MODULE-COMPLIANCE
          FROM SNMPv2-CONF

      DisplayString, TruthValue
          FROM SNMPv2-TC

      chateauCDProduct, ChateauTrapControl, ChateauEventSeverity
          FROM CHATEAUSYSTEMS-REGISTRATIONS-MIB;
```

Note the syntax punctuation. One or more definitions are imported FROM a MIB-NAME. There is no punctuation after each FROM clause. A final semicolon terminates the entire IMPORTS statement.

MIB SNMPv2-SMI contains syntax keyword definitions, including the names of SMIv2 data object base types.

> **MIB Diagnosis Hint**. Permissive compilers may not be strict about inclusion of IMPORTS of *well-known* definitions. For example, the keyword and data type definitions in SNMPv2-SMI are well known, and a compiler may not complain if they are not explicitly imported. However another compiler will complain. This is an easy edit to insert.

MIB SNMPv2-TC contains SMIv2 standard textual convention definitions (derived types—the topic of Chapter 10).

MIB SNMPv2-CONF contains syntax keyword definitions for use in the SMIv2 conformance statements—Chapter 12.

Several definitions are imported from the enterprise CHATEAUSYSTEMS-REGISTRATIONS-MIB:
- chateauCDProduct is a node definition under which nodes, data, and traps defined in the importing MIB will be organized.
- ChateauTrapControl and ChateauEventSeverity are enterprise textual convention definitions that will be used in data object SYNTAX clauses in the importing MIB.

Example of SMIv1 MIB IMPORTS

These are the equivalent IMPORTS for an SMIv1 MIB.

```
IMPORTS
  OBJECT-TYPE
      FROM RFC-1212
  TRAP-TYPE
      FROM RFC-1215
  Counter
      FROM RFC1155-SMI
  DisplayString, TruthValue
      FROM SNMPv2-TC-v1-MIB

  chateauCDProduct, ChateauTrapControl, ChateauEventSeverity
      FROM CHATEAUSYSTEMS-REGISTRATIONS-MIB;
```

The TRAP-TYPE keyword is imported instead of NOTIFICATION-TYPE.

Syntax keywords are imported from different SMIv1 MIBs than for SMIv2.

The standard textual conventions DisplayString and TruthValue are imported from an SMIv1 MIB (SNMPv2-TC-v1-MIB) that is an SMIv1 syntax equivalent to the SMIv2 MIB (SNMPv2-TC).

> Two of the standard textual conventions defined in SNMPv2-TC and in SNMPv2-TC-v1-MIB are also defined in RFC1213-MIB, and you also will encounter this in SMIv1 MIBs, as shown below:

```
IMPORTS
    DisplayString, PhysAddress
        FROM RFC1213-MIB;
```

Chateau Systems imported definitions are the same as for the SMIv2 IMPORTS.

MIB Comment Syntax

-- This is an example MIB Comment

MIB comments begin with double dashes. Comments may begin at the left, be indented, or begin following a line of valid MIB syntax.

Comments continue until the end of line, or until terminating double dashes '--' are encountered.

> **MIB Diagnosis Hint.** Some compilers do not deal well with comments that terminate with double dashes. If there is valid MIB syntax following the terminating dashes, the compiler may not recognize it. This is a simple problem to repair.

MIBs are sometimes prefaced with diagrams of OID structure, and dashed lines may be used to construct those diagrams. Such diagrams are a nice touch, but horizontal lines should be indicated with symbols different from dashes—for example, using the underline symbol.

Example—MIB header comments illustrating top-level nodes of a MIB

```
--
-- The objects defined in this MIB are located under the
-- private.enterprises subtree as shown below:
--
--
--
--   iso(1).org(3).dod(6).internet(1)
--                 |
--              private(4)
--                 |
--             enterprises(1)
--                 |
--          chateausystems(10910)
--                 |
--          _____ _|_____
--         |                            |
--   chateauExperimental(1)   chateauRegistrations(2)
--         |
```

Exercises

1. How are MIBs mapped to files?

2. What is wrong with the following syntax?

   IMPORTS vronx FROM vronxSmi.mib;

3. Name some of the types of definitions imported by MIB IMPORTS syntax.

Chapter 8

Node Definitions

Node is a term used in this book to describe an OID definition that is used to organize MIB objects into *logical categories*. Under a node, you may find yet more nodes, data objects, trap objects, or conformance statements. In the table to the right, objects defining nodes are shaded.

In the diagram below, two node definitions are shown as ovals. The top node, chateauCDProduct-MIB, is lexicographically superior to the next node, and is this MIB's top node.

The chateauCDProdControl node is defined for the organization of product control data objects beneath it. Under this node, a box contains three scalar data objects, whose name prefixes indicate their location under the *product control* node.

DEFINITIONS MY-MIB-NAME ::= BEGIN
IMPORTS syntax
MODULE-IDENTITY statement
TEXTUAL-CONVENTION definitions
Node definitions
Scalar Data Objects
Table Object
Entry Object
Table SEQUENCE statement
Table Data Objects
NOTIFICATION-TYPE Objects
OBJECT-GROUP lists
NOTIFICATION-GROUP lists
MODULE-COMPLIANCE grouping lists
END

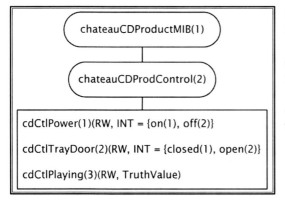

cdCtlPower is a read-write enumerated INTEGER that can be { on(1), off(2) }

cdCtlTrayDoor is a read-write enumerated INTEGER that can be { closed(1), open(2) }

cdCtlPlaying is a read-write TruthValue textual convention { true(1), false(2) }

MIB syntax provides for simple node definitions, as well as dual-purpose objects.

- MODULE-IDENTITY (SMIv2) defines a node and has multiple textual information clauses that provide useful information to the user
- OBJECT IDENTIFIER (SMIv1 and SMIv2) simple node definitions
- OBJECT-IDENTITY (SMIv2) simple node definitions
- *Table objects* and table *entry objects* (SMIv1 and SMIv2) are part of indexed table syntax, and also define nodes
- Node OID definitions can be IMPORTS'ed from other MIBs

MODULE-IDENTITY Syntax (SMIv2)

An SMIv2 MIB has exactly one MODULE-IDENTITY statement that must appear just after the IMPORTS statement.

It defines a single node, which is often the lexicographically top most node in this MIB (although other organizational models will be encountered).

It also provides important textual information about this MIB.

If an SMIv2 MIB is converted to SMIv1, MODULE-IDENTITY clauses are converted to comment lines (beginning with double dashes), and the node definition appears as an OBJECT IDENTIFIER statement.

Example syntax for MODULE-IDENTITY

```
chateauCDProductMIB  MODULE-IDENTITY
LAST-UPDATED     "200511090000Z"
ORGANIZATION     "Chateau Systems, Inc."
CONTACT-INFO
        "Customer Service email or 800# contact information."
DESCRIPTION
        "This MIB defines Nodes and Data Objects to support
        Chateau Systems CD Players.
        Copyright information and legal disclaimers are often included."
REVISION         "200511090000Z"
DESCRIPTION      "Third Release."
REVISION         "200501210000Z"
DESCRIPTION      "Second Release."
REVISION         "200412190000Z"
DESCRIPTION      "First Release."
::= { chateauCDProduct 1 }
```

chateauCDProductMIB is the top node defined in this MIB. Its parent node is chateauCD-Product. From the example in Chapter 7 describing IMPORTS, the definition of node chateauCDProduct is imported from:

CHATEAUSYSTEMS-REGISTRATIONS-MIB

The OID of chateauCDProductMIB will be the OID of chateauCDProduct **dot** 1, or:

chateauCDProduct.1

There are several Date-Time fields shown, all with format:

YYYYMMDDHHMMZ

For MIBs last revised prior to the year 2000, a shortened year field is acceptable:

YYMMDDHHMMZ

Single or multiple REVISION clauses may appear. Multiple REVISION clauses appear in reverse chronological order (the most recent first), and the most recent REVISION Date-Time should be identical to the LAST-UPDATED value.

> **MIB Diagnosis Hints**. Compilers may complain about aspects of Date-Time formats but will issue only warnings and will not inhibit MIB loading.
>
> Possible problems include:
> - Older compilers may not recognize the YYYY format.
> - Not all compilers check for valid field values. E.g. MM = 14 will slip by some.
> - REVISION clauses not in reverse chronological order.
> - Most recent REVISION and LAST-UPDATED values that are not equal.
> - Some really good compilers check current date and time against LAST-UPDATED and will complain about future dates!

OBJECT IDENTIFIER Syntax (SMIv1, SMIv2)

This syntax is valid for SMIv1 and SMIv2:

```
chateauCDProdConfig
  OBJECT IDENTIFIER
    ::= { chateauCDProductMIB 1 }
```

This defines the OID for node chateauCDProdConfig, whose parent is node chateauCDProductMIB.

The OID of chateauCDProdConfig is chateauCDProductMIB **dot** 1   or:

```
chateauCDProductMIB.1
```

Multiple descriptions (names) can be assigned to the same OBJECT IDENTIFIER value. *For example*:

```
mib     OBJECT IDENTIFIER ::=   { mgmt 1 }  -- from RFC-1156
mib-2   OBJECT IDENTIFIER ::=   { mgmt 1 }  -- from RFC-1213
```

OBJECT-IDENTITY Syntax (SMIv2)

Equivalent SMIv2-only syntax is:

```
chateauCDProdConfig OBJECT-IDENTITY
  STATUS current
   DESCRIPTION
    "CD Configuration Organizational node"
  ::= { chateauCDProductMIB 1 }
```

SMIv2 syntax adds a STATUS clause, an important addition. If this node becomes obsolete, you can change its status to obsolete, helping to ensure that the OID for this node is not reused for some other future purpose (which would be a registration rule violation).

A DESCRIPTION clause has also been added. This allows and encourages developers to add useful comments.

Multiple descriptions (names) *cannot* be assigned to the same OBJECT-IDENTITY value.

Table and Table Entry Objects

Two objects used to define indexed tables also define nodes—*Table objects* and table *entry objects*.

Example of indexed table syntax

```
cdChangerSlotTable OBJECT-TYPE              -- Table Object
    SYNTAX        SEQUENCE OF CdChangerSlotEntry
    MAX-ACCESS  not-accessible
    STATUS        current
    DESCRIPTION "CD Changer Slot Table."
    ::= { cdChangerStatus 2 }

cdChangerSlotEntry  OBJECT-TYPE              -- Entry Object
    SYNTAX        CdChangerSlotEntry
    MAX-ACCESS  not-accessible
    STATUS        current
    DESCRIPTION "An entry in cdChangerSlotTable."
    INDEX   { cdChangerSlotNbr }
    ::= { cdChangerSlotTable 1 }

CdChangerSlotEntry  ::=                      -- SEQUENCE statement
    SEQUENCE {
        cdChangerSlotNbr              Unsigned32,  -- INDEX
        cdChangerSlotStatus           INTEGER,
        cdChangerSlotCDTrackPlaying   Unsigned32,
        cdChangerCDNbrTracks          Unsigned32 }
```

Objects cdChangerSlotTable and cdChangerSlotEntry both define nodes. Detailed discussions of indexed table syntax are deferred to Chapter 13.

Exercises

1. What are MIB node definition objects used for?

2. Name the SMIv1 node objects.

3. Name the SMIv2 node objects.

Chapter 9

Data Object—Base Types

Elements of data object syntax, as well as specific descriptions of SMIv1 and SMIv2 base types, are discussed next.

Derived types (textual conventions, or TCs) will be described in Chapter 10.

Semantics are also discussed—intended uses of particular data types, and how managers are expected to process and display data.

Example MIB objects (from actual MIBs) are given for each base type. A secondary purpose of these examples is to familiarize readers with some commonly used standard MIBs. Network engineers will find this information useful in management of their networks, and developers will benefit from the concepts.

```
DEFINITIONS MY-MIB-NAME ::= BEGIN

IMPORTS syntax

MODULE-IDENTITY statement

TEXTUAL-CONVENTION definitions
Node definitions
```

Scalar Data Objects

```
Table Object
Entry Object
Table SEQUENCE statement
```

Table Data Objects

```
NOTIFICATION-TYPE Objects

OBJECT-GROUP lists
NOTIFICATION-GROUP lists
MODULE-COMPLIANCE grouping lists

END
```

MIB Diagnosis Hint. SMIv1 and SMIv2 data object syntax is similar, but subtly different. MIBs with mixed syntax are fairly common, and can be the cause of compiler complaints. Such problems are easily repaired.

For example, SMIv1 and SMIv2 both have a STATUS clause: two STATUS values are the same, one is comparable but has a different name, and SMIv1 has one STATUS value that SMIv2 does not.

Another example involves base type definitions: some types are shared, and SMIv2 introduced types that replace comparable SMIv1 types and others that are new.

Compilers look at the first few lines of a MIB to determine which syntax to judge it by. If syntax is mixed one compiler may decide it is an SMIv1 MIB, and another may decide it is SMIv2. Based on this decision, reported errors will vary.

Data Object Syntax

SMIv1 Syntax

Example of SMIv1 data object

```
cdEvCtlAgtPollFreq OBJECT-TYPE
    SYNTAX      INTEGER      -- SMIv1 and SMIv2 base type
    ACCESS      read-write   -- ACCESS is SMIv1 clue
    STATUS      mandatory    -- mandatory is SMIv1 clue
    DESCRIPTION
      "Agent polling frequency for Alarms in seconds"
    ::= { cdEventControl 1 }
```

The SYNTAX clause specifies the data type of the object. Types can be:
- SMIv1 base type
- Subtype defined within this MIB
- Subtype definition imported from a standard MIB
- Subtype definition imported from another enterprise MIB

ACCESS clause values for SMIv1 are:
- read-only
- read-write
- write-only (obsolete usage and not likely to be encountered)
- not-accessible, which applies only to indexed *table* and *entry objects*

STATUS clause values for SMIv1 can be:
- mandatory
- optional (rarely used)
- deprecated means that this object may still be supported by agents in limited circumstances. The DESCRIPTION clause should clarify usage
- obsolete is used for objects no longer supported. It is important that developers use this status value vs. editing the object out of the MIB, to ensure that this OID is not reused in the future

The DESCRIPTION clause contains textual information useful to network engineers. Any agent semantics should be described, and data nuances discussed. Good descriptions help set apart great MIBs from lesser MIBs.

> **MIB Diagnosis Hint.** When editing MIB objects (during development, or when repairing problem MIBs) a missing quote mark surrounding DESCRIPTION text will result in puzzling compiler errors usually reported many lines beyond the actual problem.

The notation:

        ::= { cdEventControl 1 }

identifies cdEventControl as the parent node for this object, and defines the OID for cdEvCtlAgtPollFreq to be equal to the OID for cdEventControl **dot** 1

    or   cdEventControl.1

SMIv2 Syntax

Example SMIv2 data object with required clauses

```
cdEvCtlAgtPollFreq OBJECT-TYPE
    SYNTAX        Unsigned32        -- SMIv2 base type
    MAX-ACCESS  read-write          -- MAX-ACCESS is SMIv2 clue
    STATUS        current           -- current is SMIv2 clue
    DESCRIPTION  "Agent polling frequency for Alarms in seconds"
    ::= { cdEventControl 1 }
```

Example SMIv2 data object showing optional clauses

```
cdEvCtlAgtPollFreq OBJECT-TYPE
    SYNTAX        Unsigned32
    UNITS         "seconds"
    MAX-ACCESS  read-write
    STATUS        current
    DESCRIPTION "Agent polling frequency for Alarms in seconds"
    REFERENCE    "Product Manual Section 2"
    DEFVAL {30}
    ::= { cdEventControl 1 }
```

The SYNTAX clause specifies the data type of the object.

- SMIv2 base type. SMIv1 and SMIv2 share some base types, some SMIv1 base types have equivalent SMIv2 counterparts, and new base types are defined by SMIv2
- Subtype defined within this MIB
- Subtype definition imported from a standard MIB, commonly from the MIB named SNMPv2-TC
- Subtype definition imported from another enterprise MIB

MAX-ACCESS clause values for SMIv2 are:

- read-only
- read-write
- not-accessible applies to indexed *table* and *entry objects* (as for SMIv1) and is also used to limit access to table index objects. Table index objects that are not-accessible cannot be viewed by managers, or be included in trap data objects.
  - Further discussions are in Chapters 13 and 19
- accessible-for-notify is used for data objects that is sent with traps but which cannot be read (*get, getnext, getbulk*) by managers
  - *Example*: object alarmSeverity is an enumerated integer that can have values { warning(2), minor(3), major(5) }
  - The value for this data object is sent with every trap, but is of no interest to a manager browsing the MIB for its current value
- read-create is for objects used in conjunction with the textual convention RowStatus to create new indexed table rows from a manager, and is discussed further in Chapter 15
- The value supplied with MAX-ACCESS is the maximum access permission.
  - Implementation considerations may not always allow maximum access. For example, read-write may be specified but a particular agent implementation may limit access to read-only

STATUS clause values for SMIv2 are:

- current (replaces SMIv1's mandatory value)
- deprecated
- obsolete

The DEFVAL clause is used to specify a default or initial value for read-write objects that is used in the absence of any user *set* value for this object.

SMIv1, SMIv2 Summary Tables

Summary of SMIv1 and SMIv2 data object clause requirements

CLAUSE example-value	SMIv1	SMIv2
SYNTAX INTEGER	required	required
UNITS "inches"		optional
ACCESS read-only	required	
MAX-ACCESS read-write		required
STATUS obsolete	required	required
DESCRIPTION "this description"	optional	required
REFERENCE "Reference Document"	optional	optional
DEFVAL { online }	optional	optional

Summary of MIB access clause values

ACCESS & MAX-ACCESS values	SMIv1	SMIv2
read-only	yes	yes
read-write	yes	yes
not-accessible	For table & entry objects	yes
accessible-for-notify		yes
read-create		yes
write-only	obsolete	

Summary of MIB status clause values

STATUS values	SMIv1	SMIv2
mandatory	yes	
current		yes
optional	yes (rarely used)	
deprecated	yes	yes
obsolete	yes	yes

Overview of Base Types

SMIv1 and SMIv2 syntax defines data *base types* and *derived types* (called *textual conventions*).

All base and derived types can be reduced to either of two kinds of data:
1. Integers
2. Hex strings of varying lengths (OCTET STRING)

   Hex string example:

   An object of type IpAddress can be assigned a value of:

   192.168.102.153

   which is represented as a hex value:

   0xC0:0xA8:0x66:0x99

Why does SNMP define so many base types and textual conventions if all are equivalent to integers and hex strings?

For a number of reasons:
  - ASN.1 (refer to Appendix D) is used to define MIB syntax. The *Abstract Syntax Notation (ASN.1)* has its own data types, and some of these are used to define MIB data types.
  - Rich data types in MIBs allow managers to display data appropriately. For example, a Gauge (based on an *integer*) might be displayed as a graphical gauge. Or a DisplayString (a textual convention based on OCTET STRING) will be displayed as text vs. hex values.
    - SMIv2 TEXTUAL-CONVENTION definitions have an optional DISPLAY-HINT clause which allows managers to display data as intended by the MIB designer.
  - This also allows agents and managers to apply semantics to data objects. For example:
    - A Gauge will clamp to defined min/max limits.
    - A Counter will always increment up and roll over at maximum value.
  - Finally, when you are reading a MIB, the data types convey semantic information.

Base Types List

SMIv1 and SMIv2 base type commonality and differences are summarized in this table.

Base Types	SMIv1	SMIv2
INTEGER	yes	yes
Integer32		yes
Unsigned32		yes
Gauge	yes	
Gauge32		yes
Counter	yes	
Counter32		yes
Counter64		yes
TimeTicks	yes	yes
OCTET STRING	yes	yes
OBJECT IDENTIFIER	yes	yes
IpAddress	yes	yes
NetworkAddress	yes	
Opaque	yes	yes
BITS		yes

Specifying Value Restrictions

Data range and size constraints can be optionally specified as part of the SYNTAX clause.

Example of value restriction for an unsigned integer

```
cdChangerNbrCdSlots   OBJECT-TYPE        -- SMIv2 Example
    SYNTAX        Unsigned32 (1..8)       -- valid values are 1 through 8
    MAX-ACCESS  read-only
    STATUS        current
    DESCRIPTION "Max number of CDs that can be loaded"
        ::= { cdChangerStatus 1 }
```

Specifying Size Restrictions

Example of size restriction for an OCTET STRING data type. In this SMIv2 example a fixed size of 2 octets is specified, but ranges can also be specified.

From RFC-4273 *Definitions of Managed Objects for BGP-4*   BGP4-MIB. (Border Gateway Protocol)

```
bgpPeerLastError OBJECT-TYPE
        SYNTAX        OCTET STRING (SIZE (2))
        MAX-ACCESS read-only
        STATUS        current
        DESCRIPTION
            "The last error code and subcode seen by this
            peer on this connection.  If no error has
            occurred, this field is zero.  Otherwise, the
            first byte of this two byte OCTET STRING
            contains the error code, and the second byte contains the
            subcode."
        REFERENCE
            "RFC-4271, Section 4.5."
        ::= { bgpPeerEntry 14 }
```

IMPORTS Requirements

MIBs need to IMPORTS the definition of the keyword OBJECT-TYPE, as well as the keywords for data types used in the MIB.

MIB Diagnosis Hint. IMPORTS problems are common. Definitions of keywords are *well known* to most compilers, and permissive compilers are forgiving about missing IMPORTS. Other compilers are more rigorous. These problems are easily repaired by editing the required IMPORTS.

The OBJECT-TYPE keyword needs to be imported for use in defining data objects.

```
IMPORTS                              -- SMIv1
    OBJECT-TYPE FROM RFC-1212;
IMPORTS                              -- SMIv2
    OBJECT-TYPE FROM SNMPV2-SMI;
```

SMIv1 MIBs import keywords for SMIv1 base data types used to define objects, but do not need to import the following three types:

INTEGER, OCTET STRING, OBJECT IDENTIFIER

Example that IMPORTS all needed SMIv1 base types

```
IMPORTS    -- SMIv1 base type keywords
    Gauge, Counter, TimeTicks, IpAddress, NetworkAddress, Opaque
        FROM RFC1155-SMI;          -- MIB defined in RFC-1155
```

SMIv2 MIBs import keywords for SMIv2 base data types used to define objects, but do not need to import the following four types:

INTEGER, OCTET STRING, OBJECT IDENTIFIER, BITS

Example that IMPORTS all needed SMIv2 base types

```
IMPORTS    -- SMIv2 base type keywords
    Integer32, Unsigned32, Gauge32, Counter32, Counter64,
    TimeTicks, IpAddress, Opaque
        FROM SNMPv2-SMI;          -- MIB defined in RFC-2678
```

Some enterprise MIBs present a third case, usually by vendors that supply SMIv1 and SMIv2 versions of the same MIB. Some vendors will convert SMIv2 base types (e.g., Integer32) to SMIv1 base types (e.g., INTEGER). However, others create a MIB file that defines SMIv2 data type keywords (e.g., Integer32) as a textual convention equivalent (e.g., to INTEGER), and this file is IMPORTS'ed by the SMIv1 MIB. This allows the SMIv1 MIB to use the *same data type keyword names* as the SMIv2 MIB.

Example

```
IMPORTS    -- SMIv2 base type keywords to be used in this SMIv1 MIB
    Integer32, Unsigned32, Gauge32, Counter32
        FROM SNMPv2-SMI-v1;  -- Enterprise created MIB
```

MIB Diagnosis Hint. You compile an enterprise MIB into your manager, which reports an error that the SNMPv2-SMI-v1 MIB needed for IMPORTS is missing. The name of the MIB looks *very official*, but you cannot find it in the RFCs. In fact, the MIB is usually defined by the same enterprise vendor that supplied the primary MIB. Enterprises will have their own versions of this MIB (and MIB names may vary).

Integrated IMPORTS Examples

SMIv1 Example

```
IMPORTS
    OBJECT-TYPE FROM RFC-1212;

IMPORTS   -- SMIv1 base type keywords
    Gauge, Counter, TimeTicks, IpAddress, NetworkAddress, Opaque
        FROM RFC1155-SMI;
```

SMIv2 Example

```
IMPORTS   -- SMIv12
    OBJECT-TYPE FROM SNMPV2-SMI;

IMPORTS   -- SMIv2 base type keywords
    Integer32, Unsigned32, Gauge32, Counter32, Counter64,
    TimeTicks, IpAddress, Opaque
        FROM SNMPv2-SMI;   -- MIB defined in RFC-2678
```

Base Type Details

INTEGER (SMIv1, SMIv2)

SMIv1 INTEGER objects are used to express signed, unsigned, and enumerated integers.

The range of an INTEGER is (-2147483648. . . 2147483647)

SMIv2 INTEGER objects are generally used to express only enumerated integers, and the new types Integer32 and Unsigned32 are used for signed and unsigned integers.

> **MIB Diagnosis Hint.** In an SMIv2 MIB, if an INTEGER is used without a range restriction validation compilers will flag errors but only warnings. The MIB is still safe to use. Range restrictions can be stated in two ways:
>
> INTEGER (1..5)
> INTEGER { okay(1), warning(2), majorFailure(5) }

Example of enumerated integer syntax from the RFC-1230 SMIv1 IEEE 802.4 Token Bus MIB

```
dot4State OBJECT-TYPE    -- SMIv1 Example
SYNTAX  INTEGER { other(1),
                  offline(2),
                  outOfRing(3),
                  enteringRing(4),
                  inRing(5) }
ACCESS  read-only
STATUS  mandatory
DESCRIPTION    "The current state of the 802.4  interface.  The value of
               other(1) is used if the state is unknown
               (e.g., due to an error condition)."
::=  { dot4Entry 3 }
```

MIB Naming Rules. SMIv1 and SMIv2 INTEGER enumerated value naming rules are somewhat different. The suggestions here will satisfy most compilers and facilitate conversion between SMIv1 and SMIv2 syntax. An enumerated value name must begin with a lower case letter, can contain numbers, should avoid hyphens and underscores, and must not exceed 64 characters. Names with fewer than 24 characters are recommended. Enumeration names within an INTEGER object definition must be unique, but MIB-wide uniqueness is not a requirement.

Enumerated values should be positive. SMIv1 values must be; SMIv2 values need not be, but should be to facilitate syntax conversion. Some compilers do not handle negative enumerations well. Values need not be consecutive.

MIB Diagnosis Hint. Negative enumerations are illegal in SMIv1, but will be accepted by some compilers—this can cause unexpected trouble. For example, a *trap* arrives with data value enumeration < 0. Some managers may interpret the value in the trap as a very large positive number and fail to match it to its equivalent textual definition for proper display and for trap filter value matching.

MIB Style Hint. The enumerated value "1" (one) commonly represents the *true, okay, enabled,* or *normal* condition. This is consistent with the TruthValue textual convention.

Another example of enumerated integer syntax from the RFC-1213, from the *snmp group* of data objects, followed by additional discussion

```
snmpEnableAuthenTraps OBJECT-TYPE
        SYNTAX  INTEGER { enabled(1), disabled(2) }
        ACCESS  read-write
        STATUS  mandatory
        DESCRIPTION
                "Indicates whether the SNMP agent process is
                permitted to generate authentication-failure
                traps.  The value of this object overrides any
                configuration information; as such, it provides a
                means whereby all authentication-failure traps may
                be disabled.
                 Note that it is strongly recommended that this
                object be stored in non-volatile memory so that it
                remains constant between re-initializations of the
                network management system."
        ::= { snmp 30 }
```

SNMP Tidbit. RFC1213-MIB contains an *snmp group* of objects that report on SNMP agent behavior. One object, snmpEnableAuthenTraps, is shown above. If set to enabled(1), any attempt by a manager to *get* or *set* data from/to this agent with an invalid SNMPv1 or SNMPv2c community string will cause the agent to send an authenticationFailure trap (one of the six generic traps) to its targeted managers.

You may recognize this object as one commonly configured directly in the agent (via GUI or a file read at startup), but it can also be configured by a *set* of a value to this MIB object.

Integer32 (SMIv2)

Defined as INTEGER (-2147483648 . . . 2147483647)

> *Example* from RFC-3805 Printer MIB v2. Note that the Integer32 type with zero to positive value limits was used for the SYNTAX.

```
prtConsoleNumberOfDisplayLines OBJECT-TYPE
    SYNTAX          Integer32 (0..65535)
    MAX-ACCESS  read-only
    STATUS          current
    DESCRIPTION
        "The number of lines on the printer's physical
        display.  This value is 0 if there are no lines on the
        physical display or if there is no physical display"
    ::= { prtGeneralEntry 11 }
```

Unsigned32 (SMIv2)

Defined as INTEGER (0 . . . 4294967295)

> *Example* from the CD-player MIB

```
cdChStPowerOnHours   OBJECT-TYPE    -- SMIv2 Example
    SYNTAX          Unsigned32
    MAX-ACCESS  read-only
    STATUS          current
    DESCRIPTION
        "The total number of hours that this CD Player
        has been powered on in its lifetime."
    ::= { cdChassisStatus 1 }
```

Gauge (SMIv1) and Gauge32 (SMIv2)

A Gauge or Gauge32 is a unsigned 32-bit integer. It is often specified with range restrictions, and actual data is clamped to those (min, max) values.

They are used for modeling objects whose values rise and fall within well known limits. *For example*: CPU loading (0–100%), speed (0–300 mph), fuel level (0–35 liters).

Example of Gauge32 from RFC-2790 HOST-RESOURCES-MIB

```
hrSystemProcesses OBJECT-TYPE   -- SMIv2 Example
      SYNTAX        Gauge32
      MAX-ACCESS    read-only
      STATUS        current
      DESCRIPTION
        "The number of process contexts currently loaded or
        running on this system."
      ::= { hrSystem 6 }
```

Counter (SMIv1) and Counter32 (SMIv2)

Counter and Counter32 are unsigned 32-bit integers that count up. They behave as modulo-32 counters which roll over at the maximum value and start counting at zero again.

MIB Diagnosis Hint: The DEFVAL clause is not valid for counter data objects.

An example of Counter from RFC-1213, from the *snmp group* of objects, followed by additional discussion

```
snmpInBadCommunityNames OBJECT-TYPE
      SYNTAX    Counter
      ACCESS    read-only
      STATUS    mandatory
      DESCRIPTION
          "The total number of SNMP Messages delivered to
          the SNMP protocol entity which used an SNMP
          community name not known to said entity."
      ::= { snmp 4 }
```

SNMP Tidbit. RFC1213-MIB contains an *snmp group* of objects that report on SNMP agent behavior. One object, snmpInBadCommunityNames, is shown above. Other objects include:

    snmpInSetRequests
    snmpOutNoSuchNames
    snmpInPkts

These statistics can be useful to network engineers setting up and debugging SNMP networks.

Counter64 (SMIv2)

Counter64 is an unsigned 64-bit integer that counts up. It behaves as a modulo-64 counter, rolls over at the maximum value, and starts counting at zero again. The Counter64 data type was introduced for applications (such as high-speed communications links) where 32-bit counters roll over too quickly. Range is INTEGER (0..18446744073709551615)

Counter64 objects cannot be converted to SMIv1, and cannot be transported using the SNMPv1 protocol. They are transportable by SNMPv2c and SNMPv3 messages.

MIB Diagnosis Hint. The DEFVAL clause is not valid for Counter64.

MIB Design Hint. Use 64-bit counters when necessary, but avoid them if not. Realize that data values can only be transported using SNMPv2c messages and SNMPv3 messages. However, a particular manager tool used by your customers may only speak SNMPv1 messages. For those customers, add a pair of 32-bit counters with equivalent functionality (high-order, low-order counters).

Example of Counter64 from RFC-2863 IF-MIB

```
-- High Capacity Counter objects.  These objects are all 64 bit versions of
-- the "basic" ifTable counters, and have the same basic semantics as
-- their 32-bit counterparts, with syntax extended to 64 bits.
ifHCInOctets OBJECT-TYPE              -- SMIv2 Example
 SYNTAX        Counter64
 MAX-ACCESS    read-only
 STATUS        current
 DESCRIPTION  "The total number of octets received on the interface,
      including framing characters.  This object is a 64-bit
      version of ifInOctets. Discontinuities in the value of this counter can
      occur at re-initialization of the management system, and at other
      times as indicated by the value of ifCounterDiscontinuityTime."
 ::= { ifXEntry 6 }
```

Trending Data for Counters

Counters are commonly used for trending *rates*. For example, the total number of parity errors is not particularly interesting, but the value of *parity errors per second* is.

Managers can be configured for trend reports, the polling for and logging of data over extended time intervals. If a Counter, Counter32, or Counter64 is trended, the manager will usually trend a rate rather than the counter values themselves. For example:

> A manager polls a counter object for parity errors every 50 seconds:
> - At T=1000 seconds, counter value = 2015
> - At T=1050 seconds, counter value = 5034
> - For the given sample period, the trend graph will record a data value change normalized to seconds:
>   = (5034 − 2015) / 50 seconds = 60 parity errors/second

A graphical illustration—if you trend the same parity error data as both Unsigned32 and as Counter32, the two trend reports would appear as shown below (where Total Parity Errors is for the Unsigned32 object, and Parity Errors per Second is for the Counter32 object):

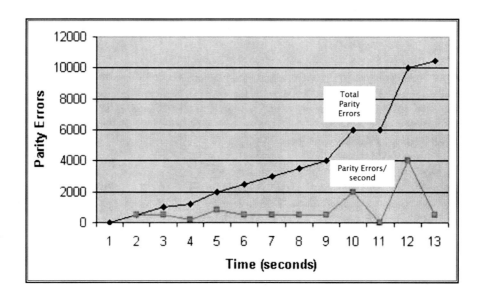

Counter Discontinuities

If counter objects are used in MIBs, care should be taken (by MIB designers and by manager logic) to handle discontinuities.

If a counter rolls over, manager polling logic should detect that the most current sampled value is less than the prior value, and calculate the true difference.

However, if counters roll over too quickly, managers may not be able to easily detect rollovers. In this case the MIB designer needs to use Counter64 objects, or high-low pairs of 32-bit counters.

Counter discontinuities may also occur because the status of the monitored device (e.g., an interface) has substantially changed (gone off-line, disappeared, etc.). In these cases the MIB should be designed with an object which, when read, notifies managers of the discontinuity.

> *Example* of a MIB object that signals a counter discontinuity event, from RFC-2863 *The Interfaces Group MIB* IF-MIB

```
ifCounterDiscontinuityTime OBJECT-TYPE
    SYNTAX       TimeStamp
    MAX-ACCESS  read-only
    STATUS       current
    DESCRIPTION
        "The value of sysUpTime on the most recent occasion at which
        any one or more of this interface's counters suffered a
        discontinuity.  The relevant counters are the specific
        instances associated with this interface of any Counter32 or
        Counter64 object contained in the ifTable or ifXTable.  If
        no such discontinuities have occurred since the last re-
        initialization of the local management subsystem, then this
        object contains a zero value."
    ::= { ifXEntry 19 }
```

The previous Counter64 example was for the ifHCInOctets object, and the DESCRIPTION field for that object discusses the use of the example just above to indicate reinitialization occurrences of the counter.

TimeTicks (SMIv1, SMIv2)

The TimeTicks data type is an unsigned 32-bit integer that rolls over at its maximum value. Each *tick* represents a hundredth of a second. The length of time between rollovers is about 497 days.

Example of TimeTicks *from RFC-1213 Management Information Base for Network Management of TCP/IP-based internets:MIB-II*   RFC1213-MIB

```
sysUpTime OBJECT-TYPE    -- SMIv1 Example
    SYNTAX   TimeTicks
    ACCESS   read-only
    STATUS   mandatory
    DESCRIPTION
        "The time (in hundredths of a second) since the
        network management portion of the system was last re-initialized."
    ::= { system 3 }
```

OCTET STRING (SMIv1, SMIv2)

The OCTET STRING type is used to specify octets (8 bits) of binary information and textual information. There are several textual convention definitions based on OCTET STRING.

SMIv2 specifies a size limit of 65535 octets, but also warns that sizes greater than 255 may encounter problems (agents and managers may not have large enough buffers to transport values longer than 255 octets).

The SIZE clause can be used to restrict the number of octets of an object.

Examples of OCTET STRING SIZE *limitations*

```
OCTET STRING (SIZE(0..255)      -- zero to 255 octets
OCTET STRING (SIZE(8))          -- exactly 8 octets
OCTET STRING (SIZE(8|11))       -- exactly 8 or exactly 11 octets
                                -- used by the DateAndTime
                                -- textual convention
```

Example of OCTET STRING from RFC-2790 HOST-RESOURCES-MIB

```
hrPartitionID OBJECT-TYPE        -- SMIv2 Example
    SYNTAX          OCTET STRING
    MAX-ACCESS      read-only
    STATUS          current
    DESCRIPTION
        "A descriptor which uniquely represents this partition
        to the responsible operating system.  On some systems,
        this might take on a binary representation."
    ::= { hrPartitionEntry 3 }
```

OBJECT IDENTIFIER (SMIv1, SMIv2)

This type defines MIB objects of type OID. Typical uses are:

- Pointer to another MIB object. The standard Entity MIB has examples of this.
- Pointer to a table row.
- Globally unique enumeration definition. Similar to enumerated INTEGER use, but universally unique.

OID

1.3.6.1.2.1.1.1

Example of OBJECT IDENTIFIER from RFC-1213 RFC1213-MIB, an entry in the system table. The value assigned to this object uniquely defines the type of equipment being managed. Managers poll for this value and use it to select an icon representing this object in its device map.

```
sysObjectID OBJECT-TYPE          -- SMIv1 Example
        SYNTAX      OBJECT IDENTIFIER
        ACCESS      read-only
        STATUS      mandatory
        DESCRIPTION
            "The vendor's authoritative identification of the
            network management subsystem contained in the
            entity.  This value is allocated within the SMI
            enterprises subtree (1.3.6.1.4.1) and provides an
            easy and unambiguous means for determining `what
            kind of box' is being managed.  For example, if
            vendor `Flintstones, Inc.' was assigned the
            subtree 1.3.6.1.4.1.4242, it could assign the
            identifier 1.3.6.1.4.1.4242.1.1 to its `Fred Router'."
        ::= { system 2 }
```

> **SNMP Tidbit.** The SMIv2 standard textual convention TDomain is another example of using OID types for enumerations. See Chapter 10.
>
> **SNMP Tidbit.** There are two SMIv2 TCs that use the OID type to define pointers: RowPointer and VariablePointer. See Chapter 10.

NetworkAddress (SMIv1)

NetworkAddress specifies a string of four octets. Its use is discouraged, and for many uses the base type IpAddress is preferred. The full discussion of available network address types and subtypes appears in Chapter 10.

There are subtle issues if NetworkAddress is used as an SMIv1 table INDEX, and the MIB is converted to SMIv2. This issue is discussed in Chapter 14.

> *Example* of NetworkAddress from RFC-1213 RFC1213-MIB, which is used as a secondary INDEX for the Address Translation Table

```
atNetAddress OBJECT-TYPE      -- SMIv1 Example
        SYNTAX  NetworkAddress
        ACCESS  read-write
        STATUS  deprecated       -- NOTE deprecated use of this object
        DESCRIPTION "The NetworkAddress (e.g., the IP address)
             corresponding to the media-dependent `physical' address."
        ::= { atEntry 3 }
```

IpAddress (SMIv1, SMIv2)

This type specifies an IP address as four octets encoded in network byte order.

> *Example* of IpAddress from RFC-1213 RFC1213-MIB, which is used as the INDEX in the IP address Table

```
ipAdEntAddr OBJECT-TYPE    -- SMIv1 Example
        SYNTAX  IpAddress
        ACCESS  read-only
        STATUS  mandatory
        DESCRIPTION "The IP address to which this entry's addressing
             information pertains."
        ::= { ipAddrEntry 1 }
```

RFC-4181 *Guidelines for Authors and Reviewers of MIB Documents* states that the IpAddress type should not be used in new MIB modules. The InetAddress and InetAddressType textual conventions defined in RFC-4001 should be used instead. These, and other network address related textual conventions are discussed in Chapter 10.

Opaque (SMIv1, SMIv2)

The Opaque type is equivalent to OCTET STRING and encodes arbitrary binary information. SMIv2 sets a limit of 65535 bytes, but warns about possible manager–agent compatibility issues if the size exceeds 255 octets.

It is rarely used, but can find usefulness when the manager and agents are both designed and used by the same enterprise.

Example of Opaque type adapted from an enterprise MIB

```
rcf400fpu    OBJECT-TYPE    -- SMIv1 Example
    SYNTAX       Opaque
    ACCESS       read-only
    STATUS       mandatory
    DESCRIPTION "Encoding is documented in VRONX PUB 1504, which describes
            product cards and ports in the VRONX Ruxer product."
    :: = { vronxRuxerConfig 13 }
```

BITS (SMIv2)

The BITS type is based on OCTET STRING, and is used for collections of labeled bits. BITS are numbered starting with zero and must be contiguous. SMIv2 warns of compatibility problems for sizes greater than 255 bits.

MIB Naming Rules. A BITS object bit label can have 1 to 64 letters and numbers, must begin with a lower-case letter, and cannot contain hyphens or underscores. Labels for individual bits in a BITS object must be unique. Bit labels in different BITS objects need not be unique.

Example of BITS from the SONET-MIB defined in RFC-2558 *Definitions of Managed Objects for the SONET/SDH Interface Type*

```
sonetMediumLoopbackConfig OBJECT-TYPE  -- SMIv2 Example
   SYNTAX      BITS { sonetNoLoop(0),
                      sonetFacilityLoop(1),
                      sonetTerminalLoop(2),
                      sonetOtherLoop(3) }
   MAX-ACCESS  read-write
   STATUS      current
   DESCRIPTION "The current loopback state of the SONET/SDH interface.
      The values mean:
      sonetNoLoop
              Not in the loopback state. A device that is not
              capable of performing a loopback on this interface
              shall always return this value.
      sonetFacilityLoop
              The received signal at this interface is looped back out
              through the corresponding transmitter in the return direction.
      sonetTerminalLoop
              The signal that is about to be transmitted is connected
              to the associated incoming receiver.
      sonetOtherLoop
              Loopbacks that are not defined here."
   ::= { sonetMediumEntry 8 }
```

Floating-Point Numbers

Neither SMIv1 nor SMIv2 supports a floating-point data type. However, there are work-around examples.

Create an object typed as DisplayString, and communicate all floating-point values as readable text. Clever managers can decode this DisplayString value for use in arithmetic expressions (e.g., to build a custom table, or for trend reports).

Define an object typed as Integer32 or Unsigned32, and use the UNITS clause to specify decimal point information. *For example*:

    UNITS "microamps"

Some MIBs define floating-point information in two objects, as a DisplayString and as a scaled Integer32, in an attempt to accommodate varying user needs and managers.

Encode the floating-point object as an Opaque type. Managers will need custom scripting to decode and use these values. A UC Davis MIB provides an example of such a textual convention definition.

Example of textual convention definition of a floating-point type from UCD-SNMP-MIB. This is an example of the use of the Opaque data type to create a subtype.

```
-- Define the Float Textual Convention
--   This definition was written by David Perkins.

Float ::= TEXTUAL-CONVENTION is
    STATUS      current
    DESCRIPTION
        "A single precision floating-point number.  The semantics
        and encoding are identical for type 'single' defined in
        IEEE Standard for Binary Floating-Point, ANSI/IEEE Std 754-1985.
        The value is restricted to the BER serialization of the following ASN.1 type:
            FLOATTYPE ::= [120] IMPLICIT FloatType
        (note: the value 120 is the sum of '30'h and '48'h)
        The BER serialization of the length for values of
        this type must use the definite length, short encoding form.
        For example, the BER serialization of value 123
        of type FLOATTYPE is '9f780442f60000'h.  (The tag
        is '9f78'h; the length is '04'h; and the value is
        '42f60000'h.) The BER serialization of value
        '9f780442f60000'h of data type Opaque is
        '44079f780442f60000'h. (The tag is '44'h; the length
        is '07'h; and the value is '9f780442f60000'h."
    SYNTAX Opaque (SIZE (7))
```

Exercises

1. Name a common cause of MIB compiler complaints.

2. MIB data object syntax includes a SYNTAX clause. What information follows the keyword SYNTAX?

3. Explain how the MAX-ACCESS accessible-for-notify value is used, and how it differs from other possible access values.

4. What are the two very general types of MIB data that all base and derived data types can be reduced to?

5. MIB syntax allows restriction of data base type *sizes* and *values*. Explain the difference between the two.

6. Which SMIv2 base type cannot be transported in SNMPv1 messages?

7. Are there any SMIv1 or SMIv2 base types that cannot be transported in SNMPv3 messages?

8. The DEFVAL clause is not appropriate for which base data types?

9. The mib-2 system table includes the data object sysObjectId. What is its data type, and what is this object used for (by managers)?

10. Neither SMIv1 nor SMIv2 syntax defines a floating-point number base type. What options does a MIB developer have to represent floating-point values?

Chapter 10

Data Object—Derived Types

Derived data types (textual conventions) are used in the SYNTAX clause of data objects, just as are base types.

SMIv2 formalizes the concept of derived data types—the definition of a new type based on a base type. This formalization uses the new TEXTUAL-CONVENTION syntax.

SMIv1 also provides for definition of subtypes using a less formal notation.

Textual conventions (TCs) define a new type based on a base type:
- With a new type name that is descriptive of its specific purpose.
- Often with data size or value restrictions.
- And may have detailed semantics (agent behavior in managing this object), discussed in the DESCRIPTION clause.

```
DEFINITIONS MY-MIB-NAME ::= BEGIN

IMPORTS syntax

MODULE-IDENTITY statement
─────────────────────────────────
TEXTUAL-CONVENTION definitions
Node definitions
─────────────────────────────────
Scalar Data Objects

Table Object
Entry Object
Table SEQUENCE statement
─────────────────────────────────
Table Data Objects

NOTIFICATION-TYPE Objects

OBJECT-GROUP lists
NOTIFICATION-GROUP lists
MODULE-COMPLIANCE grouping lists

END
```

Textual conventions can be defined in:
- The MIB in which they are used. There are examples of this in standard MIBs and in enterprise MIBs.
- MIBs outside of the MIB in which they are used. Such definitions must be imported using the IMPORTS statement.
  - There are standard TCs, such as those contained in the SNMPv2-TC MIB defined by RFC-2579.
  - Enterprises often define TCs intended for common use by all of an organization's MIBs.

Example MIB objects (from actual MIBs) are given for each standard textual convention discussed. A secondary purpose of these examples is to familiarize the reader with some commonly used standard MIBs.

TEXTUAL-CONVENTION Syntax

This is the syntax used by SMIv2 to define data subtypes.

Example of a standard textual convention defined by RFC-2579 in the SNMPv2-TC MIB. DisplayString can be used in a data object SYNTAX clause to specify *data type*. Note the DISPLAY-HINT provided.

```
DisplayString ::= TEXTUAL-CONVENTION
   DISPLAY-HINT "255a"
   STATUS          current
   DESCRIPTION
      "The value must conform to the NVT
      ASCII character set which consists of
      the 7-bit ASCII displayable characters
      and a few control characters as defined
      in RFC-854."
   SYNTAX  OCTET STRING (SIZE (0..255))
```

Example of an enterprise SMIv2 textual convention definition. ChateauTrapControl can be used in a data object SYNTAX clause to specify *data type*.

```
ChateauTrapControl ::= TEXTUAL-CONVENTION
   STATUS    current
   DESCRIPTION
      "Used to enable or disable specific Traps."
   SYNTAX    INTEGER
         {
            trapEnable(1),
            trapDisable(2)
         }
```

Syntax for equivalent SMIv1 definitions

```
DisplayString ::= OCTET STRING (SIZE(0..255))

ChateauTrapControl ::= INTEGER
            {
                trapEnable(1),
                trapDisable(2)
            }
```

SMIv2 TEXTUAL-CONVENTION general case syntax (showing optional clauses)

```
ucName "::=" "TEXTUAL-CONVENTION"
    ["DISPLAY-HINT" chrStr]
    "STATUS" <statusV2>
    "DESCRIPTION" chrStr
    ["REFERENCE" chrStr]
    "SYNTAX" <syntaxDescr>
```

If a MIB uses the TEXTUAL-CONVENTION construct, it must contain the following IMPORTS

```
IMPORTS
        TEXTUAL-CONVENTION
            FROM SNMPv2-TC;
```

DISPLAY-HINT Clause Brief Discussion

RFC-2579 *Textual Conventions for SMIv2* discusses syntax for display hints over several pages. It's fairly tedious, and the RFC is a good reference for the exceptional individual seeking more detail.

Example of DISPLAY-HINT from RFC-2579 is repeated here

```
Hundredths ::= TEXTUAL-CONVENTION
    DISPLAY-HINT "d-2"
    ...
    SYNTAX     INTEGER (0..10000)

-- suggests that a Hundredths value of 1234 be rendered as "12.34"
```

The DisplayString TC definition shown previously also provides a DISPLAY-HINT clause example.

When the SMIv2 standard TC for DateAndTime is discussed, yet another example of a DISPLAY-HINT is shown.

TEXTUAL-CONVENTION and Base Types

A strict reading of RFC-2578 supports the rule that any new SMIv2 TEXTUAL-CONVENTION definition should be based on an SMIv2 base type and not on another textual convention definition. There has been some controversy on this topic—many compilers follow this rule, but others do not.

MIB Diagnosis Hint. If you encounter a MIB with this problem, you can edit the TC definition to be based on a base type. The following example may be useful.

Example of problem subtyping of a textual convention—basing a TC on a previously defined TC

```
ChateauProductID ::= TEXTUAL-CONVENTION
    STATUS    current
    DESCRIPTION
       "Specifies unique Chateau Systems Product Identifier as text."
    SYNTAX    DisplayString (SIZE(8))    -- Cannot base TC definition on a TC!
```

Equivalent legal textual convention definition—based on a base type. This is the same as the DisplayString TC definition, but with a different SIZE restriction.

```
ChateauProductID ::= TEXTUAL-CONVENTION
    DISPLAY-HINT "255a"  -- Note same display hint as for DisplayString
    STATUS          current
    DESCRIPTION
            "Specifies unique Chateau Systems Product Identifier as text."
    SYNTAX  OCTET STRING (SIZE (8))
```

SNMPv2-TC Standard Textual Conventions

Standard *Textual Conventions for SMIv2* are defined in RFC-2579 in the SNMPv2-TC MIB. Use of these TCs is very common in standard and enterprise MIBs.

The rest of this chapter discusses details of these definitions.

TruthValue	RowStatus	PhysAddress
TimeStamp	DisplayString	MacAddress
TimeInterval	DateAndTime	AutonomousType
StorageType	VariablePointer	TDomain
TestAndIncr	RowPointer	TAddress

Additional (to the right) network address-related textual convention definitions defined outside of SNMPv2-TC will also be discussed. These are available as options to the IpAddress base type as well as to the TDomain and TAddress SNMPv2-TC definitions.

Deciding which is most appropriate requires some study on the part of developers.

InetAddressType
InetAddress
TransportDomain
TransportAddressType
TransportAddress

IMPORTS Requirements

Any of these definitions used in a MIB must appear in an IMPORTS statement.

> **MIB Diagnosis Hint.** These TC definitions are *well known,* and a permissive compiler may process a MIB lacking needed IMPORTS without errors. More restrictive compilers will balk without the proper IMPORTS—this problem is easily repaired by adding the required IMPORTS information.

Example SMIv2 IMPORTS statement

```
IMPORTS                -- need to import subtypes used
    DisplayString, TruthValue, DateAndTime
        FROM SNMPv2-TC;
```

Example of equivalent SMIv1 IMPORTS statement

```
IMPORTS                  -- need to import subtypes used
    DisplayString, TruthValue, DateAndTime
        FROM SNMPv2-TC-v1-MIB;
```

MIB Diagnosis Hint. The MIB SNMPv2-TC-v1-MIB looks *official* (i.e., like a standard MIB) but is usually supplied by the enterprise supplying the importing MIB. This file can be created by:

- ○ Passing MIB SNMPv2-TC through an SMIv2-to-SMIv1 conversion tool
- ○ Hand editing
- ○ Obtaining it from various enterprise MIB vendors

TruthValue

TruthValue defines an enumerated Boolean type with values:

INTEGER { true(1), false(2) }

Example of TruthValue—with decent agent semantics description

```
cdCtlPlaying   OBJECT-TYPE
    SYNTAX        TruthValue
    MAX-ACCESS  read-write
    STATUS        current
    DESCRIPTION
        "CD Player 'play' status.
        Can be modified by the user.
        If cdCtlPower = off
        OR cdCtlTrayDoor = open,
        then the user cannot modify this value."
    ::= { chateauCDProdControl 3 }
```

Note that true is equal to 1. MIB INTEGER enumerations commonly use the value "1" to describe *okay, enabled,* or *normal* states or conditions.

TimeStamp

TimeStamp resolves to TimeTicks in hundredths of a second, and is a snapshot of the value of mib-2's sysUpTime object when a particular event occurred.

Example of TimeStamp from the DS1-MIB defined in RFC-3895

```
dsx1LineStatusLastChange OBJECT-TYPE
    SYNTAX          TimeStamp
    MAX-ACCESS      read-only
    STATUS          current
    DESCRIPTION
        "The value of MIB II's sysUpTime object at the
        time this DS1 entered its current line status
        state.  If the current state was entered prior to
        the last re-initialization of the proxy-agent,
        then this object contains a zero value."
    ::= { dsx1ConfigEntry 16 }
```

TimeInterval

TimeInterval is an integer in hundredths of a second.

Example of TimeInterval from RFC-2789 *Mail Monitoring MIB* MTA-MIB

```
mtaGroupLastInboundActivity OBJECT-TYPE
    SYNTAX          TimeInterval
    MAX-ACCESS      read-only
    STATUS          current
    DESCRIPTION
        "Time since the last time that this group had an active
        inbound association for purposes of message reception."
    ::= {mtaGroupEntry 17}
```

StorageType

StorageType is used with manager row-create logic, discussed in Chapter 15. Very briefly, for some objects, managers can add a row of values to an indexed table (where the columns identify the objects). StorageType allows the manager to *set* a value that specifies how the new table row is to be stored in memory by the agent.

StorageType resolves to an enumerated INTEGER, and takes values:

```
INTEGER
{
        other(1),
        volatile(2),
        nonvolatile(3),
        permanent(4),
        readOnly(5)
}
```

Example of StorageType from RFC-3414 *User-based Security Model (USM) for version 3 of the Simple Network Management Protocol (SNMPv3).* SNMP-USER-BASED-SM-MIB is defined in this RFC, and this example is an entry in the row-create table usmUserTable, which lists all users that are allowed access to this platform. Note: the DESCRIPTION has been truncated.

```
usmUserStorageType OBJECT-TYPE
    SYNTAX      StorageType
    MAX-ACCESS  read-create
    STATUS      current
    DESCRIPTION "The storage type for this conceptual row.
            Conceptual rows having the value 'permanent' must
            allow write-access at a minimum to: . . .

            . . .

            It is an implementation issue to decide if a SET for
            a readOnly or permanent row is accepted at all. In some
            contexts this may make sense, in others it may not. If
            a SET for a readOnly or permanent row is not accepted
            at all, then a 'wrongValue' error must be returned."
    DEFVAL     { nonVolatile }
    ::= { usmUserEntry 12 }
```

TestAndIncr

TestAndIncr resolves to an integer >= 0, and is used by agents for logic managing simultaneous write access to MIB objects from multiple managers.

From a software viewpoint, it functions similarly to a semaphore.

When a manager attempts to *set* an integer value to this object, if the value to be *set* is the same as the existing value, the operation succeeds and the existing value is then incremented. If the value to be *set* is different from the existing value, the *set* operation fails and an *error = inconsistentValue* is returned to the manager.

The value of the MAX-ACCESS clause for this object should be read-write or read-create.

> *Example* of TestAndIncr from the same SNMPv3 MIB shown previously in the StorageType example. *Command Generator Application* is SNMPv3 terminology for a *manager.*

```
usmUserSpinLock  OBJECT-TYPE
    SYNTAX        TestAndIncr
    MAX-ACCESS  read-write
    STATUS        current
    DESCRIPTION "An advisory lock used to allow several cooperating
                Command Generator Applications to coordinate their
                use of facilities to alter secrets in the
                usmUserTable."
    ::= { usmUser 1 }
```

RowStatus

RowStatus is also used with manager row-create logic (Chapter 15). It resolves to an enumerated INTEGER. RowStatus values are:

```
INTEGER
{
    -- the following two values are states: values which may be read or written
        active(1), notInService(2),
    -- the following value is a state: a value that may be read but not written
        notReady(3),
    -- the following three values are actions: may be written but are never read
        createAndGo(4), createAndWait(5), destroy(6)
}
```

Example of RowStatus from RFC-4560 *Definitions of Managed Objects for Remote Ping, Traceroute, and Lookup Operations,* DISMAN-PING-MIB. A manager (platform A) can remotely add a row to the pingCtlTable in this MIB (on platform B). When this row is set to active by the manager the agent in platform B will *ping* platform C, and record the results in the table, which are then retrieved by the manager.

The Ping MIB is discussed further in Chapter 15.

```
pingCtlRowStatus OBJECT-TYPE
    SYNTAX        RowStatus
    MAX-ACCESS    read-create
    STATUS        current
    DESCRIPTION
        "This object allows entries to be created and deleted  in the
        pingCtlTable.
        Deletion of an entry in this table results in the deletion of all
        corresponding (same
        pingCtlOwnerIndex and pingCtlTestName index values)
        pingResultsTable and pingProbeHistoryTable entries.

        A value MUST be specified for pingCtlTargetAddress
        prior to acceptance of a transition to active(1) state.

        When a value for pingCtlTargetAddress is set,
        the value of object pingCtlRowStatus changes from
        notReady(3) to notInService(2).

        Activation of a remote ping operation is controlled
        via pingCtlAdminStatus, not by changing this object's
        value to active(1).

        Transitions in and out of active(1) state are not allowed while
        an entry's pingResultsOperStatus is active(1),
        with the exception that deletion of an entry in this
        able by setting its RowStatus object to destroy(6) will stop an
        active ping operation.

        The operational state of a ping operation can be determined by
        examination of its pingResultsOperStatus object."

    ::= { pingCtlEntry 23 }
```

DisplayString

DisplayString is a commonly used subtype for textual data. It assumes values from the ASCII printable character set (and a few control characters).

Example of DisplayString from the SMIv1 MIB defined in RFC-1213
RFC1213-MIB, an entry in the system table

```
sysLocation OBJECT-TYPE
        SYNTAX  DisplayString (SIZE (0..255))
        ACCESS  read-write
        STATUS  mandatory
        DESCRIPTION
            "The physical location of this node (e.g.,
            `telephone closet, 3rd floor')."
        ::= { system 6 }
```

DisplayString Alternatives

Some newer MIBs use the SnmpAdminString textual convention rather than DisplayString. This new definition in RFC-3411 facilitates internationalization, and represents information using the ISO/IEC IS 10646-1 character set, encoded as an octet string using the UTF-8 transformation format. RFC-3411 is also one of the SNMPv3 definitional documents.

MIB Diagnosis Hint. If you encounter SnmpAdminString in an IMPORTS statement, you may need to *mstrip* or *smistrip* the SNMP-FRAMEWORK-MIB from RFC-3411.

If you intend to use SnmpAdminString TC in a new MIB, you need to include the following:

IMPORTS SnmpAdminString FROM SNMP-FRAMEWORK-MIB;

Example of SnmpAdminString from *RFC-4133 Entity MIB (Version 3)* ENTITY-MIB, from the entPhysicalTable

```
entPhysicalName OBJECT-TYPE
    SYNTAX      SnmpAdminString
    MAX-ACCESS  read-only
    STATUS      current
    DESCRIPTION  -- abbreviated description
        "The textual name of the physical entity.  The value of this
        object should be the name of the component as assigned by
        the local device and should be suitable for use in commands
        entered at the device's `console'.  This might be a text
        name (e.g., `console') or a simple component number (e.g.,
        port or module number, such as `1'), depending on the
        physical component naming syntax of the device.

        If there is no local name, or if this object is otherwise
        not applicable, then this object contains a zero-length string."

    ::= { entPhysicalEntry 7 }
```

Other alternatives to DisplayString are also available.

In RFC-2278 *Definitions of System-Level Managed Objects for Applications*, SYSAPPL-MIB, contains two textual convention definitions intended for internationalization of text:

*   Utf8String OCTET STRING (SIZE(0..255))
*   LongUtf8String OCTET STRING (SIZE(0..1024))

Other MIBs (such as the standard Printer MIB) define their own versions of text string textual conventions.

DateAndTime

DateAndTime resolves to an OCTET STRING (SIZE(8|11)).

This is a date/time specification that has exactly 8 octets, or exactly 11 with the optional time zone offset.

Encoding

Octets	Contents
1-2	year
3	month
4	day
5	hour
6	minutes
7	seconds
8	deci-seconds
9	direction from UTC "+/-"
10	hours from UTC
11	minutes from UTC

The DateAndTime syntax has a DISPLAY-HINT "2d-1d-1d,1d:1d:1d.1d,1a1d:1d"

For example, Tuesday, May 26, 1992, at 1:30:15 PM EDT would be displayed as:

1992-5-26,13:30:15.0,-4:0

Example of DateAndTime from RFC-4560 *Definitions of Managed Objects for Remote Ping, Traceroute, and Lookup Operations* DISMAN-PING-MIB

```
pingResultsLastGoodProbe OBJECT-TYPE
    SYNTAX        DateAndTime
    MAX-ACCESS    read-only
    STATUS        current
    DESCRIPTION
        "Date and time when the last response was received for
        a probe."
    ::= { pingResultsEntry 10 }
```

Network Address Textual Convention Choices

Chapter 9, *Data Object–Base Types* discusses NetworkAddress (SMIv1) and IpAddress (SMIv2), along with the preference for using IpAddress.

SMIv2 also introduced two standard textual conventions used in pairs:

{ TDomain, TAddress }

that allows a MIB to define pairs of domain-type and address.

Subsequent RFCs have introduced yet more network address modeling choices, which are summarized in the table below, and explained in the following sections. Note that these textual conventions are used in pairs or in tuples.

Textual Convention Name	RFC	MIB
TDomain	2579	SMIv2-TC-MIB
TAddress	2579	SMIv2-TC-MIB
InetAddressType	4001	INET-ADDRESS-MIB
InetAddress	4001	INET-ADDRESS-MIB
TransportDomain	3419	TRANSPORT-ADDRESS-MIB
TransportAddressType	3419	TRANSPORT-ADDRESS-MIB
TransportAddress	3419	TRANSPORT-ADDRESS-MIB

Network engineers should be aware of what they may encounter and where to find needed IMPORTS MIBs.

Developers need to be aware of their choices and make good decisions in modeling network addresses.

TDomain

TDomain describes types of transport services, and resolves to type OBJECT IDENTIFIER.

This an example of using OID values as globally unique enumerations.

{ TDomain, TAddress } pairs are used to identify SNMP transport endpoints. The format of TAddress is determined by the specified TDomain.

TDomain *valid OID enumerations (others are defined as needed in other MIBs)*

OID	Transport Domain	RFC Reference
1.3.6.1.6.1.1	snmpUDPDomain	RFC-3417
1.3.6.1.6.1.2	snmpCLNSDomain	RFC-3417
1.3.6.1.6.1.3	snmpCONSDomain	RFC-3417
1.3.6.1.6.1.4	snmpDDPDomain	RFC-3417
1.3.6.1.6.1.5	snmpIPXDomain	RFC-3417
1.3.6.1.6.1.6	snmpIeee802Domain	RFC-4789

Example of TDomain from RFC-2742 *Definitions of Managed Objects for Extensible SNMP Agents* AGENTX-MIB

```
agentxConnTransportDomain OBJECT-TYPE
    SYNTAX       TDomain          -- assumes OID values shown in table above
    MAX-ACCESS   read-only
    STATUS       current
    DESCRIPTION
     "The transport protocol in use for this connection to the
       subagent. "
    ::= { agentxConnectionEntry 3 }
```

SNMP Tidbit. RFC-2741 *Agent Extensibility (AgentX) Protocol Version 1* defines the *AgentX* protocol for standard communications between master agents and subagents. Prior to *AgentX*, master agent-to-subagent protocols were proprietary (and continue to be maintained by agent SDK vendors along with *AgentX*).

RFC-2742 defines an AGENTX-MIB which reports protocol statistics, which can be useful for debugging SNMP networks.

Much earlier than AgentX, the SMUX protocol attempted to provide similar capabilities. RFC-1227 (HISTORIC) describes SMUX.

TAddress

TAddress resolves to an OCTET STRING and specifies a transport address in a format consistent with a paired value of TDomain, which defines the transport service.

In addition to the TAddress TC there are additional, closely related, textual conventions defining specific address types in RFC-3417 *Transport Mappings for the Simple Network Management Protocol (SNMP)* in the SNMPv2-TM MIB.

For example, for a TDomain = snmpUDPDomain, UDP has 6 bytes—the first 4 bytes are the IP address in network-byte order, and the last 2 bytes are the UDP port in network-byte order. The refined TAddress TC is:

```
SnmpUDPAddress ::= TEXTUAL-CONVENTION
    DISPLAY-HINT "1d.1d.1d.1d/2d"
    STATUS      current
    DESCRIPTION
        "Represents a UDP over IPv4 address:

        octets   contents       encoding
         1-4     IP-address     network-byte order
         5-6     UDP-port       network-byte order
        "
    SYNTAX      OCTET STRING (SIZE (6))
```

Other { TDomain, TAddress } pairs defined in RFC-3417 are:

TDomain OID Enumeration	TAddress Textual Convention
snmpUDPDomain	SnmpUDPAddress
snmpCLNSDomain	SnmpOSIAddress
snmpCONSDomain	SnmpOSIAddress
snmpDDPDomain	SnmpNBPAddress
snmpIPXDomain	SnmpIPXAddress

TransportDomain, TransportAddressType, TransportAddress

The suggested alternative to (TDomain, TAddress) pairs are the TCs defined in RFC-3419 *Textual Conventions for Transport Addresses*, in the TRANSPORT-ADDRESS-MIB:

(TransportDomain, TransportAddressType, TransportAddress)

TransportDomain is defined as an object with type OID, and is a globally unique identifier.

```
TransportDomain ::= TEXTUAL-CONVENTION
    STATUS     current
    DESCRIPTION
        "A value that represents a transport domain.

        Some possible values, such as transportDomainUdpIpv4, are
        defined in this module.  Other possible values can be
        defined in other MIB modules."

    SYNTAX     OBJECT IDENTIFIER
```

Example definitions for two possible OID enumerated values for a TransportDomain object

```
transportDomainTcpIpv4 OBJECT-IDENTITY
    STATUS     current
    DESCRIPTION
        "The TCP over IPv4 transport domain.  The corresponding
        transport address is of type TransportAddressIPv4 for
        global IPv4 addresses."
    ::= { transportDomains 5 }

transportDomainTcpIpv6 OBJECT-IDENTITY
    STATUS     current
    DESCRIPTION
        "The TCP over IPv6 transport domain.  The corresponding
        transport address is of type TransportAddressIPv6 for
        global IPv6 addresses."
    ::= { transportDomains 6 }
```

TransportAddressType is defined as an enumerated INTEGER.

```
TransportAddressType ::= TEXTUAL-CONVENTION
    STATUS      current
    DESCRIPTION
        "A value that represents a transport domain. This is the
         enumerated version of the transport domain registrations
         in this MIB module. ... (description is abbreviated ...)"
    SYNTAX      INTEGER {
                unknown(0),
                udpIpv4(1),
                udpIpv6(2),
                udpIpv4z(3),
                udpIpv6z(4),
                tcpIpv4(5),
                tcpIpv6(6),
                tcpIpv4z(7),
                tcpIpv6z(8),
                sctpIpv4(9),
                sctpIpv6(10),
                sctpIpv4z(11),
                sctpIpv6z(12),
                local(13),
                udpDns(14),
                tcpDns(15),
                sctpDns(16)
            }
```

TransportAddress is defined as a generic object of type OCTET STRING.

```
TransportAddress ::= TEXTUAL-CONVENTION
    STATUS      current
    DESCRIPTION
        "Denotes a generic transport address.
         .. description abbreviated for this example ... "

    SYNTAX      OCTET STRING (SIZE (0..255))
```

Additional TransportAddress TCs are defined for specific values of TransportAddressType. *For example*

```
TransportAddressIPv4 ::= TEXTUAL-CONVENTION
   DISPLAY-HINT "1d.1d.1d.1d:2d"
   STATUS      current
   DESCRIPTION
     "Represents a transport address consisting of an IPv4
      address and a port number (as used for example by UDP,
      TCP and SCTP):

      octets     contents      encoding
       1-4       IPv4 address  network-byte order
       5-6       port number   network-byte order

      This textual convention SHOULD NOT be used directly in object
      definitions since it restricts addresses to a specific format.
      However, if it is used, it MAY be used either on its own or
      in conjunction with TransportAddressType or TransportDomain
      as a pair."
   SYNTAX      OCTET STRING (SIZE (6))
```

RFC-3419 has a good multiple page comparison of these definitions, with alternatives.

InetAddressType, InetAddress

A suggested alternative to IpAddress is InetAddressType and InetAddress, textual conventions defined by RFC-4001 and which always appear in pairs.

InetAddress is an OCTET STRING (SIZE(0..255). The encoding of InetAddress is dependent on the value of InetAddressType.

InetAddressType is an enumerated INTEGER with values:

   { unknown(0), ipv4(1), ipv6(2), ipv4z(3), ipv6z(4), dns(16) }

For each of these values, the MIB also defines an additional TC which is the actual encoding of InetAddress for that type.

For example, for an InetAddressType value of ipv6

```
InetAddressIPv6 ::= TEXTUAL-CONVENTION
   DISPLAY-HINT "2x:2x:2x:2x:2x:2x:2x:2x"
   STATUS      current
   DESCRIPTION
      "Represents an IPv6 network address:

         Octets   Contents         Encoding
          1-16    IPv6 address     network-byte order

      The corresponding InetAddressType value is ipv6(2).

      This textual convention SHOULD NOT be used directly in object
      definitions, as it restricts addresses to a specific format.
      However, if it is used, it MAY be used either on its own or in
      conjunction with InetAddressType, as a pair."
   SYNTAX      OCTET STRING (SIZE (16))
```

Note the additional DISPLAY-HINT example above.

PhysAddress

PhysAddress is a physical memory address and resolves to OCTET STRING.

Example of PhysAddress from RFC-1213, an object in the interface table ifTable

```
ifPhysAddress OBJECT-TYPE
   SYNTAX  PhysAddress
   ACCESS  read-only
   STATUS  mandatory
   DESCRIPTION
      "The interface's address at the protocol layer
       immediately `below' the network layer in the
       protocol stack.  For interfaces which do not have
       such an address (e.g., a serial line), this object
       should contain an octet string of zero length."
   ::= { ifEntry 6 }
```

MacAddress

MacAddress is an IEEE 802.1a MAC address in canonical order, and resolves to a 6-byte OCTET STRING.

> *Example* of MacAddress from RFC-4188 *Definitions of Managed Objects for Bridges* BRIDGE-MIB

```
dot1dBaseBridgeAddress OBJECT-TYPE
    SYNTAX        MacAddress
    MAX-ACCESS    read-only
    STATUS        current
    DESCRIPTION
      "The MAC address used by this bridge when it must be
      referred to in a unique fashion.  It is recommended
      that this be the numerically smallest MAC address of
      all ports that belong to this bridge.  However, it is only
      required to be unique.  When concatenated with
      dot1dStpPriority, a unique BridgeIdentifier is formed,
      which is used in the Spanning Tree Protocol."
    REFERENCE
      "IEEE 802.1D-1998: clauses 14.4.1.1.3 and 7.12.5"
    ::= { dot1dBase 1 }
```

AutonomousType

AutonomousType resolves to OBJECT IDENTIFIER, and is an identification value that has general usage. For example, it could identify a MIB object or sub-tree, or might define hardware-type enumerations.

> *Example* of AutonomousType from RFC-4133 *Entity MIB (Version 3)* ENTITY-MIB. The Entity MIB is used to model containment structures (e.g., a chassis contains slots, which contain modules, which contain daughter boards and ports).

```
entPhysicalVendorType OBJECT-TYPE
    SYNTAX        AutonomousType
    MAX-ACCESS  read-only
    STATUS        current
    DESCRIPTION
        "An indication of the vendor-specific hardware type of the
        physical entity.  Note that this is different from the
        definition of MIB-II's sysObjectID.

        An agent should set this object to an enterprise-specific
        registration identifier value indicating the specific
        equipment type in detail.  The associated instance of
        entPhysicalClass is used to indicate the general type of
        hardware device.

        If no vendor-specific registration identifier exists for
        this physical entity, or the value is unknown by this agent,
        then the value { 0 0 } is returned."
    ::= { entPhysicalEntry 3 }
```

Chapter 16 *Elements of Advanced MIB Complexity* contains examples of entPhysicalVendorType values and interpretation for a managed Cisco product.

VariablePointer

VariablePointer resolves to OBJECT IDENTIFIER and points to a specific MIB data object instance.

For example, it might contain the OID.instance of (and therefore point to):

sysContact.0 *or to* ifInOctets.3

Example of VariablePointer from RFC-3231 *Definitions of Managed Objects for Scheduling Management Operations* DISMAN-SCHEDULE-MIB.

schedVariable is an object in a row-create scheduling table (row-create details are in Chapter 15), indexed by { schedOwner, schedName }.

When the scheduler invokes an action, a schedValue will be written by the agent to the object.instance pointed to by schedVariable.

Syntax for both objects is shown below.

```
schedVariable OBJECT-TYPE
      SYNTAX          VariablePointer
      MAX-ACCESS      read-create
      STATUS          current
      DESCRIPTION
        "An object identifier pointing to a local MIB variable
          which resolves to an ASN.1 primitive type of INTEGER."
      DEFVAL     { zeroDotZero }
      ::= { schedEntry 11 }
```

```
schedValue OBJECT-TYPE
      SYNTAX          Integer32
      MAX-ACCESS      read-create
      STATUS          current
      DESCRIPTION
        "The value which is written to the MIB object pointed to by
          schedVariable when the scheduler invokes an action. The
          implementation shall enforce the use of access control
          rules when performing the set operation on schedVariable.
          This is accomplished by calling the isAccessAllowed abstract
          service interface as defined in RFC-2571.

          Note that an implementation may choose to issue an SNMP Set
          message to the SNMP engine and leave the access control
          decision to the normal message processing procedure."
      DEFVAL     { 0 }
      ::= { schedEntry 12 }
```

RowPointer

RowPointer is the OID.instance of the first accessible object in the row of an indexed table, and resolves to OBJECT IDENTIFIER.

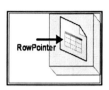

Example of RowPointer from RFC-3201 *Definitions of Managed Objects for Circuit to Interface Translation* CIRCUIT-IF-MIB, an object in the Circuit Interface Circuit Table ciCircuitTable. This is another example of a manager row-create table (Chapter 15).

```
ciCircuitObject OBJECT-TYPE
        SYNTAX        RowPointer
        MAX-ACCESS    not-accessible      -- because this is also an INDEX
        STATUS        current
        DESCRIPTION
          "This value contains the RowPointer that uniquely
          describes the circuit that is to be added to this table.
          Any RowPointer that will force the size of OBJECT
          IDENTIFIER of the row to grow beyond the legal limit
          MUST be rejected.

          The purpose of this object is to point a network manager
          to the table in which the circuit was created as well as
          define the circuit on which the interface is defined.

          Valid tables for this object include the frCircuitTable
          from the Frame Relay DTE MIB(FRAME-RELAY-DTE-MIB), the
          frPVCEndptTable from the Frame Relay Service MIB
          (FRNETSERV-MIB), and the aal5VccTable from the ATM MIB
          (ATM MIB).  However, including circuits from other MIB
          tables IS NOT prohibited."
        ::= { ciCircuitEntry 1 }
```

Complete List of Current Standard TCs

A complete list of current and useful standard textual conventions can be found at:

www.ops.ietf.org/mib-common-tcs.html

A partial list is shown in the screen capture below.

Generic and Common Textual Conventions (TCs)

Appendix B in "Guidelines for Authors and Reviewers of MIB Documents [RFC4181, BCP111]", lists an initial set of Commonly used Textual Conventions. This web page is intended to keep that list up-to-date with the most commonly used TCs. If you have any suggestions for changes or additions, pls send an email to the OPS AD maintaining this page, Dan Romascanu.

The following TCs are defined in SNMPv2-TC [RFC2579]:

```
    DisplayString           OCTET STRING (SIZE (0..255))
    PhysAddress             OCTET STRING
    MacAddress              OCTET STRING (SIZE (6))
    TruthValue              enumerated INTEGER
    TestAndIncr             INTEGER (0..2147483647)
    AutonomousType          OBJECT IDENTIFIER
    VariablePointer         OBJECT IDENTIFIER
    RowPointer              OBJECT IDENTIFIER
    RowStatus               enumerated INTEGER
    TimeStamp               TimeTicks
    TimeInterval            INTEGER (0..2147483647)
    DateAndTime             OCTET STRING (SIZE (8 | 11))
    StorageType             enumerated INTEGER
    TDomain                 OBJECT IDENTIFIER
    TAddress                OCTET STRING (SIZE (1..255))

    Note 1.  InstancePointer is obsolete and MUST NOT be used.

    Note 2.  DisplayString does not support internationalized text.
             It MUST NOT be used for objects that are required to
```

This list cross-references the RFCs and MIBs where TCs are defined.

Enterprise MIB authors should consult this list for useful definitions before defining unique enterprise TCs.

When network engineers encounter these definitions in a MIB, this reference site will be useful in locating the required IMPORTS MIB files.

Exercises

1. What is a textual convention?

2. How are textual conventions defined in SMIv2 MIBs?

3. Is there any way to define textual conventions in SMIv1 MIBs?

4. What values can the TruthValue textual convention assume?

5. The textual convention TestAndIncr is intended for use in a manner similar to what common software mechanism?

6. What is wrong with the following SMIv2 textual convention definition?

```
UserAlias ::= TEXTUAL-CONVENTION
   STATUS          current
   DESCRIPTION
      "User Assigned name for the entity."
   SYNTAX  DisplayString (SIZE (6..24))
```

7. You have just taken delivery of an updated MIB. The previous version compiled with no problem, but the new one compiles with unresolved IMPORTS. The new MIB deprecates old objects of base data type IpAddress, and uses the new InetAddress and InetAddressType textual conventions defined in RFC-4001 to define equivalent objects.

   Go to the IETF web site, copy RFC-4001 to your computer, and use one of the tools *mstrip* or *smistrip* (command-line or web-based) to strip out the required INET-ADDRESS-MIB, and load it into your manager.

Chapter 11

Trap Objects

SNMP agents send unsolicited event messages (called *traps* or *notifications*) to targeted managers.

Targeted managers are defined as part of the agent configuration process, and consist of pairs of:

    { trapCommunityString, targetAddress }

For an IP network, targetAddress will be the IP address, with default UDP port 162 assumed, or with a different port specified:

    { targetIPAddr:udpPort }

Agents can be configured to target one or more managers. The size of the targeted manager list is agent-implementation dependent.

```
DEFINITIONS MY-MIB-NAME ::= BEGIN

IMPORTS syntax

MODULE-IDENTITY statement

TEXTUAL-CONVENTION definitions
Node definitions

Scalar Data Objects

Table Object
Entry Object
Table SEQUENCE statement
Table Data Objects

TRAP-TYPE Objects (SMIv1)
NOTIFICATION-TYPE Objects (SMIv2)

OBJECT-GROUP lists
NOTIFICATION-GROUP lists
MODULE-COMPLIANCE grouping lists

END
```

Events are called *traps* for SMIv1 and *notifications* for SMIv2. However, common terminology is to describe all events as *traps*, *events*, or sometimes *alarms* (although not all *traps* are truly *alarms*—for example, a *trap* may be *informational*).

The concept of a trap is simple. Trap objects have names that reflect the nature of the event, and normally contain data values that provide important details to managers (although data is not required to be sent). Any data value sent in a trap must have a corresponding data object definition in a MIB.

SMIv1 TRAP-TYPE syntax is different from SMIv2 NOTIFICATION-TYPE syntax. Both representations convey equivalent information, and (properly coded) SMIv2 objects can be translated to equivalent SMIv1 objects.

This chapter discusses syntax issues, although there is considerably more to good trap design— Part 5 *Advanced Trap Topics* is important reading for developers (how to design useful traps) and for network engineers (recognizing different trap models, and understanding how to design appropriate manager trap filters).

SMIv1 syntax will be presented first, followed by SMIv2, which looks similar to syntax for other types of MIB objects.

TRAP-TYPE SMIv1 Syntax

SMIv1 trap object syntax looks a little different than other object syntax.

Example of SMIv1 trap object syntax from MIB managing a CD-player

```
cdPowerSupplyEv TRAP-TYPE              -- trap name
    ENTERPRISE chateauCDProdEvents     -- name of ENTERPRISE node
    VARIABLES                          -- data objects sent with this trap
    {
        cdDynCfgUserAlias,
        cdStCfgModel,
        cdChStPowerSupply,
        cdEvSeverity,
        cdEvDescription
    }
    DESCRIPTION
        "Sent when cdChStPowerSupply changes from okay to voltageError,
         or from voltageError to okay.
         This trap can be disabled by setting
         cdPowerSupplyEvTrapEn = trapDisable."
    REFERENCE "Optional Reference Clause"
    ::= 20                             -- NOTE! A little different
```

Observations regarding SMIv1 syntax for this example:
- Keyword TRAP-TYPE
- The name of this trap object is cdPowerSupplyEv
- ENTERPRISE clause identifies an existing MIB node named chateauCDProdEvents
- VARIABLES clause contains a list of data object names whose values will be transported by this trap. A brief discussion of the objects sent with this trap:
  - cdDynCfgUserAlias is a read-write textual object that allows end-users to assign an alias for this CD player (e.g., "Main Dining Room")
  - cdStCfgModel is the CD player model information
  - cdChStPowerSupply is the enumerated INTEGER status of the power supply (e.g., voltageError(2))

- ◦ cdEvSeverity is the enumerated INTEGER severity of this trap (e.g., warning(2))
    - ◦ cdEvDescription is a text object that supplies additional information to the user
- There is no STATUS clause (that might be used to deprecate or obsolete this trap object). If an SMIv1 trap object is deprecated or obsolete, it should be so noted in an amended DESCRIPTION clause.
- The parent node for this trap object is not obvious, and is discussed next.

```
The parent node of trap cdPowerSupplyEv is
        chateauCDProdEvents.0

The OID of cdPowerSupplyEv is
        chateauCDProdEvents.0.20
```

The SMIv1 compiler inserts the ".0" after the enterprise node as shown above. In SMIv2 syntax, an explicit ".0" node must be coded which does not appear in the equivalent SMIv1 MIB.

> **SNMP Tidbit**. Uses of the ENTERPRISE keyword can be confusing. The term *enterprise* was previously described as the OID assigned by IANA (Internet Assigned Numbers Authority), but usage with trap objects is a little different—it is the name of a MIB node superior to the trap OID.
>
> For a specific MIB organizational style, the IANA enterprise OID and the trap enterprise OID *can* be the same. Enterprise SMIv1 MIB styles exist that define traps as objects under a node that is identical with the vendor's IANA assigned enterprise OID. The enterprise may define a multitude of MIBs, but all traps are organized under the enterprise's OID. In this style of MIB organization, the ENTERPRISE clause specifies a node that is exactly the same as the vendor's enterprise OID.
>
> *For example*, for the mythical enterprise Vronx with IANA enterprise OID = vronx, traps would be organized as

```
vronx.0.modelXpowerSupplyEv
vronx.0.modelYpowerSupplyEv
vronx.0.modelXchassisTempEv
vronx.0.modelZoilPressureHighEv
vronx.0.modelQsituationNormalEv
        and so on
```

Appendix E, *Enterprise Definitions,* expands this discussion.

NOTIFICATION-TYPE SMIv2 Syntax

SMIv2 syntax looks more familiar.

Example of SMIv2 trap object syntax for a MIB managing a CD player

```
cdPowerSupplyEv NOTIFICATION-TYPE        -- notification name
    OBJECTS                              -- data sent with this notification
    {
        cdDynCfgUserAlias,
        cdStCfgModel,
        cdChStPowerSupply,
        cdEvSeverity,
        cdEvDescription
    }
    STATUS  current
    DESCRIPTION
        "Sent when cdChStPowerSupply changes from okay to voltageError,
        or from voltageError to okay.
        This trap can be disabled by setting
        cdPowerSupplyEvTrapEn = trapDisable."
    ::= { cdEventList 20 }
```

Observations regarding SMIv2 example syntax (equivalent to the SMIv1 trap example above):

- Keyword NOTIFICATION-TYPE replaces TRAP-TYPE
- No ENTERPRISE clause
- OBJECTS clause replaces VARIABLES clause but identifies the same data objects to be sent with the event
- A new STATUS clause allows specification of this object as current, deprecated or obsolete
- Node parentage is clearer—cdEventList is the parent node (and must itself have an OID extension of ".0")
    - cdPowerSupplyEv ::= { cdEventList 20 }
    - The node cdEventList *does not appear* in an equivalent SMIv1 MIB!

When coding a new SMIv2 MIB, a node with an OID extension of ".0" should always be the parent of a list of notifications. Another way of stating this is that the next-to-last sub-identifier for a NOTIFICATION-TYPE OID must be zero.

If this is not done, translating the SMIv2 notification to SMIv1 trap syntax will result in a trap object with an OID that is different.

SNMP Tidbit. Agent software code is based on an SMIv2 trap definition, whose parent node does *not* end in .0. The SMIv2 MIB is translated to SMIv1 for loading into a manager tool that only accepts SMIv1 MIBs. When the agent sends traps to the manager tool, they will be logged as *unknown traps.* This is a serious problem.

Equivalent SMIv1 and SMIv2 Syntax

Example. SMIv1 and SMIv2 equivalent node and event object syntax. The OIDs for both trap objects will be the same.

SMIv1	SMIv2

```
chateauCDProdEvents
   OBJECT IDENTIFIER
::= { chateauCDProductMIB 10 }
```

```
chateauCDProdEvents  OBJECT-IDENTITY
   STATUS current
   DESCRIPTION
      "CD Player Event Data
      and Trap Definitions are
      organized under this node."
   ::= { chateauCDProductMIB 10 }


cdEventList  OBJECT-IDENTITY
   STATUS current
   DESCRIPTION
      "Notification Objects are
      organized under this node."
   ::= { chateauCDProdEvents 0 }
```

```
cdPowerSupplyEv TRAP-TYPE
   ENTERPRISE chateauCDProdEvents
   VARIABLES
   {
      cdDynCfgUserAlias,
      cdStCfgModel,
      cdChStPowerSupply,
      cdEvSeverity,
      cdEvDescription
   }
   DESCRIPTION "etc"
   ::= 20
```

```
cdPowerSupplyEv NOTIFICATION-TYPE
   OBJECTS
   {
      cdDynCfgUserAlias,
      cdStCfgModel,
      cdChStPowerSupply,
      cdEvSeverity,
      cdEvDescription
   }
   STATUS  current
   DESCRIPTION "etc"
   ::= { cdEventList 20 }
```

The OIDs for both objects are the same, and are equal to:

1.3.6.1.4.1.10910.2.2.3.1.1.10.0.20

If you use a MIB browser that displays MIB object properties, both objects will show:

Trap ENTERPRISE = chateauCDProdEvents

Exercises

1. What is the minimum number of VARIABLES clause data objects that must be defined in SMIv1 TRAP-TYPE syntax, and sent with SNMPv1 traps?

2. When designing an SMIv2 NOTIFICATION-TYPE, what important issue must be addressed to ensure it can be re-coded as an equivalent SMIv1 TRAP-TYPE?

Chapter 12

Conformance Objects (SMIv2)

Conformance objects are different from the MIB objects discussed so far.

Node objects provide MIB structure. *Data objects* supply values that managers can *get* and *set*. *Trap objects* define unsolicited notifications sent from agents to managers. Each of these objects is assigned a unique OID.

Conformance objects in MIBs are also assigned OIDs. However managers cannot *get* information about conformance objects, nor do agents directly supply any information about conformance objects.

Conformance statements provide additional information (to the MIB reader) about data objects and trap objects. They are used to organize *groups* of data and trap objects, and then to specify each *group* as *mandatory, conditional,* or *optional* as per agent implementation.

```
DEFINITIONS MY-MIB-NAME ::= BEGIN

IMPORTS syntax

MODULE-IDENTITY statement

TEXTUAL-CONVENTION definitions
Node definitions

Scalar Data Objects

Table Object
Entry Object
Table SEQUENCE statement
Table Data Objects

TRAP-TYPE Objects (SMIv1)
NOTIFICATION-TYPE Objects (SMIv2)

OBJECT-GROUP lists
NOTIFICATION-GROUP lists
MODULE-COMPLIANCE grouping lists

END
```

Conformance statements apply only to SMIv2 MIBs, and RFC-2580 *Conformance Statements for SMIv2* is a good supplement to this chapter.

Conformance Object Uses

RFC-3805 *Printer MIB v2* contains the Printer-MIB, which defines objects which model printers and their status. Printer technologies vary and not all objects apply to all printers. Conformance statements categorize data and trap objects into mandatory, conditional, or optional agent implementation.

A screen capture of Printer MIB organization appears to the right, showing high-level data and trap organizational nodes. Conformance objects are organized at the end of the MIB (which is common) under the prtMIBConformance node.

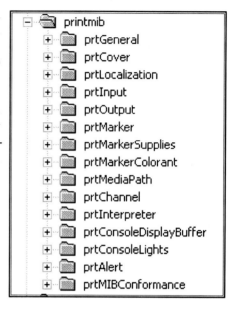

A printer manufacturer will implement an agent that supports all mandatory objects as well as any conditional objects that apply to their printer technology. They can then claim *full compliance* with the Printer MIB.

In addition to the standard Printer MIB, vendors typically supply proprietary enterprise MIBs to ensure detailed and comprehensive management of their printer product.

Conformance statements can also be viewed as a sort of *contract* between the MIB designers and agent implementors, which may be two different groups.

All new RFC-based standard MIBs are required to provide conformance statements.

Enterprise MIB designers often include conformance statements, particularly if a MIB describes a family of products, or a product with options. Mandatory groups support the core product, and conditional or optional groups provide support for particular product family members, or for optional features. This allows developers to support only one version of a MIB rather than a family of MIBs with small differences.

Conformance statements are useful to network engineers in understanding agent product support capabilities.

If a MIB is to pass MIB validation compilers at the strictest levels, conformance statements must be included. However validation compiler complaints about missing conformance statements will not prevent a MIB from loading successfully into managers.

Conformance Object Syntax

There are three MIB objects which appear commonly, and a fourth that is less common. The three common objects are OBJECT-GROUP, NOTIFICATION-GROUP, and MODULE-COMPLIANCE.

- Data objects are assigned to an OBJECT-GROUP

- Trap objects are assigned to a NOTIFICATION-GROUP
- MODULE-COMPLIANCE objects refer to object and trap groups and designate them as mandatory, conditional, or optional
- Less commonly used, AGENT-CAPABILITIES describes agent semantic issues

The screen capture at the right shows multiple Printer MIB conformance data object groups and one trap group, the prtAlertTrapGroup.

Each of the data object groups contains multiple data objects.

For example

```
prtResponsiblePartyGroup OBJECT-GROUP
    OBJECTS { prtGeneralCurrentOperator,
            prtGeneralServicePerson }
    STATUS  current
    DESCRIPTION
      "The responsible party group contains
      contact information for
      humans responsible for the printer."
    ::= { prtMIBGroups 2 }
```

The prtAlertTrapGroup includes only the single trap defined in the MIB:

      printerV2Alert

which is discussed in some detail in Chapter 18, *Trap Models*.

Additional examples below are from RFC-3418 *Management Information Base (MIB) for the Simple Network Management Protocol (SNMP)*, which contains SNMPv2-MIB definitions. Included are re-definitions from the RFC1213-MIB *system group* and *snmp group*. (These should be familiar from examples in previous chapters.)

Strict adherence to the RFCs requires that all MIB data and trap objects be a member of at least one OBJECT-GROUP, and IETF MIBs must reference all groups in a MODULE-COMPLIANCE object.

OBJECT-GROUP

OBJECT-GROUP syntax organizes data objects into groups that are then referenced in a MODULE-COMPLIANCE object.

Example of OBJECT-GROUP syntax from the SNMPv2-MIB

```
snmpGroup OBJECT-GROUP
    OBJECTS { snmpInPkts,
        snmpInBadVersions,
        snmpInASNParseErrs,
        snmpSilentDrops,
        snmpProxyDrops,
        snmpEnableAuthenTraps }
    STATUS  current
    DESCRIPTION
        "A collection of objects providing basic instrumentation
        and control of an SNMP entity."
    ::= { snmpMIBGroups 8 }
```

The OBJECTS clause lists data objects contained in the snmpGroup. All data objects defined in a MIB with a MAX-ACCESS clause with a value other than not-accessible must be included in at least one object group.

NOTIFICATION-GROUP

NOTIFICATION-GROUP syntax organizes notification objects into groups that are then referenced in a MODULE-COMPLIANCE object.

Example of NOTIFICATION-GROUP syntax from the SNMPv2-MIB

```
snmpBasicNotificationsGroup NOTIFICATION-GROUP
    NOTIFICATIONS { coldStart, authenticationFailure }
    STATUS      current
    DESCRIPTION
        "The basic notifications implemented by an SNMP entity
        supporting command responder applications."
    ::= { snmpMIBGroups 7 }
```

MODULE-COMPLIANCE

MODULE-COMPLIANCE syntax describes mandatory, conditional, or optional implementation (by agents) of data object and notification groups.

Example of MODULE-COMPLIANCE syntax from the SNMPv2-MIB

```
snmpBasicCompliance MODULE-COMPLIANCE
    STATUS  deprecated
    DESCRIPTION
        "The compliance statement for SNMPv2 entities which
        implement the SNMPv2 MIB.

        This compliance statement is replaced by
        snmpBasicComplianceRev2."
    MODULE  -- this module
      MANDATORY-GROUPS {
          snmpGroup,
          snmpSetGroup,
          systemGroup,
          snmpBasicNotificationsGroup }

      GROUP   snmpCommunityGroup
      DESCRIPTION
        "This group is mandatory for SNMPv2 entities which
        support community-based authentication."

    ::= { snmpMIBCompliances 2 }
```

Note that in this example, STATUS is deprecated, and a new, preferred compliance statement exists (snmpBasicComplianceRev2) as described in the DESCRIPTION clause.

The MODULE clause can be used repeatedly to name each MIB module (by name or by OID) for which compliance statements are being specified. If compliances apply only to this MIB, the name can be omitted as shown above (MODULE -- this module).

The optional MANDATORY-GROUPS clause lists those data and notification object groups which are unconditionally mandatory. All agents claiming *full compliance* must support these objects.

The GROUP clause is optional and can be used to name conditionally mandatory groups or unconditionally optional groups. Multiple GROUP clauses may appear in one compliance object. The DESCRIPTION clause following a GROUP clause describes any conditions.

An optional REFERENCE clause, not shown in the example, can also be used.

Example of MODULE-COMPLIANCE syntax from RFC-3805 *Printer MIB v2,* the Printer-MIB, with additional discussion following

```
prtMIBCompliance MODULE-COMPLIANCE
    STATUS  current
    DESCRIPTION
        "The compliance statement for agents that implement the
        printer MIB as defined by RFC-1759."
    MODULE -- this module
    MANDATORY-GROUPS { prtGeneralGroup, prtInputGroup,
                prtOutputGroup,
                prtMarkerGroup, prtMediaPathGroup,
                prtChannelGroup, prtInterpreterGroup,
                prtConsoleGroup, prtAlertTableGroup }
    OBJECT    prtGeneralReset          -- SEE NOTES BELOW
    SYNTAX    INTEGER {
            notResetting(3),
            resetToNVRAM(5)
            }
    DESCRIPTION
        "It is conformant to implement just these two states in this
        object.  Any additional states are optional."

    OBJECT    prtConsoleOnTime          -- SEE NOTES BELOW
    MIN-ACCESS  read-only
    DESCRIPTION
        "It is conformant to implement this object as read-only"

    OBJECT    prtConsoleOffTime
    MIN-ACCESS  read-only
    DESCRIPTION
        "It is conformant to implement this object as read-only"
    ::= { prtMIBConformance 1 }
```

This longer example illustrates two additional features.

OBJECT prtGeneralReset is an enumerated INTEGER. It is mandatory that this subset of two enumeration values be supported by all compliant agents, as stated in the DESCRIPTION.

OBJECT prtConsoleOnTime is a read-write object. However, the MIN-ACCESS clause states that a conformant agent needs to implement only read-only access, as stated in the DESCRIPTION.

AGENT-CAPABILITIES

AGENT-CAPABILITIES statements are seldom encountered and may be contained in a separate file.

An abbreviated *example* of AGENT-CAPABILITIES syntax from RFC-2580 is shown below, along with commentary paraphrased from the RFC. The RFC itself describes a more comprehensive example.

```
exampleAgent AGENT-CAPABILITIES
    PRODUCT-RELEASE     "ACME Agent release 1.1 for 4BSD."
    STATUS          current
    DESCRIPTION       "ACME agent for 4BSD."

    SUPPORTS        IF-MIB
      INCLUDES        { ifGeneralGroup, ifPacketGroup }

      VARIATION       ifAdminStatus
        SYNTAX      INTEGER { up(1), down(2) }
        DESCRIPTION "Unable to set test mode on 4BSD."

      VARIATION       ifOperStatus
        SYNTAX      INTEGER { up(1), down(2) }
        DESCRIPTION "Information limited on 4BSD."

    ::= { acmeAgents 1 }
```

This agent supports one MIB module: the IF-MIB.

For the IF-MIB, the ifGeneralGroup and ifPacketGroup groups are supported, but only restricted syntax is supported for objects ifAdminStatus and ifOperStatus.

Exercises

1. Conformance objects were introduced in SMIv2 MIB syntax. What corresponding SNMPv2 message types were added to allow managers to obtain conformance object information from agents?

Part 4

Complex MIBs

So far basic MIB organization has been described, along with the syntax of MIB objects. The next chapters describe complex MIBs.

Indexed Tables, described in Chapter 13, are very common, and are a level of complexity beyond scalar objects. Indexed tables can have single or multiple indexes, can share indexes, and may augment (extend with additional objects) existing tables.

Chapter 14 discusses *Index Data Types.* Integer indexes feel quite comfortable to most, but other data type choices are available (object identifiers, display strings, and a few others). The choice of index data type impacts data object instance values, lexicographical ordering of data, manager trap filtering, ease of agent development, and SNMP message contents.

Chapter 15 talks about *Row-Create Tables.* Most SNMP references limit this discussion to manager row creation, but this chapter also discusses agent row creation (and deletion).

Elements of Advanced Complexity are described in Chapter 16. Such *elements* facilitate more elegant and complex MIB models. Object relationships are represented using OID pointers, index pointers, and tag-lists. For example, linked-lists are easily modeled.

All of these mechanisms are common in standard MIBs, and fairly common in enterprise MIBs.

A few examples of standard MIBs that employ *complex models* are also briefly described.

> The *Entity MIB* finds common usage in describing network appliance products. It allows the definition of containers and contents. For example, a chassis contains slots, which contain modules, which may have daughter boards or I/O ports. Physical relationships can be described as well as logical relationships. The mapping of logical entities to physical entities can be modeled.

SNMPv3 is the secure version of SNMP. Configuring agents to provide this security is done by configuring *SNMPv3 Configuration MIBs* on the agent platform. The user interface for this configuration may be a GUI, or editing a text file read at startup, but ultimately involves setting values to configure the SNMPv3 MIBs.

The *RMON and RMON2 MIBs* allow users to configure *probes* on remote platforms that provide detailed network operational statistics (vs. just device data). For example, a manager on *Platform BASE* configures an RMON agent on *Platform REMOTE* to collect network statistics, and to report back to the manager.

Advanced complexity is important for network engineers wishing to take full advantage of the MIBs and monitoring agents at their disposal.

Developers should understand the opportunities complex MIBs offer in modeling their products.

Chapter 13

Indexed Tables

This chapter discusses indexed table syntax, along with multi-indexed tables and sharing of indexes among tables. SMIv1 and SMIv2 table definition syntax is similar.

Indexed tables are quite common in MIBs. In discussing tables, *columns* refer to the named data objects in a table, and *rows* refer to the indexed *instances* of each data object.

Syntax for data objects contained within indexed tables is identical to that of scalar data objects. However, each such object must be identified in the table definition SEQUENCE statement.

This chapter and the next one continue the discussion of object instances—in indexed tables the *instance value* is equal to the *index value*. This chapter confines its discussions to integer index types.

```
DEFINITIONS MY-MIB-NAME ::= BEGIN

IMPORTS syntax

MODULE-IDENTITY statement

TEXTUAL-CONVENTION definitions
Node definitions

Scalar Data Objects

Table Object
Entry Object
Table SEQUENCE statement
Table Data Objects

TRAP-TYPE Objects (SMIv1)
NOTIFICATION-TYPE Objects (SMIv2)

OBJECT-GROUP lists
NOTIFICATION-GROUP lists
MODULE-COMPLIANCE grouping lists

END
```

Chapter 14 discusses additional index data types.

INDEX	Name	Rank	Serial Number
1	Parker	private	12345
2	Smith	private	23456
3	Snoopy	major	34567
4	Walsh	corporal	45678
5	Ng	private	56789

To the left is an example of a single integer-indexed table containing three data objects, and five rows.

Tables can have single indexes or multiple indexes, and indexes can be shared with other tables.

SNMP MIB syntax does not support the concept of *tables of tables* (or, in more familiar terms to "C" programmers *struct of struct*). This constrains a MIB designer's modeling choices, but can be overcome by the clever use of shared indexes and object pointers.

Indexed Table Syntax

The syntax for SMIv1 and SMIv2 tables is similar, varying in just a few details:
- SMIv1 *table object* and table *entry object* definitions employ the ACCESS clause.
- SMIv2 *table* and *entry object* definitions employ the equivalent MAX-ACCESS clause.
- SMIv1 and SMIv2 tables use the INDEX clause to identify table index objects.
- SMIv2 *entry objects* can replace the INDEX clause with the new AUGMENTS clause to indicate an extension of a previously defined table, sharing its index definitions.
- SMIv2 *entry objects* occasionally make use of the optional IMPLIED keyword. There is some controversy surrounding use of IMPLIED, and this discussion is deferred until Chapter 14.

An indexed table is defined by three MIB syntactic elements:
- *Table object* which also defines a node.
  - The *table object* is also referred to as a *conceptual table object*.
- *Entry object* syntax follows the *table object* (its parent node), and also defines a node.
  - An *entry object* is also referred to as a *conceptual row object*.
- SEQUENCE statement follows the *entry object* and has no OID assignment.
  - This statement lists all of the data objects (by name and data type) that are included in the table.

Following the table definition syntax elements are the definitions of the table data objects themselves. These definitions are all identified in the SEQUENCE statement and have the *entry object* as their parent, but do not otherwise differ from syntax for scalar data objects.

Data object names and types must be the same as specified in the SEQUENCE statement.

SMIv2 example of indexed table syntax from the CHATEAU-CD-PRODUCT-MIB, followed by discussion

```
cdChangerSlotTable OBJECT-TYPE          -- the table object
    SYNTAX      SEQUENCE OF CdChangerSlotEntry
    MAX-ACCESS  not-accessible
    STATUS      current
    DESCRIPTION
        "CD Changer Slot Table."
    ::= { cdChangerStatus 2 }

cdChangerSlotEntry  OBJECT-TYPE          -- the entry object
    SYNTAX      CdChangerSlotEntry
    MAX-ACCESS  not-accessible
    STATUS      current
    DESCRIPTION
        "An entry in cdChangerSlotTable."
    INDEX   { cdChangerSlotNbr }
    ::= { cdChangerSlotTable 1 }

CdChangerSlotEntry  ::=                  -- the SEQUENCE statement
    SEQUENCE {
        cdChangerSlotNbr            Unsigned32,
        cdChangerSlotStatus         INTEGER,
        cdChangerSlotCDTrackPlaying Unsigned32,
        cdChangerCDNbrTracks        Unsigned32 }

-- Data Objects declared in SEQUENCE follow here
```

This table contains data objects for the CD changer: *slot number, slot status, current track playing*, and the *number of tracks* on the CD in the slot.

Table object syntax
- cdChangerSlotTable is its name, and its parent node is cdChangerStatus.
  ○ The OID of cdChangerSlotTable is cdChangerStatus.2
- SYNTAX SEQUENCE OF *Label-of-the-SEQUENCE-statement*
  ○ The label CdChangerSlotEntry is repeated (and must be identical) in the *table object*, the table *entry object*, and the SEQUENCE statement.
  ○ The label must begin with a capital letter and can be any name.
  ○ However, the common naming convention is that it be the name of the *entry object*, modified to begin with a capital letter, as shown in the example.
- ACCESS (SMIv1) or MAX-ACCESS (SMIv2) value must be not-accessible.
- STATUS clause also allows the table to be deprecated or obsolete if necessary.

Table *entry object* syntax

- cdChangerSlotEntry is its name, and its parent node is the *table object* cdChangerSlotTable
    - ○ The OID of cdChangerSlotEntry is cdChangerSlotTable.1
- SYNTAX *Label-of-the-SEQUENCE-statement*
- ACCESS or MAX-ACCESS must have a value not-accessible.
- STATUS clause allows the table to be deprecated or obsolete.
- INDEX clause identifies the index (or indexes) for this table.
    - ○ In this case the INDEX is a data object defined as part of the table, cdChangerSlotNbr.
    - ○ In more complex tables, a table index may be defined elsewhere in the MIB (or even in a different MIB).
- An AUGMENTS clause (SMIv2) may replace the INDEX clause, discussed later in this chapter.

SEQUENCE statement syntax

- The *Label-of-the-SEQUENCE-statement* is that referenced in the *table object* syntax and the *entry object* syntax.
- Has no OID assignment (is not a node or a MIB object)
- Lists pairs of:
    - ○ { dataObjectName   DataType }
    - ○ These are the data objects which populate the table (i.e., the table columns).
    - ○ DataType can be a base type or a derived type (textual convention). Note that SIZE or range limits are not specified, even if limits are specified in the actual definition of the data object.
    - ○ Subsequent data object declarations must match in name and type.

These three elements are followed by definitions of the actual MIB data objects contained in the table, all under the *entry object* node. The syntax of these objects is identical to that of scalar data objects.

Continuing the Example. These are the MIB data objects that follow the Table, Entry, and SEQUENCE statements. The parent node for all of these objects is cdChangerSlotEntry.

```
cdChangerSlotNbr   OBJECT-TYPE
   SYNTAX      Unsigned32 (1..8)
   MAX-ACCESS  not-accessible
   STATUS      current
   DESCRIPTION
      "Slot number and table index."
   ::= { cdChangerSlotEntry 1 }


cdChangerSlotStatus   OBJECT-TYPE
   SYNTAX      INTEGER
           { containsCD(1), empty(2) }
   MAX-ACCESS  read-only
   STATUS      current
   DESCRIPTION
      "CD Changer Slot Status."
   ::= { cdChangerSlotEntry 2 }


cdChangerSlotCDTrackPlaying   OBJECT-TYPE
   SYNTAX      Unsigned32
   MAX-ACCESS  read-only
   STATUS      current
   DESCRIPTION
      "If a CD is currently playing, this is the Track Number.
      This is also the value of cdChangerCDTrackNbr for the CD that is playing.
      = 0 if no CD is currently playing."
   ::= { cdChangerSlotEntry 3 }


cdChangerCDNbrTracks   OBJECT-TYPE
   SYNTAX      Unsigned32
   MAX-ACCESS  read-only
   STATUS      current
   DESCRIPTION
      "The number of Tracks on this CD.
      This is also the size the sub-table cdChangerCDTrackTable
      for this CD - ie, the maximum value of cdChangerCDTrackNbr."
   ::= { cdChangerSlotEntry 4 }
```

Indexed Table Example Diagrams

Diagrams of the CD changer slot table example are shown in several formats:
- MIB diagram (a subset of the diagram shown in Appendix H)
- MIB browser showing MIB structure
- Table matrix with data examples

CD changer slot table diagram showing nodes and data objects. Two parent nodes of the table are shown, then the *table* and *entry objects*, followed by the data objects contained within the table.

```
chateauCDProdStatus(3)

cdChangerStatus(2)

cdChangerSlotTable(2)

cdChangerSlotEntry(1)
INDEX = cdChangerSlotNbr
```

```
cdChangerSlotNbr(1)(NA, uint32)

cdChangerSlotStatus(2)(RO, INT =
    {containsCD(1), empty(2) })

cdChangerSlotCDTrackPlaying(3)(RO, uint32)
    -- = cdChangerCDTrackNbr of song playing
    -- = 0 if no track  playing

chChangerCDNbrTracks(4)(RO, uint32)
    -- = number of tracks on the CD
    -- = size of cdChangerCDTrackTable
```

The next page has further illustrations of the cdChangerSlotTable.

SNMPc MIB browser screen capture showing node progression to the cdChangerSlot-Table, cdChangerSlotEntry, and Slot Table data objects

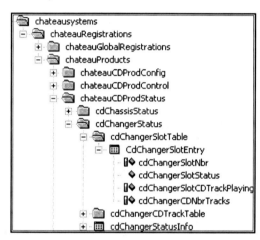

cdChangerSlotTable data objects with example data—trackPlaying = '0' means *not playing*

cdChangerSlotNbr	CdChangerSlotStatus	cdChangerTrackPlaying	cdChangerNbrTracks
1	containsCD	0	12
2	empty	0	0
3	containsCD	2	7
4	containsCD	0	8

properties of the cdChangerSlotTable object

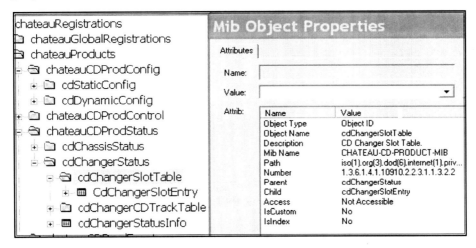

- The object name cdSlotChangerSlotTable is shown.
- The DESCRIPTION can be viewed.
- The numeric OID of the object is available, as well as the equivalent name.
- The child object's name cdChangerSlotEntry object is given.

properties of the cdChangerSlotEntry object

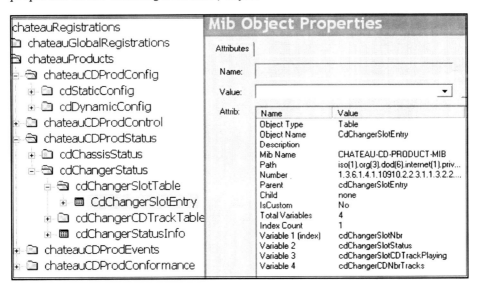

- Additional information includes the number and names of all table objects, and identifies the index object.

Selecting INDEX Objects

Lexicographical Ordering

MIB designers must keep in mind that agents respond to *getnext* requests by return-ing data in lexicographical order. That is, for an object in an indexed table, data will be displayed in index order. For tables with integer indexes, this will be in integer-index order.

Choosing INDEX objects is somewhat of a style issue—what ordering will look best to the user? In the CD changer example, cdChangerSlotNumber was chosen, and *getnext* requests will return table data values in slot-number order.

> For a two-slot changer, *getnext* returned values will be ordered as shown below—the *instance values* shown are the cdChangerSlotNbr *index val-ues.*

```
cdChangerSlotStatus.1
cdChangerSlotStatus.2
cdChangerSlotCDTrackPlaying.1
cdChangerSlotCDTrackPlaying.2
cdChangerSlotCDNbrTracks.1
cdChangerSlotCDNbrTracks.2
```

ACCESS (MAX-ACCESS) Values for INDEXes

The access allowed for an index object can influence the choice of the index.

cdChangerSlotNbr is the INDEX for the example table above. Note that its MAX-ACCESS is not-accessible, which means that a MIB browser cannot *get* this value, it cannot be speci-fied as one of the trap definition OBJECTS, and so values cannot be sent with *traps.*

The rule that INDEX values should be not-accessible in SMIv2 MIBs is relatively recent. The reasoning is that if a manager *gets* any other table value (e.g., cdChangerSlotStatus), the returned message binding:

> PDU = { OID.instance, value }

will contain the INDEX:

INDEX = instance = cdChangerSlotNbr

and cdChangerSlotNbr value can be parsed from the instance value by the manager.

This reasoning is also consistent with observations of programming languages. If an indexed table is declared in the "C" language, the index is not usually also accessible as an element within the table.

If you perform a table-*get* for data from a manager, indeed the index values will still be displayed as expected.

What happens if the INDEX *is* accessible (such as read-only)? A validating compiler will flag warnings, but only if advanced severity checking is specified. MIBs will load successfully into managers.

However, there is an issue concerning *traps* that needs to be considered. If an INDEX object reflects physical configuration (slot number, port number, textual name, etc.) and is not-accessible, those values cannot be sent as data OBJECTS in traps. When the network engineer designs trap filters in a manager, *value matching logic* for these objects may not be possible. And while it is also true that managers can be coded to parse out these values from the instance values of other OBJECTS sent with the *trap*, not all currently have this capability.

From a practical standpoint, MIB developers may want to consider:

1. Make the table index accessible (read-only), and include index objects in trap OBJECTS as needed. Decide not to worry about validating the MIB at higher severity settings.

2. Define an arbitrary INDEX of type Unsigned32, which is not-accessible, and which has no physical meaning. Include cdChangerSlotNbr as read-only data within the table. This allows any data needed for trap filter matching to be sent as OBJECTS with *traps*, and also allows the MIB to pass all validation testing.

    With an arbitrary index, agent semantics can be defined to still return *getnext* values in slot-number order.

This important issue is revisited using an expanded example in Chapter 19, *More on Trap Syntax*.

Multiple and Shared Indexes

Multiple Indexes

There is no specific limit to the number of indexes for a table. However each index adds instance values to the OID, and the encoded *OID.instance* length can have no more than 128 elements. Integer indexes add one element to the instance, but other index types (see Chapter 14) add more than one element.

SMIv2 example of multiple indexes from the CD player MIB. For each slot, there is a CD with multiple tracks. The cdChangerCDTrackTable has two indexes; the first is shared with the cdChangerSlotTable.

```
cdChangerCDTrackTable OBJECT-TYPE
    SYNTAX        SEQUENCE OF CdChangerCDTrackEntry
    MAX-ACCESS  not-accessible
    STATUS        current
    DESCRIPTION  "Changer Track Table for a single CD."
    ::= { cdChangerStatus 3 }

cdChangerCDTrackEntry  OBJECT-TYPE
    SYNTAX        CdChangerCDTrackEntry
    MAX-ACCESS  not-accessible
    STATUS        current
    DESCRIPTION  "An entry in cdChangerCDTrackTable."
    INDEX  { cdChangerSlotNbr, cdChangerCDTrackNbr }        -- 2 INDEXES
    ::= { cdChangerCDTrackTable 1 }

CdChangerCDTrackEntry  ::=
    SEQUENCE {
        cdChangerCDTrackNbr              Unsigned32,
        cdChangerCDTrackPlaying         TruthValue,
        cdChangerCDTrackLengthSecs      Unsigned32,
        cdChangerCDTrackLengthStr       DisplayString,
        cdChangerCDTrackTitle           DisplayString,
        cdChangerCDTrackArtist          DisplayString }
```

The diagram below shows values for cdChangerCDTrackTable, for the INDEX cdChangerCDTrackNbr = 3 and INDEX trackNumber = 1..7). Track data object names have been abbreviated, and not all table objects are shown.

cdChangerSlotNbr	CdChangerSlotStatus	cdChangerTrackPlaying	cdChangerNbrTracks		cdChangerSlotNbr	trackNbr	trackPlaying	trackLengthSecs	trackTitle
1	containsCD	0	12		3	1	false	120	"Ours is no OID-inary love"
2	empty	0	0		3	2	true	122	"Confusin' me with version 3"
3	containsCD	2	7		3	3	false	129	"Love is a tender trap"
4	containsCD	0	8		3	4	false	94	"Always SMI-ling at my mib-2"
					3	5	false	200	"I can't get enough of you"
					3	6	false	99	"Whose love will I getnext?"
					3	7	false	170	"Forgive me for my MIB-stakes"

AUGMENTS Clause (SMIv2)

In SMIv2 MIBs the AUGMENTS clause can be used to extend a previously defined table with additional data objects.

AUGMENTS replaces the INDEX clause. The extension is one-to-one (i.e., each index in the base table has existence in the extension table).

An example is given on the next page.

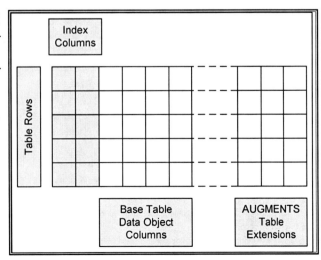

Example of the AUGMENTS clause from RFC-2863 *The Interfaces Group MIB* IF-MIB, the Interfaces Extension Table. There is a one-to-one relationship between entries in the ifTable and the ifXTable. The extension objects are named in the SEQUENCE statement.

```
ifXTable        OBJECT-TYPE
    SYNTAX         SEQUENCE OF IfXEntry
    MAX-ACCESS  not-accessible
    STATUS         current
    DESCRIPTION "List of interface entries.  Number of entries = ifNumber.
        This table contains additional objects for the interface table."
    ::= { ifMIBObjects 1 }

ifXEntry        OBJECT-TYPE
    SYNTAX         IfXEntry
    MAX-ACCESS  not-accessible
    STATUS         current
    DESCRIPTION
        "Entry of additional mgmt info  applicable to a particular interface."
    AUGMENTS    { ifEntry }
    ::= { ifXTable 1 }

IfXEntry ::=                                    -- List of the augmenting objects
    SEQUENCE { ifName              DisplayString,
        ifInMulticastPkts          Counter32,
        ifInBroadcastPkts          Counter32,
        ifOutMulticastPkts         Counter32,
        ifOutBroadcastPkts         Counter32,
        ifHCInOctets               Counter64,
        ifHCInUcastPkts            Counter64,
        ifHCInMulticastPkts        Counter64,
        ifHCInBroadcastPkts        Counter64,
        ifHCOutOctets              Counter64,
        ifHCOutUcastPkts           Counter64,
        ifHCOutMulticastPkts       Counter64,
        ifHCOutBroadcastPkts       Counter64,
        ifLinkUpDownTrapEnable     INTEGER,
        ifHighSpeed                Gauge32,
        ifPromiscuousMode          TruthValue,
        ifConnectorPresent         TruthValue,
        ifAlias                    DisplayString,
        ifCounterDiscontinuityTime TimeStamp }
```

Sparse Table Extensions

If there is a sparse relationship between the extension table and the base table, the AUGMENTS clause is not appropriate, and an INDEX clause must be used which repeats the index object name (or names) specified by the INDEX clause in the base table.

The table extension may define new data objects that apply only to specific equipment types, where the equipment type is defined by one of the base table data objects. For example, extension table objects might apply only to Ethernet interfaces.

In the diagram below, the base table has two indexes. The INDEX clause for the extension table will name the same two index data objects.

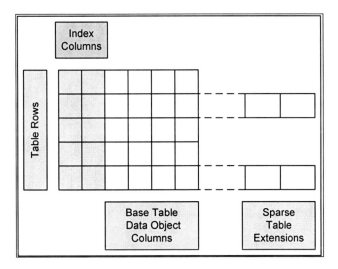

An example of a sparse table extension appears on the next page.

Example of sparse table extension from RFC-2358 EtherLike-MIB. The dot-3ControlTable extends the dot3StatsTable, but only for interfaces which implement the MAC Control sub-layer.

```
dot3ControlTable OBJECT-TYPE
        SYNTAX        SEQUENCE OF Dot3ControlEntry
        MAX-ACCESS  not-accessible
        STATUS        current
        DESCRIPTION "A table of descriptive and status information
            about the MAC Control sub-layer on the ethernet-like
            interfaces attached to a particular system. There
            will be one row in this table for each ethernet-like
            interface in the system which implements the MAC
            Control sublayer.  If some, but not all, of the
            ethernet-like interfaces in the system implement the
            MAC Control sublayer, there will be fewer
            rows in this table than in the dot3StatsTable."
        ::= { dot3 9 }

    dot3ControlEntry OBJECT-TYPE
        SYNTAX        Dot3ControlEntry
        MAX-ACCESS  not-accessible
        STATUS        current
        DESCRIPTION "An entry in the table, containing information
            about the MAC Control sublayer on a single
            ethernet-like interface."
        INDEX      { dot3StatsIndex }        -- Index from the dot3StatsTable
        ::= { dot3ControlTable 1 }

    Dot3ControlEntry ::=
        SEQUENCE { dot3ControlFunctionsSupported  BITS,
            dot3ControlInUnknownOpcodes              Counter32,
            dot3HCControlInUnknownOpcodes            Counter64 }
```

Note that the INDEX object dot2StatsIndex does not appear in this table's SEQUENCE statement but is used from the definition in the table being extended.

Enterprise Extensions to Standard MIB Tables

Enterprise MIBs can extend standard MIB indexed tables to define enterprise-specific managed objects.

For example, a vendor might define enterprise-specific extensions to the interface table ifTable defined in the standard RFC1213-MIB.

This can be done in either of two ways. In both approaches, the extension objects to the standard ifTable will be defined within the enterprise's OID space (*not* in the IETF standard MIB space).

> *Example-1.* IMPORTS ifIndex and uses it in the table entry INDEX clause. This approach is suitable for sparse extensions—i.e., a subset of rows will support values in the extension columns.

```
IMPORTS ifIndex FROM RFC1213-MIB;
. . . . . . . . . .

vronxInterfaceEntry  OBJECT-TYPE
    SYNTAX        VronxInterfaceEntry
    MAX-ACCESS  not-accessible
    STATUS        current
    DESCRIPTION
      "An entry in vronxInterfaceTable."
    INDEX   { ifIndex }
    ::= { vronxInterfaceTable 1 }


VronxInterfaceEntry ::=
    SEQUENCE                          -- the list of vronx extension data objects
        {
        vronxInterfaceUserAlias     DisplayString,
        vronxInterfaceType          INTEGER
        }
```

Example-2. IMPORTS ifEntry and uses it in the table entry AUGMENTS clause (SMIv2). This approach is suitable for dependent extensions—i.e., all indexes in the ifTable are supported by values in the extension objects.

```
IMPORTS ifEntry FROM RFC1213-MIB;
. . . . . . . . . .


vronxInterfaceEntry  OBJECT-TYPE
    SYNTAX        VronxInterfaceEntry
    MAX-ACCESS  not-accessible
    STATUS        current
    DESCRIPTION
       "An entry in vronxInterfaceTable."
    AUGMENTS   { ifEntry }
    ::= { vronxInterfaceTable 1 }



VronxInterfaceEntry  ::=
    SEQUENCE {                         -- the list of vronx extension data objects
               vronxInterfaceUserAlias      DisplayString,
               vronxInterfaceType           INTEGER
           }
```

Exercises

1. In SNMP indexed tables, what do the columns represent? What do the rows represent?

2. Explain the relationship of table index values to data object OID instance values.

3. Name the three syntactic elements needed to define an SNMP indexed table.

4. Which of the three elements contains the INDEX object declarations?

5. What is lexicographical ordering? How does the selection of the INDEX affect this ordering?

6. What is the preferred ACCESS (SMIv1) or MAX-ACCESS (SMIv2) value for INDEX data objects?

7. You need to define a table with two indexes. How do you code this syntax?

8. Extensions of existing tables can be coded using either:

   INDEX { name-of-index-object-from-base-table }, or

   AUGMENTS { name-of-something }

   What is the name-of-something?

   How do these two methods differ?

Index Data Types

An integer data type is the most commonly encountered SYNTAX for INDEX objects in tables.

This chapter elaborates on the use of integer indexes and introduces additional data types also used as indexes:

- IP addresses
- Network addresses (SMIv1)
- Octet strings (including text strings)
- Object identifiers

Remember that a table data object's *index* is also the *instance* value that is appended to the OID. Thus, index data types such as strings or object identifiers will result in instances that have multiple dotted integer elements.

The maximum number of elements in an OID.instance is 128. This is a consideration in choosing index data types. For example, very long DisplayString object index values could result in OID.instance values that exceed this size limit.

```
DEFINITIONS MY-MIB-NAME ::= BEGIN

IMPORTS syntax

MODULE-IDENTITY statement

TEXTUAL-CONVENTION definitions
Node definitions

Scalar Data Objects

Table Object
Entry Object INDEX Clause
Table SEQUENCE statement
Table Data Objects

TRAP-TYPE Objects (SMIv1)
NOTIFICATION-TYPE Objects (SMIv2)

OBJECT-GROUP lists
NOTIFICATION-GROUP lists
MODULE-COMPLIANCE grouping lists

END
```

An SMIv2 INDEX clause can contain the optional IMPLIED keyword, which is confusing but which will be explained. Lexicographical ordering for tables with non-integer indexes is discussed, and is affected by use of the IMPLIED keyword.

Integer Indexes

Chapter 13 provided examples of integer index use.

Although often typed as INTEGER in SMIv1 MIBs and as Integer32 in SMIv2 MIBs, integer index values cannot be negative.

Values of zero are valid, but are discouraged (an *index* or *instance* of zero looks a lot like a scalar object instance, and can be confusing to users).

However, if the index object is based on the physical realization of something that has a zero value, then zero is acceptable.

> *For example,* routerPortNumber has values (0..15), and could be used as a table index.

Enumerated INTEGER objects can also be used as table indexes.

Index values do not need to be contiguous, and often are not. Tables may be very sparsely populated, with index values widely separated.

Example of Host Resources MIB table showing software processes with non-contiguous indexes

hrSWRunIndex	hrSWRunName	hrS\
1	System Idle Process	▲
8	System	
164	smss.exe	
196	csrss.exe	
216	winlogon.exe	
244	services.exe	
256	lsass.exe	
356	svchost.exe	
428	svchost.exe	
460	spoolsv.exe	
488	avgamsvr.exe	

If using an integer index, it is sensible to declare it as INTEGER, Integer32, or Unsigned32. Declarations of other integer-based types (Counter, Gauge) may result in compiler complaints.

IpAddress Indexes

An IpAddress index type is a special case of the more general OCTET STRING, in that it is exactly 4 octets in size. The instance value for an IpAddress index type is exactly the IP address (encoded in hex).

Example of IpAddress index from the *RFC1213-MIB,* INDEX is ipAdEntAddr of type IpAddress

```
ipAddrTable OBJECT-TYPE
    SYNTAX      SEQUENCE OF IpAddrEntry
    ACCESS      not-accessible
    STATUS      mandatory
    DESCRIPTION "Table of addressing information relevant to this
                    entity's IP addresses."
    ::= { ip 20 }


ipAddrEntry OBJECT-TYPE
    SYNTAX  IpAddrEntry
    ACCESS  not-accessible
    STATUS  mandatory
    DESCRIPTION "Addressing information for one of this
                    entity's IP addresses."
    INDEX   { ipAdEntAddr }
    ::= { ipAddrTable 1 }


IpAddrEntry ::=
    SEQUENCE {
    ipAdEntAddr             IpAddress,      -- the INDEX object
    ipAdEntIfIndex          INTEGER,        -- xref value of ifIndex for a row in ifTable
    ipAdEntNetMask          IpAddress,
    ipAdEntBcastAddr        INTEGER,
    ipAdEntReasmMaxSize     INTEGER (0..65535) }


ipAdEntAddr OBJECT-TYPE
    SYNTAX  IpAddress
    ACCESS  read-only
    STATUS  mandatory
    DESCRIPTION "IP address to which this entry's addressing
                    information pertains."
    ::= { ipAddrEntry 1 }
```

For index ipAdEntAddr = 198.245.15.101 the instance value for ipAdEntNetMask is:

ipAdEntNetMask.instance = ipAdEntNetMask.C6.F5.0F.65

Note that there is no *octet count* preceding the four IP address octets (as there is for other OCTET STRING based index types).

Example of multi-indexed table using four indexes of types INTEGER and IpAddress. From RFC-4292 *IP Forwarding Table MIB*, the IP-FORWARD-MIB, containing the ipForwardTable.

```
ipForwardEntry OBJECT-TYPE
    SYNTAX        IpForwardEntry
    MAX-ACCESS    not-accessible
    STATUS        obsolete
    DESCRIPTION
        "A particular route to a particular destination,
         under a particular policy."
    INDEX {
            ipForwardDest,
            ipForwardProto,
            ipForwardPolicy,
            ipForwardNextHop }
    ::= { ipForwardTable 1 }


IpForwardEntry ::= SEQUENCE {
        ipForwardDest       IpAddress,       -- Index1
        ipForwardMask       IpAddress,
        ipForwardPolicy     Integer32,       -- Index3
        ipForwardNextHop    IpAddress,       -- Index4
        ipForwardIfIndex    Integer32,
        ipForwardType       INTEGER,
        ipForwardProto      INTEGER,         -- Index2 (enumeration)
        ipForwardAge        Integer32,
        ipForwardInfo       OBJECT IDENTIFIER,
        ipForwardNextHopAS  Integer32,
        ipForwardMetric1    Integer32,
        ipForwardMetric2    Integer32,
        ipForwardMetric3    Integer32,
        ipForwardMetric4    Integer32,
        ipForwardMetric5    Integer32 }
```

For this table definition, a *MIB-walk* screen capture of instance and object values looks like

```
ipForwardDest.0.0.0.0.3.0.192.168.1.1=0.0.0.0
ipForwardDest.127.0.0.0.2.0.127.0.0.1=127.0.0.0
ipForwardAge.0.0.0.0.3.0.192.168.1.1=24465
ipForwardAge.127.0.0.0.2.0.127.0.0.1=24489
ipForwardAge.192.168.1.0.2.0.192.168.1.46=24472
ipForwardAge.192.168.1.46.2.0.127.0.0.1=24472
ipForwardAge.192.168.1.255.2.0.192.168.1.46=24472
ipForwardAge.224.0.0.0.2.0.192.168.1.46=24472
ipForwardAge.255.255.255.255.2.0.192.168.1.46=24511
ipForwardInfo.0.0.0.0.3.0.192.168.1.1=0.0
```

where the indexes for the highlighted line are:

index1 = ipForwardDest	= 192.168.1.46	
index2 = ipForwardProto	= 2 (enumerated value = local (2))	
index3 = ipForwardPolicy	= 0	
index4 = ipForwardNextHop	= 127.0.0.1	

and the value of:

ipForwardAge.index1.index2.index3.index4 = 24472 seconds

properties of the IpForwardEntry object, identifying the index objects

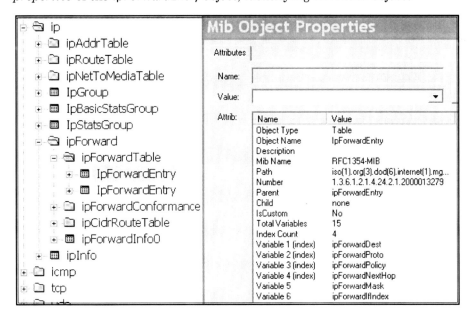

NetworkAddress Indexes (SMIv1)

SMIv1 NetworkAddress index objects provide for multiple address *types*, but only the IP address *type* is actually defined (and its *type* is encoded by the preceding '1' in the instance value).

An example object encoding for an IP NetworkAddress value of 198.245.15.101 would be (with instance octets shown in decimal):

tableDataObject.1.198.245.15.101

This is the subtle SMIv2 conversion issue mentioned when NetworkAddress syntax, and its use as an index, was previously discussed (Chapter 9).

> **SNMP Tidbit.** If NetworkAddress is used as an index object, its instance value will have a preceding '1'. If this MIB is converted to SMIv2, the NetworkAddress object will be converted to an IpAddress type.
>
> IpAddress objects used as indexes do *not* have a '1' preceding the instance value. This results in differences in returned instances and lexicographical ordering, depending on which MIB syntax version is supported.

Most SMIv1 MIBs that used a NetworkAddress type as a table index have since deprecated that usage and replaced it with an IpAddress object.

OCTET STRING and DisplayString Indexes

OCTET STRING and DisplayString objects are both represented as hex strings, and their usage as indexes are similar.

There are two cases to discuss:
1. Fixed-length strings
2. Variable-length strings

Fixed Length Strings

Example of fixed length OCTET STRING object syntax

```
vronxLanguageIndex OBJECT-TYPE
    SYNTAX        OCTET STRING (SIZE(2))      -- exactly two octets
    MAX-ACCESS  read-only
    STATUS        current
    DESCRIPTION
      "A two character ASCII code specifying the language.
       Examples en, fr, de."
    ::= { vronxEntry 2 }
```

A fixed length string (used as an index) with length 'n' will have 'n' dotted decimal components in the *index* or *instance* extension.

if vronxLanguageIndex = "fr"

> *then* table object OID and instance for vronxStatus are:

> > vronxStatus.index = vronxStatus.f.r
> > vronxStatus.index = vronxStatus.102.114

Variable Length Strings

Example of variable length DisplayString object syntax

```
vronxLanguageIndex OBJECT-TYPE
    SYNTAX        DisplayString(SIZE(2..32))       -- 2 to 32 octets
    MAX-ACCESS  read-only
    STATUS        current
    DESCRIPTION
      "Text string naming the language to be used. EG 'french'"
    ::= { vronxEntry 2 }
```

A variable length string (used as an index) with length 'n' will have 'n+1' components in the *index* or *instance* extension, where the first element = 'n' is the size of the string (the count of octets following).

if vronxLanguageIndex = "french"

> *then* table object OID and instance values are (numbers shown in decimal)

> vronxStatus.index = vronx.6.f.r.e.n.c.h
> = vronxStatus.6.102.114.101.110.99.104

The inclusion of the IMPLIED keyword in an INDEX clause affects this encoding, and will be discussed soon—but first OBJECT IDENTIFIER indexes are covered.

OBJECT IDENTIFIER Indexes

An OBJECT IDENTIFIER can be used as an index and is encoded as a variable length OCTET STRING (discussed above).

> *Example* of OBJECT IDENTIFIER syntax

```
vronxLanguageIndex OBJECT-TYPE
    SYNTAX        OBJECT IDENTIFIER
    MAX-ACCESS  read-only
    STATUS        current
    DESCRIPTION
      "Globally unique identifier for the language to be used,
       as defined in vronx document 'Stuff You Need to Know'
       and in the vronx STUFF-MIB.
       For example vronxLanguageIndex can assume a value of:
        'french' is an enumerated OID = 1.3.6.1.4.1.10910.2.1.16.3
        "
    ::= { vronxEntry 2 }
```

An object typed as an OBJECT IDENTIFIER (used as an index) with length 'n' will have 'n+1' components in the *index* or *instance* extension, where the first element is the size of the OID value (the count of octets following).

if vronxLanguageIndex (the OID enumeration for french):

> = 1.3.6.1.4.1.10910.2.1.16.3
> the number of octets in this OID value is 11

and table object and instances will be (instances shown in decimal):

> vronxStatus.index = vronxStatus.11.1.3.6.1.4.1.10910.2.1.16.3

The inclusion of the IMPLIED keyword in an INDEX clause affects the encoding, and is discussed next.

INDEX Clause with the IMPLIED Keyword

In SMIv2 MIBs you may encounter the IMPLIED keyword within an INDEX clause.

Before the use of IMPLIED is described, here's a quote from RFC-3216 *SMIng Objectives (2001)*. SMIng stands for *SMI new generation*. This is an INFORMATIONAL RFC.

> 4.1.36 Deprecate Use of IMPLIED Keyword
>
> Type: fix
> From: WG
> Description: The SMIng SNMP mapping must deprecate the use of the
>   IMPLIED indexing schema.
> Motivation: IMPLIED is confusing and most people don't understand it.
>   The solution (IMPLIED) is worse than the problem it is trying to
>   solve and therefore for the sake of simplicity, the use of IMPLIED
>   should be deprecated.

The Problem IMPLIED Attempts to Fix

Octet strings of variable length (including the OID type) are lexicographically sorted not just by values of the index itself, but including index value *length* encodings (i.e. the 'n' count of octets that precede the index octets themselves). From one of the previous examples:

```
vronxLanguageIndex OBJECT-TYPE
    SYNTAX    DisplayString(SIZE(2..32))
```

Alphabetically (actually, *ascii-betically*) ordered values for vronxLanguage-Index are:
```
        english
        french
        greek
```

However lexicographical ordering for the vronxStatus object for these *instance* values will be

5.g.r.e.e.k	*or*	5.103.114.101.101.107
6.f.r.e.n.c.h	*or*	6.102.114.101.110.99.104
7.e.n.g.l.i.s.h	*or*	7.101.110.103.108.105.115.104

The IMPLIED Keyword Solution

The IMPLIED keyword is a compiler directive that encodes index values as if they were fixed length, without the preceding 'n' octet count, and allows objects to be lexicographically sorted as expected (*ascii-betically* with no concern for octet length).

Example of the IMPLIED keyword from RFC-3413 *Simple Network Management Protocol (SNMP) Applications* (one of the SNMPv3 Definitional RFCs), the SNMP-PROXY-MIB

```
snmpProxyEntry OBJECT-TYPE
    SYNTAX        SnmpProxyEntry
    MAX-ACCESS    not-accessible
    STATUS        current
    DESCRIPTION
        "A set of translation parameters used by a proxy forwarder
        application for forwarding SNMP messages.

        Entries in the snmpProxyTable are created and deleted
        using the snmpProxyRowStatus object."
    INDEX { IMPLIED snmpProxyName }
    ::= { snmpProxyTable 1 }
```

In this example INDEX snmpProxyName is of type SnmpAdminString (textual values, equivalent to type DisplayString).

Good goals! However:

A few limitations are discussed in RFC-2578 *Structure of Management Information Version 2 (SMIv2)*

> Note that the IMPLIED keyword can only be present for an object
> having a variable-length syntax (e.g., variable-length strings or
> object identifier-valued objects), Further, the IMPLIED keyword can
> only be associated with the last object in the INDEX clause.
> Finally, the IMPLIED keyword may not be used on a variable-length
> string object if that string might have a value of zero-length.

And, finally, from RFC-4181 *Guidelines for Authors and Reviewers of MIB Documents*

> Use of the IMPLIED keyword is NOT RECOMMENDED for any index
> object that may appear in the INDEX clause of an expansion table.
> Since this keyword may be associated only with the last object in
> an INDEX clause, it cannot be associated with the same index
> object in a primary table and an expansion table. This will
> cause the sort order to be different in the primary table and any
> expansion tables. As a consequence, an implementation will be
> unable to reuse indexing code from the primary table in expansion
> tables, and data structures meant to be extended might actually have
> to be replicated.
> Designers who are tempted to use IMPLIED
> should consider that the resulting sort order rarely meets user
> expectations, particularly for strings that include both
> uppercase and lowercase letters, and it does not take the user language
> or locale into account.

Summary of INDEX Object Choices

MIB designers choosing INDEX objects must consider:

- For single or multiple indexes, will the resultant lexicographical ordering be what a user is expecting to see from *getnext* operations (especially for non-integer indexes)?
- Will agent software developers understand the lexicographical order requirements for non-integer indexes and have the time to code this more complicated logic?
  - We all agree that they *should* understand, and *should* take the time—but there are existing faulty deployments.
  - If project schedules are tight, it may be better to produce a simpler, correct agent than a complex, faulty agent by coding the MIB with integer indexes.
- Any index types other than integers (e.g., DisplayString) will add multiple dotted integer values to express an instance value. Is it possible that such a choice will result in an illegal OID.instance size greater than 128 octets?
- INDEX accessibility issues are mentioned in Chapter 13 and will be discussed further in Chapter 19; a synopsis of these issues:
  - If the INDEX object has physical relevance, is it acceptable that a manager cannot *get* this not-accessible value.
  - INDEX objects with ACCESS or MAX-ACCESS not-accessible are not available for inclusion in trap OBJECTS or VARIABLES.
  - If values for such objects may be useful for configuring trap filters, do targeted managers support parsing this information out of *instance* values bound with other trap OBJECTS sent with the trap from the same table?
  - Some of the issues above can be resolved by specifying MAX-ACCESS read-only. Is it acceptable that this MIB will not pass this MIB validation test?

Exercises

1. Index types include integers. How do integer index values map to data object instance values?

2. Index types also include several based on OCTET STRING. How do these index values map to data object instance values?

Chapter 15

Row-Create Tables

This chapter discusses a special case of indexed tables that finds use in quite a few standard MIBs and in some enterprise MIBs.

First discussed is the ability of *agents* to add rows to tables. This common logic is interesting, but is not the primary topic of this chapter.

Next, the ability of *managers* to create new rows in tables managed by agents on remote platforms is presented.

Remember that table *rows* represent instances of objects. When a new *row* is added to a table, a new indexed set of table objects (the columns of the table) is added.

Manager row creation utilizes syntax presented in previous chapters. It will be useful for the reader to review these two items before proceeding with this chapter.

```
DEFINITIONS MY-MIB-NAME ::= BEGIN

IMPORTS syntax

MODULE-IDENTITY statement

TEXTUAL-CONVENTION definitions
Node definitions

Scalar Data Objects

Table Object
Entry Object
Table SEQUENCE statement
Table Data Objects

TRAP-TYPE Objects (SMIv1)
NOTIFICATION-TYPE Objects (SMIv2)

OBJECT-GROUP lists
NOTIFICATION-GROUP lists
MODULE-COMPLIANCE grouping lists

END
```

1. The MAX-ACCESS read-create values discussed in Chapter 9.
2. The TEXTUAL-CONVENTION RowStatus discussed in Chapter 10.

The example given in Chapter 10 for pingCtlRowStatus object in the DISMAN-PING-MIB will be expanded in this chapter. This expansion also provides additional examples of:

- A multi-indexed table
- A text string (SnmpAdminString) used as an index
- BITS data type usage

Agent Row Creation

When SNMP literature mentions row-create logic, it always refers to manager row creation logic, which is the primary topic of this chapter. But first the ability of an agent (on its own initiative) to manage indexed table row existence is discussed.

Agents commonly create new rows within indexed tables.

For example, for the ifTable defined in RFC-1213, agents responsible for managing this table periodically inspect the hardware, determine how many interfaces are present, and populate the ifTable with a number of rows that is exactly the number of interfaces.

Another example is for a simple MIB that models a chassis containing slots. If a slot is occupied by a module, the agent creates a table row with the table index value = slotNumber. If a module is removed, the agent removes that row from the table.

This diagram shows an agent adding a row to this simple table

slotNumber	moduleType	serialNbr
1	powerSupply	12345
4	processor	23456
7	ethernetIf	34567

slotNumber	moduleType	serialNbr
3	expander	45678

New Row

In this example, choice of the slotNumber as table index guarantees ordered index assignments.

However, in situations where the index may be arbitrary (no physical or logical significance), agent logic to add and remove rows should maintain orderly index values—index values for persistent rows should not change (be reassigned) by the agent when another is added or removed.

Alternate MIB Models for Chassis-slot Management

A brief digression from row creation—to discuss a common modeling problem, how to model chassis-slot architectures. This discussion also applies to modeling the logical number of active interfaces, the number of active ports on a module, etc.

Agent row creation is one way for MIB/agent designers to model chassis slots. If a slot is occupied by a module, create a corresponding row. If a module is removed, delete a row. Module insertion and removal may be an event of interest to managers and can be reported by traps.

Two alternate modeling methods involve knowing the maximum number of slots, which is always the table size.

1. Define a new enumerated INTEGER object slotStatus for all rows (1..16) with values:
   { empty(1), modulePresent(2) }

2. Expand the ModuleType enumeration definitions to include a value for empty. The full list would look like:
   { empty(1), powerSupply(2), processor(3), ethernetIf(4), expander(5) }

In both of these alternatives, sending traps when modules are inserted or removed may be appropriate.

Manager Row Creation

With properly designed MIBs and agents, managers can *also* create new rows of data in tables managed by agents on remote platforms. They accomplish this by instructing the agent to add (or delete) rows, and by providing the agent with appropriate data values to populate objects in the new row.

In the next graphical example, a simple MIB access control table is defined which allows manager platforms identified by IP addresses MIB access privileges. An accessPriv = privileged is required to create and delete rows in the control table itself.

A manager performs a *set* operation to the agent, supplying values for accessIpAddr, accessPriv, and rowStatus = createAndGo(4) (a RowStatus textual convention value—Chapter 10).

A test value for table Index is supplied as the *instance value* for the three objects. If the manager is already privileged, and if the Index value is not in use, the agent will create the new row, store the values, and then modify the rowStatus value to active.

Manager row-create example

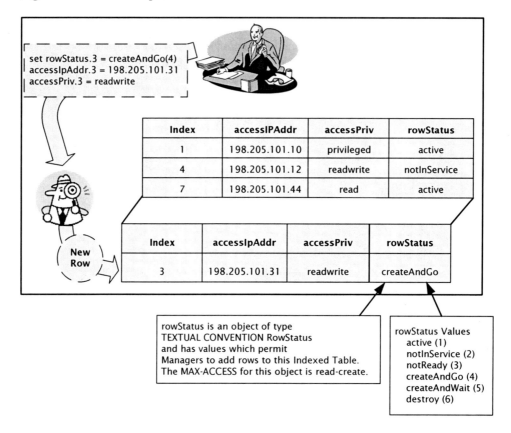

RFC-2579 *Textual Conventions for SMIv2* provides extensive descriptions of the RowStatus TEXTUAL-CONVENTION and how managers can manipulate this value to create and otherwise manage table rows. Briefer descriptions appear here, followed by several more examples.

For a table with an integer index, a manager selects a random positive integer, and uses it as an *instance* value (*index*) to *set* the rowStatus object to a value of either createAndGo(4) or createAndWait(5).

> rowStatus.randomIntegerIndex = value

> createAndGo(4) is appropriate if the manager simultaneously *sets* all table column values along with the rowStatus object

> createAndWait(5) is appropriate if the manager initially *sets* values for a subset of the table column objects, followed by *sets* for additional object values, and finally by a *set* of the rowStatus to active(1)

If the specified *index* value is already in use by the targeted agent, this initial attempt to create a new row fails, and the manager must try again with a different *index* value.

Once a row has been successfully created, the manager can control its status (and existence) by *sets* to the rowStatus with values:

active(1), notInService(2), destroy(6)

The rowStatus object must have a MAX-ACCESS of read-create. All other columnar objects must have access of:
- read-create
- read-only
- accessible-for-notify
- not-accessible
- A value of read-write is not allowed

Agent semantics should be defined.
- If the agent restarts, what happens to row existence?
  - This can be controlled by adding a StorageType (*textual convention*— Chapter 10) object to the table, or by augmenting the DESCRIPTION clause.
- If the agent is also able to independently add or delete rows, this logic should be described.

Several standard MIB examples are shown on the following pages:
- Standard Ping MIB
- A comparable Cisco Ping MIB is referenced
- SNMPv3 Agent Configuration MIB
- RMON/RMON2 MIBs are mentioned
- Scheduling MIB

Standard PING MIB Example

Example of row creation from RFC-4560 *Definitions of Managed Objects for Remote Ping, Traceroute, and Lookup Operations* the DISMAN-PING-MIB

```
pingCtlTable OBJECT-TYPE
    SYNTAX        SEQUENCE OF PingCtlEntry
    MAX-ACCESS    not-accessible
    STATUS        current
    DESCRIPTION  "(description deleted for this example)."
    ::= { pingObjects 2 }

pingCtlEntry OBJECT-TYPE
    SYNTAX        PingCtlEntry
    MAX-ACCESS    not-accessible
    STATUS        current
    DESCRIPTION "(description deleted for this example, to fit)"
    INDEX { pingCtlOwnerIndex, pingCtlTestName }
    ::= { pingCtlTable 1 }

PingCtlEntry ::=
    SEQUENCE {
        pingCtlOwnerIndex            SnmpAdminString,      -- Index 1
        pingCtlTestName              SnmpAdminString,      -- Index 2
        pingCtlTargetAddressType     InetAddressType,
        pingCtlTargetAddress         InetAddress,
        pingCtlDataSize              Unsigned32,
        pingCtlTimeOut               Unsigned32,
        pingCtlProbeCount            Unsigned32,
        pingCtlAdminStatus           INTEGER,
        pingCtlDataFill              OCTET STRING,
        pingCtlFrequency             Unsigned32,
        pingCtlMaxRows               Unsigned32,
        pingCtlStorageType           StorageType,
        pingCtlTrapGeneration        BITS,
        pingCtlTrapProbeFailureFilter Unsigned32,
        pingCtlTrapTestFailureFilter Unsigned32,
        pingCtlType                  OBJECT IDENTIFIER,
        pingCtlDescr                 SnmpAdminString,
        pingCtlSourceAddressType     InetAddressType,
        pingCtlSourceAddress          InetAddress,
        pingCtlIfIndex               InterfaceIndexOrZero,
        pingCtlByPassRouteTable      TruthValue,
        pingCtlDSField               Unsigned32,
        pingCtlRowStatus             RowStatus  }          -- Row Status
```

Manager on platform A can remotely add a row to the pingCtlTable in this MIB (managed by an agent on platform B). When this row is set to active(1) by the manager, the agent on platform B will *ping* the agent on the manager-specified platform C, and record the results in a separate pingResultsTable (not shown), which can then be retrieved by manager *get* operations.

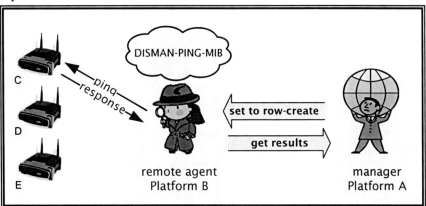

This is a nicely designed MIB offering lots of *ping test* flexibility. Some of its features are described here using a simple test setup example.

The pingCtlTable has two indexes (both text strings)—pingCtlOwnerIndex and pingCtlTestName. This makes it easy to create a row with unique index values (on the first try) and also serves to nicely document the test.

To create a new row (a new ping test), the manager will *set* pingCtlRow-Status (with an instance value corresponding to the two chosen index values) to a value of createAndWait(5). *For example*:

pingCtlRowStatus."OwnerWalsh"."Test9Feb" = createAndWait(5)

pingCtlRowStatus.10.O.w.n.e.r.W.a.l.s.h.8.T.e.s.t.9.F.e.b = createAndWait(5)

If a row is successfully created (and it probably will be, given the uniqueness of the two index values), the manager will next perform *sets* for other data in the control table. All objects in the table have MAX-ACCESS read-create. Some objects are required, many have default values, and others are optional.

pingTargetAddressType will default to a value of ipv4(1)

set pingCtlTargetAddress to the IP address of the ping target

> *set* pingCtlDataSize to the size of the ping data portion (octets)
>
> *set* pingCtlTimeOut to a value in seconds (defaults to 3 seconds)
>
> *set* pingCtlProbeCount to the number of pings that comprise a single test (defaults to 1)
>
> *set* pingCtlTrapGeneration BITS to generate traps for various test result conditions (probeFailure(0), testFailure(1), testCompletion(2)), or set all BITS = 0 for no traps
>
> *set* pingCtlRowStatus to active(1)
>
> *set* pingCtlAdminStatus to enabled(1) to start the test
>
> *set* pingCtlAdminStatus to disabled(2) to halt a test

After a test is complete, the row can be deleted by:

> *set* pingCtlRowStatus to value destroy(6)

Cisco PING MIB

Cisco also has its own enterprise CISCO-PING-MIB that is a bit simpler to configure than the standard Ping MIB and is supported by agents on many Cisco products.

Row creation involves selecting a single unique integer index, and test results are contained within the created row rather in a separate table.

Copies of this MIB can be found on the Cisco web site or on the MIB Depot web site.

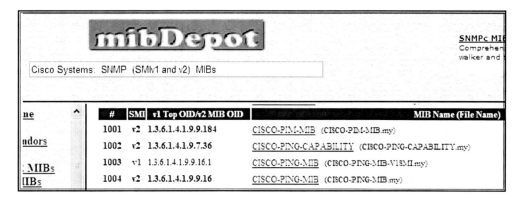

SNMPv3 Agent Configuration Example

Version 3 agents on managed devices may be configured locally using GUI interfaces, by editing text files read at agent startup, using a command-lines interface, etc.

Regardless of configuration method, all agent configuration objects have their existence in MIB definitions. As a result, managers can also configure SNMPv3 agents remotely using *set* operations to those MIB data objects.

Example of row creation from RFC-3413, containing the SNMPv3 SNMP-TARGET-MIB and defining snmpTargetAddrTable. This table is used to specify agent trap target addresses (managers to which traps will be sent), as well as to limit access (for *gets* and *sets*) to specified manager addresses.

```
snmpTargetAddrTable OBJECT-TYPE
    SYNTAX          SEQUENCE OF SnmpTargetAddrEntry
    MAX-ACCESS      not-accessible
    STATUS          current
    DESCRIPTION
      "A table of transport addresses to be used in the generation of
       SNMP messages."
    ::= { snmpTargetObjects 2 }

snmpTargetAddrEntry OBJECT-TYPE
    SYNTAX          SnmpTargetAddrEntry
    MAX-ACCESS      not-accessible
    STATUS          current
    DESCRIPTION
      "A transport address to be used in the generation
       of SNMP operations.
       Entries in the snmpTargetAddrTable are created and
       deleted using the snmpTargetAddrRowStatus object."
    INDEX { IMPLIED snmpTargetAddrName }
    ::= { snmpTargetAddrTable 1 }

SnmpTargetAddrEntry ::= SEQUENCE {
    snmpTargetAddrName        SnmpAdminString,  -- Index
    snmpTargetAddrTDomain     TDomain,
    snmpTargetAddrTAddress    TAddress,
    snmpTargetAddrTimeout     TimeInterval,
    snmpTargetAddrRetryCount  Integer32,
    snmpTargetAddrTagList     SnmpTagList,
    snmpTargetAddrParams      SnmpAdminString,
    snmpTargetAddrStorageType StorageType,
    snmpTargetAddrRowStatus   RowStatus }        -- Row Status
```

A manager creates a new target address by providing a new, unique index value (snmpTargetAddrName), along with an appropriate value for snmpTargetAddrRowStatus.

Other entries need to be filled in (e.g, snmpTargetAddrTAddress), and snmpTargetAddr-RowStatus is finally set to active(1).

> **SNMP Tidbit.** The snmpTargetAddrTable illustrates topics discussed elsewhere in this book.
>
> The INDEX object is a text string of type SnmpAdminString.
>
> The IMPLIED keyword appears as part of the index specification.
>
> The *Tag-List* concept is involved with how a particular target row is selected for transmission of a particular trap, and will be explained in Chapter 16, *Elements of Advanced MIB Complexity.*
>
> snmpTargetAddrParams is a pointer to another table (not shown) that defines additional parameters needed for trap transmission.

RMON and RMON2 MIBs Example

Many of the RMON and RMON2 (Remote Monitoring) MIBs are also configured by remote manager row-create logic. RMON2 is an extension to RMON and does not replace it—they are used together.

RMON defines a local textual convention definition called EntryStatus that is an equivalent precursor to SMIv2's RowStatus textual convention.

RMON2 uses the SMIv2 RowStatus textual convention.

Our example below is from the RMON MIB and uses EntryStatus which takes values:

> { valid, createRequest, underCreation, invalid }
>
> which are similar to those for RowStatus.

Example of row creation from RFC-2819 *Remote Network Monitoring MIB*, the RMON-MIB and the etherStatsTable

```
etherStatsTable OBJECT-TYPE
    SYNTAX       SEQUENCE OF EtherStatsEntry
    MAX-ACCESS not-accessible
    STATUS       current
    DESCRIPTION  "A list of Ethernet statistics entries."
    ::= { statistics 1 }

etherStatsEntry OBJECT-TYPE
    SYNTAX       EtherStatsEntry
    MAX-ACCESS not-accessible
    STATUS       current
    DESCRIPTION
        "A collection of statistics kept for a particular
        Ethernet interface.  As an example, an instance of the
        etherStatsPkts object might be named etherStatsPkts.1"
    INDEX { etherStatsIndex }
    ::= { etherStatsTable 1 }

EtherStatsEntry ::= SEQUENCE {
    etherStatsIndex                 Integer32,      -- read-create INDEX
    etherStatsDataSource            OBJECT IDENTIFIER,  -- read-create
    etherStatsDropEvents            Counter32,
    etherStatsOctets                Counter32,
    etherStatsPkts                  Counter32,
    etherStatsBroadcastPkts         Counter32,
    etherStatsMulticastPkts         Counter32,
    etherStatsCRCAlignErrors        Counter32,
    etherStatsUndersizePkts         Counter32,
    etherStatsOversizePkts          Counter32,
    etherStatsFragments             Counter32,
    etherStatsJabbers               Counter32,
    etherStatsCollisions            Counter32,
    etherStatsPkts64Octets          Counter32,
    etherStatsPkts65to127Octets     Counter32,
    etherStatsPkts128to255Octets    Counter32,
    etherStatsPkts256to511Octets    Counter32,
    etherStatsPkts512to1023Octets   Counter32,
    etherStatsPkts1024to1518Octets  Counter32,
    etherStatsOwner                 OwnerString,
    etherStatsStatus                EntryStatus }   -- read-create
```

Discussion continues for the RMON etherStatsTable example on the previous page.

Three read-create objects are identified above by comments. All other objects are read-only and will contain data collection results.

A manager *sets* etherStatsStatus.randomInteger to the value createRequest. If successful, the manager continues to *set* two additional object values. If unsuccessful, the manager will attempt another createRequest with a different randomInteger instance value.

The manager *sets* etherStatsOwner to a textual string value. This is typed as a textual convention OwnerString OCTET STRING (SIZE(0..127)). The possible size of zero indicates that setting a value for this object is optional.

The manager *sets* a value for etherStatsDataSource, an OBJECT IDENTIFIER pointer to an entry in RFC-1213 interface table. That is, it will contain an:
  ○ OID.instance value
  ○ That is the same as an entry ifEntry.index
  ○ Which is known to be an Ethernet interface

Finally the manager *sets*:

etherStatsStatus.successfulRandomInteger = valid

and the agent begins to populate the table with Ethernet statistics, which can later be retrieved by the manager.

RFC-3231 Scheduling MIB

RFC-3231 *Definitions of Managed Objects for Scheduling Management Operations* contains the DISMAN-SCHEDULE-MIB, which defines the table schedTable.

This MIB allows managers to create table rows, which enable scheduling of actions—one-shot, periodic, or calendar/time based.

An example of two objects from this table is shown in Chapter 10, *Data Object–Derived Types*, in the discussion for VariablePointer.

Exercises

1. Explain agent row creation vs. manager row-create logic.

2. Use your manager to view the RFC-1213 ifTable managed by the agent installed on your workstation or laptop. How many rows did the agent create to populate the table? Are the table's integer index values consecutive?

3. Alternately, use command-line tools to perform *getnext* requests for ifTable entries. How many rows did the agent create to populate the table?

4. Investigate the CISCO-PING-MIB. Find the MIB on the MIB Depot web site, and view the SMIv2 version in text format. What Cisco IMPORTS need to be satisfied? Load the MIB onto your manager, and use your manager's interface to set up a remote ping test using row-create capabilities.

5. Name some IETF standard MIBs that are dependent on manager row-create logic.

Chapter 16

Elements of Advanced MIB Complexity

Advanced complexity is mostly about pointers, often defining relationships among indexed tables, and facilitating solutions to more complicated network management problems.

For the novice, this chapter is not essential. Read it later following some hands-on SNMP experience.

However if you are planning to use RMON and RMON2 MIBs, the Entity MIB, or SNMPv3 configuration MIBs, reading this chapter will be useful.

Complex MIBs are common, particularly among standard MIBs—less common among enterprise MIBs. Examples in previous chapters have already introduced some of these concepts. Rather than an abstract discussion of design principles, a number of examples are presented.

Pointers are of two basic types, *object identifier pointers,* and *index pointers.*

Object identifier pointers
> The OBJECT IDENTIFIER base type and SMIv2 textual convention subtypes VariablePointer, RowPointer, and AutonomousType are used to define relationships among tables and objects. All three resolve to an OID.instance value.

Index pointers
> A scalar or entry in an indexed table may contain an index value as a pointer or reference to a particular row in an indexed table. Any of the possible index data types (discussed in Chapter 14) may be used.

Tag-lists are a special case of complexity and are described first.

Tag-Lists

A Tag-List (textual convention) object is defined within a table. The value of this object is multiple strings of text, with each string separated from the next by a delimiter (a delimiter can be a space, tab, CR, or LF).

An example Tag-List object value:

"apple orange banana lime"

Another object (elsewhere in the MIB) is defined as a Tag (which may be a scalar or be defined within another table), and contains a single textual item (no embedded delimiters).

For example:

"lime"

If "lime" matches any string value in a Tag-List object contained in a table row, that row is selected for further processing by the agent.

Expanding the example, Table-A below has four rows. Each of those rows has a Tag-List object (in addition to other objects that are not detailed here).

Row Index	Tag-List Object	(other table objects...)
1	"bolt orange banana lime"	
2	"avocado basil parsley"	
3	"lime lettuce tomatoe"	
4	"thyme banana apple boat"	

Agent logic processing the Tag value "lime" will select:

(row 1) and (row 3) in Table-A

and other row objects (non-Tag objects) in those two rows will be further processed by the agent.

SNMPv3 Trap Target Table Example

The following example shows only table SEQUENCE statements—the *table* and *entry objects* are omitted for brevity.

Example of Tag-List use from RFC-3413, the SNMP-TARGET-MIB containing snmpTargetAddrTable (a row-create table).

Object snmpTargetAddrTagList contains the tag list.

```
SnmpTargetAddrEntry ::= SEQUENCE {
    snmpTargetAddrName          SnmpAdminString,      -- Index
    snmpTargetAddrTDomain       TDomain,
    snmpTargetAddrTAddress      TAddress,             -- Trap Target Address
    snmpTargetAddrTimeout       TimeInterval,
    snmpTargetAddrRetryCount    Integer32,
    snmpTargetAddrTagList       SnmpTagList,          -- Tag List
    snmpTargetAddrParams        SnmpAdminString,
    snmpTargetAddrStorageType   StorageType,
    snmpTargetAddrRowStatus     RowStatus
    }
```

Example of a Tag-Object whose value is used to select a row in table snmpTargetAddrTable (above).

From RFC-3413, the SNMP-NOTIFICATION-MIB, snmpNotifyTable (a row-create table)

```
SnmpNotifyEntry ::= SEQUENCE {
    snmpNotifyName          SnmpAdminString,      -- Index
    snmpNotifyTag           SnmpTagValue,         -- Tag Value
    snmpNotifyType          INTEGER,
    snmpNotifyStorageType   StorageType,
    snmpNotifyRowStatus     RowStatus
    }
```

When an agent detects an *event* condition, it traverses all entries in the snmpNotifyTable (above) and compares each entry snmpNotifyTag value with snmpTargetAddrTagList entries in the snmpTargetAddrTable to select rows. Selected rows contain other objects that identify the manager addresses to send *traps* to, along with transmission parameters (e.g., the address of each targeted manager).

Index Pointers

Indexes of any type can be used to describe table relationships. The next example is based on a simple integer index.

Linked List Example

Transponder MIB objects in an indexed table without linked-list organization

```
transponderObjects OBJECT-IDENTITY
   STATUS current
   DESCRIPTION
      "Node under which Transponder Data Objects are organized."
   ::= { vronxProducts 11 }


transponderCount   OBJECT-TYPE
   SYNTAX       Unsigned32
   MAX-ACCESS  read-only
   STATUS        current
   DESCRIPTION
      "The current number of Transponders.
        The number of Transponder Table Entries."
   ::= { transponderObjects 1 }

transponderTable OBJECT-TYPE
   SYNTAX        SEQUENCE OF TransponderEntry
   MAX-ACCESS  not-accessible
   STATUS        current
   DESCRIPTION  "Transponder Table"
   ::= { transponderObjects 10 }

transponderEntry  OBJECT-TYPE
   SYNTAX        TransponderEntry
   MAX-ACCESS  not-accessible
   STATUS        current
   DESCRIPTION  "An entry in Transponder Table."
   INDEX   { transponderIndex }
   ::= { transponderTable 1 }


TransponderEntry  ::=
   SEQUENCE {   transponderIndex        Unsigned32,
                      transponderModel       DisplayString,
                      transponderAlias        DisplayString }
```

The same table augmented to become a linked-list

```
transponderObjects OBJECT-IDENTITY
   STATUS current
   DESCRIPTION
     "Node under which Transponder Data Objects are organized."
   ::= { vronxProducts 11 }


transponderCount  OBJECT-TYPE
   SYNTAX       Unsigned32
   MAX-ACCESS read-only
   STATUS       current
   DESCRIPTION "The current number of Transponders."
   ::= { transponderObjects 1 }


-- pointer to index of head of linked list
transponderLinkedListHead   OBJECT-TYPE
   SYNTAX          Unsigned32
   MAX-ACCESS      read-only
   STATUS          current
   DESCRIPTION
     "Contains the 'transponderIndex' value corresponding to
       the first entry in the Transponder Linked List."
   ::= { transponderObjects 2 }


transponderTable OBJECT-TYPE
   SYNTAX       SEQUENCE OF TransponderEntry
   MAX-ACCESS not-accessible
   STATUS       current
   DESCRIPTION "Transponder Table"
   ::= { transponderObjects 10 }


transponderEntry  OBJECT-TYPE
   SYNTAX       TransponderEntry
   MAX-ACCESS not-accessible
   STATUS       current
   DESCRIPTION "An entry in Transponder Table."
   INDEX  { transponderIndex }
   ::= { transponderTable 1 }


TransponderEntry  ::=
   SEQUENCE {
          transponderIndex         Unsigned32,
          transponderModel         DisplayString,
          transponderAlias         DisplayString,
          transponderNextLink      Unsigned32 -- index of next Linked entry }
```

Entity MIB List Example

Example of an index pointer from RFC-4133 *Entity MIB (Version 3)* ENTITY-MIB, entPhysicalTable. Only a subset of the table's SEQUENCE statement is shown (and then discussed).

```
EntPhysicalEntry ::= SEQUENCE {
    entPhysicalIndex         PhysicalIndex,         -- Integer Index
    entPhysicalDescr         SnmpAdminString,       -- text
    entPhysicalContainedIn   PhysicalIndexOrZero    -- pointer to different row
    entPhysicalClass         PhysicalClass          -- enumerated integer
    }
```

This table lists all of the physical objects being modeled, along with container relationships.

entPhysicalClass is an enumerated INTEGER with values =
    { other,
    unknown,
    chassis,
    backplane,
    container,
    powerSupply,
    fan,
    sensor,
    module,
    port,
    stack }

entPhysicalContainedIn is an integer that contains the value of entPhysicalIndex that this entry is contained within—it is a pointer to another row in this same table.

For example

entPhysicalIndex	entPhysicalDescr	entPhysicalContainedIn	entPhysicalClass
1	"acme chassis"	0	chassis
2	"std Slot"	1	container
3	"I/O Module"	2	module
4	"serial port"	3	port

Table entries show that this product consists of a chassis, that has a slot (container), that has a module, that has a port. The "serial port(4)" is contained in the "I/O Module (3)", which is contained in the "std Slot (2)", which is contained in the "acme chassis(1)".

SNMPc screen capture of Entity MIB data from a Cisco product. This is the same table (but different data) shown in the previous example, with the manager displaying simplified column object names, and also displaying more columns from the actual MIB. This provides an inventory of product components.

Index	Descr	VendorType	ContainedIn	Class	Pare
1	mwr1900 chassis, Hw	ciscoModules.3.1.3.374	0	chassis	-1
2	MWR1941-DC Chassis	ciscoModules.3.1.5.1	1	container	0
3	MWR1941 Motherboard	ciscoModules.3.1.9.5.61	2	module	0
4	MWR1941-DC	ciscoModules.3.1.5.2	3	container	0
5	MWR1941-DC	ciscoModules.3.1.5.2	3	container	1
6	MWR1941-DC	ciscoModules.3.1.5.2	3	container	2
7	MWR1941-DC Chassis	ciscoModules.3.1.5.1	1	container	1
8	One Port Ethernet	ciscoModules.3.1.9.3.19	7	module	1

Note the "Vendor Type" column of data—the full name is of this object is entPhysicalVendorType.

Chapter 10 contains a syntax example for exactly this object, and its SYNTAX is AutonomousType (i.e., an OID value). These are global enumerations of the Cisco Vendor Type definitions for each module.

Using the Cisco Navigator Tool (Chapter 5) we can search for any of these definitions.

Several results are shown below:

Object Identifier	Module Name
ciscoModules.3.1.3.374	cevChassisMWR1941DC
ciscoModule.3.1.5.1	cevContainerSlot
ciscoModule.3.1.10.16	cevPortFEIP

The Cisco Navigator Tool also discloses which Cisco MIBs these OID enumerations are contained in. If those MIBs are loaded into the manger, the OID values displayed above will change to the Cisco designated module names.

As an exercise, research some of the other OID enumerations.

OBJECT IDENTIFIER Pointers

RMON-MIB Example

Chapter 15's example from RFC-2819 *Remote Network Monitoring MIB*, the RMON-MIB. Only a subset of the SEQUENCE statement objects are shown here.

```
EtherStatsEntry ::= SEQUENCE {
    etherStatsIndex           Integer32,              -- read-create INDEX
    etherStatsDataSource      OBJECT IDENTIFIER,      -- read-create
    etherStatsDropEvents      Counter32,
    etherStatsOwner           OwnerString,
    etherStatsStatus          EntryStatus             -- read-create
}
```

The interface table ifTable defined in RFC-1213 is very commonly referenced from the many MIBs that model extended details of interfaces.

In this example the object etherStatsDataSource is an OBJECT IDENTIFIER that takes the value of the:

> OID.instance of an ifEntry.index of interest

i.e., the RMON MIB table entry is pointing to a row in the interface table.

Once the RMON row is created, Ethernet statistics will be collected for that interface.

RowPointer and VariablePointer Examples

RowPointer and VariablePointer are textual conventions based on OBJECT IDENTIFIER.

Mention of these is here for completeness—examples for both of these were previously presented in Chapter 10, *Data Object–Derived Types*, as part of RowPointer and VariablePointer syntax discussions.

AutonomousType Example

AutonomousType is a textual convention which is also based on OBJECT IDENTIFIER.

> *Example* of AutonomousType pointer from RFC-4133 Entity MIB (Version 3)
> ENTITY-MIB entLogicalTable. Only the SEQUENCE statement from the table
> definition is shown.

```
EntLogicalEntry ::= SEQUENCE {
    entLogicalIndex              Integer32,              -- Index
    entLogicalDescr              SnmpAdminString,
    entLogicalType               AutonomousType,         -- enumerator and pointer
    entLogicalCommunity          OCTET STRING,
    entLogicalTAddress           TAddress,
    entLogicalTDomain            TDomain,
    entLogicalContextEngineID    SnmpEngineIdOrNone,
    entLogicalContextName        SnmpAdminString  }
```

The Entity MIB also models *logical entities* (in addition to *physical entities* as shown in a previous example).

Logical table object entLogicalType is typed as an SMIv2 textual convention AutonomousType.

AutonomousType is usually reserved for globally unique enumeration definitions. And indeed, it is used here in that manner. However, it can *also* be used to point to a MIB (or branch of a MIB) that is used to model or manage this logical entity.

> *Example* AutonomousType syntax for this object use is shown below—the
> DESCRIPTION clause provides additional details.

```
entLogicalType OBJECT-TYPE
    SYNTAX      AutonomousType
    MAX-ACCESS  read-only
    STATUS      current
    DESCRIPTION "An indication of the type of logical entity.  This will
        typically be the OBJECT IDENTIFIER name of the node in the
        SMI's naming hierarchy which represents the major MIB module, or the
        majority of the MIB modules, supported by the logical entity.  For example:
            a logical entity of a regular host/router -> mib-2
            a logical entity of a 802.1d bridge -> dot1dBridge
            a logical entity of a 802.3 repeater -> snmpDot3RptrMgmt
        If an appropriate node in the SMI's naming hierarchy cannot
        be identified, the value 'mib-2' should be used."
    ::= { entLogicalEntry 3 }
```

SNMPv3 Configuration MIBs Example

The diagram below is a diagram of moderately complex relationships among SNMPv3 MIBs used to configure Version 3-compliant agents. Index entries are shaded, with arrows indicating entries in one table used to reference (or select) rows in another table. Some of the index values are supplied from values parsed from the SNMPv3 message itself.

For example, the usmUserTable is indexed by usmUserEngineID and usmUserName (values for both are parsed from an incoming SNMPv3 message header). A row selected by the two indexes produces a value for usmUserSecurityName which is then used as the second index into table vacmSecurityToGroupTable. And so on.

SNMPv3 is an advanced topic, and you don't (yet) have to understand the *why* of this logic. Just be aware that such complexities exist.

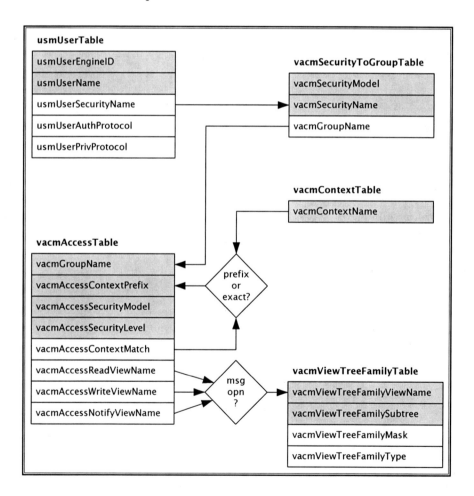

Exercises

1. Modify the Linked List example to include an object that allows managers to direct agents to return list data in either lexicographical order or in linked-list order.

Part 5

Advanced Trap Topics

Chapter 11 discussed SMIv1 and SMIv2 syntax for trap objects. It is pretty easy to define traps and to code them in one of the two formats, and to properly validate that syntax.

It takes more thought to design traps that are *really useful* in managing networks.

It may also be difficult for network engineers to *fully understand what they have* and to best configure trap filters for their manager.

Trap design problems include:
- Traps not easily categorized (and logged) into severities
- Traps not easily auto-acknowledged (by subsequent stateful traps)
- Incomprehensible trap definitions
- Too many trap definitions for a particular product
- Too few trap definitions
- Insufficient data sent with a trap
- Irrelevant data sent with a trap
- Agent semantic issues

Chapter 17, *Trap Filter Configuration,* describes capabilities of typical managers, and what network engineers can expect to accomplish. This needs to be understood prior to reviewing trap models.

Chapter 18, *Trap Models,* talks about the various models network engineers encounter when they configure trap filters. There are good and bad design models, and some apparently differing models are actually equivalent.

Chapter 19, *More on Trap Syntax,* elaborates on material presented in earlier chapters.

Chapter 20, *Trap Semantics for Agents,* discusses agent support for MIB trap objects, good design practices, and MIB data affecting agent semantics.

Chapter 17

Trap Filter Configuration

Trap filter configuration details vary among managers, in criteria (scope of filter rules), in methods (GUIs, scripting), and in resultant manager actions.

Filtering Goals

Prioritize critical network issues. This sounds pretty obvious, but also implies the need to ignore non-important traps. One white paper available on the web discusses a large network that was generating 500,000 traps a day, of which only 200 required corrective actions. Filters are one method used to bring critical events to the forefront and to ignore events of little or no importance.

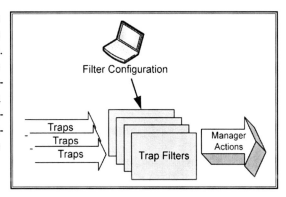

Related topics are *event correlation* and *root cause analysis*. Traps can be highly correlated. For example, a television broadcast studio contains equipment that processes a video stream. If the video stream is disconnected somewhere along the stream, downstream studio devices will all generate redundant *signal lost* events. Even within a single processing device multiple traps might be generated for this one cause.

Root cause analysis logic attempts to correlate events and to report only one event that is the root cause of the problem.

Within a single device, traps should be defined, and agents coded, to send only root-cause traps rather than a multiplicity of traps for a single problem. This is an example of *good agent semantics*.

Correlating traps (and identifying root causes) from multi-vendor equipment requires a high-end manager, or high-end plug-ins, as well as a talented manager configuration specialist.

Take appropriate actions. Event filters allow a manager to sort traps to generate appropriate actions. For example, forward trap to a specialized manager station (which may process the trap or poll the agent for additional data), send email or pages to responsible individuals, execute a programmed response (e.g., automatically switch to an alternate video input stream).

Log events. Trap filters can be configured to categorize traps into severities (e.g., *informational, normal, warning, minor, major, critical*), with each severity associated with a meaningful color (e.g., *blue, green, yellow, orange, red, magenta*). Trap logs (text describing the trap) can be sorted into severity categories so that all current *critical* events, or *warning* events, etc., can be easily viewed in separate files.

Device severity maps. Mapped device icons take on the color of the most severe unacknowledged trap received from that device. Subnet icons are configured to group multiple devices, and take on the color of the most severely impacted device within the subnet. Subnets of subnets can also be configured, and a high-level map view will indicate the color/severity of the most severe problem in the network.

When a trap is acknowledged (cleared) manually, or automatically by a compensating trap, device icon colors are also reset.

Filtering Criteria

Filtering criteria vary among mangers—typical examples are discussed next.

Platform IP address. Multiple platforms may support the same MIBs, but traps from those platforms may be handled differently, depending on the functionality or importance of a platform.

> *For example*:
> - A *loss-of-signal trap* from a router feeding a television station transmitter will be *critical*.
> - The same *loss-of-signal trap* from the same type of router feeding an off-line editing suite may be simply a *warning*.

Platform type. Managers may allow configuration of devices into types (e.g., router, printer, web server, switch), and to use this categorization as filtering criteria. For example, CPU usage problems on a web server will be more *critical* than for a workstation.

Trap identity. This one is pretty obvious. Filtering on the trap name (or OID) is usually the first thing a filter is based on.

Trap data objects. The data object values sent with a trap (SMIv1 VARIABLES clause, SMIv2 OBJECTS clause) are important to filtering.

For example, a status object defined as an enumerated:

    INTEGER csiVideoSignal { okay(1), lost(2) }

can be used to filter an arriving trap into a *normal* (okay(1)) or *critical* (lost(2)) event with appropriate actions.

Mapping of Traps to Filters

It is common to configure multiple filters for a single trap. For example, a particular trap may result in different actions depending on the agent's IP address, or on the data contained within the trap (e.g., what is the actual chassis temperature, or on what is the enumerated status being reported).

The Most Common Trap Filter

The most common trap filter, probably already familiar to many readers, is the configuration of event logs using manager-specific *script*. For example:

For a trap definition from the Chateau Systems CHATEAU-CD-PRODUCT-MIB

```
cdPowerSupplyEv NOTIFICATION-TYPE
  OBJECTS
  {  cdDynCfgUserAlias,        -- DisplayString
     cdStCfgModel,             -- DisplayString
     cdChStPowerSupply,        -- status = { okay(1), voltageError(2) }
     cdEvSeverity,             -- enumerated integer
     cdEvDescription           -- DisplayString }
  STATUS  current
  DESCRIPTION "Sent when cdChStPowerSupply changes from okay to
     voltageError, or from voltageError to okay. This trap can be disabled
     by setting cdPowerSupplyEvTrapEn = trapDisable."
  ::= { cdEventList 20 }
```

For this trap, a user might configure log message script in the manager (where $n will log the value of the n-th data object sent with the trap) as:

    "$1 Failure STATUS:$3 SEVERITY:$4"

If this trap is sent with the following OBJECTS values:

>   cdDynCfgUserAlias = "Backup CD Player"
>   cdStCfgModel = "CsiCd202"
>   cdChStPowerSupply = voltageError(2)
>   cdEvSeverity = major(4)
>   cdEvDescription = "Call vendor tech"

the following message will be logged:

>   "Backup CD Player Failure STATUS:voltageError SEVERITY:major"

Pseudo-Script Examples

A slightly more complicated filter could be created for the same trap definition. The pseudo-script below illustrates additional logic.

> We can create multiple filters for this single trap, each with a unique name. A simple filter for cdChStPowerSupply = voltageError(2) can be described by the following logic.
>
> This filter simply logs a *priority major event (red),* and clears any previous *voltage okay event (green)* from the log. The log message will be as shown previously.

```
FILTER NAME: cdPowerSupplyEv-voltageError
WHEN (TRAP: cdPowerSupplyEv)
{
    IF (cdChStPowerSupply == voltageError(2))
    {
        Log Event at Priority = major (red);
        Clear Event Log: cdPowerSupplyEv-psOkay;
    }
}
```

A yet more complicated filter could also be crafted

```
FILTER NAME: cdPowerSupplyEv-voltageError
WHEN (TRAP: cdPowerSupplyEv)
{
    IF (cdChStPowerSupply == voltageError)
    {
        IF (cdStCfgModel == "Model8091AS")
        {
            IF (SourceNodeGroup == Webserver)
            {
                Log Event at Priority = major(red);
                Send Page to EngineerLucky;
                Send Email to SupervisorLucy;
                Forward to: SNMPManagerOhio;
                Clear Event Log: cdPowerSupplyEv-psOkay;
            }
        }
    }
}
```

With these basic filtering concepts in mind, the next chapter describing *Trap Models* will make more sense.

Exercises

1. Trap filters, configured in a manager, filters on what types of information?

2. Trap filters allow managers to respond to specific trap conditions with specific actions. Name some of those actions.

Chapter 18

Trap Models

This chapter describes a variety of *trap design models*—these are not formal models, but styles encountered in standard and enterprise MIBs. Some of the most creative efforts in MIB design are apparent in the design of trap objects. The discussions in this chapter attempt to point out pros and cons of various approaches—in a style similar to conversations that might occur in a design meeting. As in many meetings, these discussions ramble a bit.

It is important for developers to adopt trap models that are appropriate and usable by network engineers, and to propagate a similar style throughout their company's MIBs. The goal of this chapter is to provide ideas and guidelines—there is no single *best* solution.

It is equally important for network engineers to realize that such models exist, to know what to expect, and to have a sense of how to configure appropriate trap filters for each.

As you review more MIBs on your own, you will discover additional creative ideas.

Trap Design Guidelines

There are two trap design guidelines to consider:

> *Is this trap something the network engineer needs to respond to, and if so, what specific actions should be taken?*

> > If there is no clear answer to this, perhaps the information would better be defined as MIB poll-able status objects, and not be the basis for a trap.

> *Will the customer understand the significance of this trap?*

> > If not, reconsider including it in the MIB.

Communication from a *network engineer*

"We were receiving one frequent trap we didn't understand. The trap description clause did not provide much information. We contacted customer support, but they didn't know what the trap was signalling either. So we were put in touch with engineering—apparently the software engineer that designed the MIB and agent no longer worked there, and we were told 'not to worry' about the trap. We never did find out what it was signalling, nothing bad happened, so it couldn't have been important."

Common Trap Models

For developers, review of these common models is a good first step in designing traps for new MIBs. For network engineers, familiarity with these commonly encountered models will be useful.

Pros and cons are discussed—but many of these are arguable and conditional. The intent here is to provide information, not to promote one model over the other. However, an important criteria is:

How easy will it be for network engineers to configure useful manager trap filters for each of a MIB's traps?

Trap–No Data

Traps are sent with data defined in the SMIv1 VARIABLES clause or the SMIv2 OBJECTS clause. Occasionally you will encounter trap definitions that do not send data.

Example from RFC-3418 *Management Information Base (MIB) for the Simple Network Management Protocol (SNMP)* SNMPv2-MIB—one of the generic trap definitions (as redefined in SMIv2 syntax)

```
authenticationFailure NOTIFICATION-TYPE
    STATUS  current
    DESCRIPTION
        "An authenticationFailure trap signifies that the SNMP
        entity has received a protocol message that is not
        properly authenticated.  While all implementations
        of SNMP entities MAY be capable of generating this
        trap, the snmpEnableAuthenTraps object indicates
        whether this trap will be generated."
    ::= { snmpTraps 5 }
```

An authenticationFailure trap is sent by an agent if an SNMP entity (possibly a hacker, but more likely another manager on the network running a *discovery process*) attempts to *get* or *set* MIB data with an invalid SNMPv1 or SNMPv2c community string.

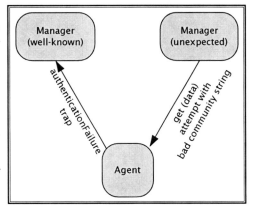

This trap is sent without data, but would be more useful if it sent a data value for the IpAddress of the offending platform, and perhaps with the value of the incorrect community string.

Interestingly, Cisco has redefined this trap in their SMIv1 CISCOTRAP-MIB to include additional data

```
authenticationFailure TRAP-TYPE
     ENTERPRISE  snmp
     VARIABLES  { authAddr }    -- SYNTAX IpAddress
     DESCRIPTION
          "An authenticationFailure trap signifies that
          the sending protocol entity is the addressee
          of a protocol message that is not properly
          authenticated.  While implementations of the
          SNMP must be capable of generating this trap,
          they must also be capable of suppressing the
          emission of such traps via an implementation-
          specific mechanism."
     ::= 4
```

This is not to say that trap definitions without data objects are deficient.

Example of a simple enterprise trap without data. Network engineers will find comfort in finding this trap in their logs each morning.

```
vronxHealthCheckOkay NOTIFICATION-TYPE
     STATUS  current
     DESCRIPTION
          "An automatic health check is performed each day.
          If there are no problems, this event is generated.
          Appropriate error events are sent if health is not okay."
     ::= { vronxSmiTraps 7 }
```

Or it might be more appropriate to provide a vronxHealth object that managers could poll when they needed to know.

Example from the Entity MIB. The Entity MIB contains a single trap definition that is sent if equipment configuration changes. A manager responds to this trap by polling the agent for updated provisioning information from the MIB.

Note agent semantics DESCRIPTION discussing *throttling the trap rate*— more on this later.

```
entConfigChange NOTIFICATION-TYPE
    STATUS          current
    DESCRIPTION
            "An entConfigChange notification is generated when the value
            of entLastChangeTime changes.  It can be utilized by an NMS
            to trigger logical/physical entity table maintenance polls.

            An agent should not generate more than one entConfigChange
            'notification-event' in a given time interval (five seconds
            is the suggested default).  A 'notification-event' is the
            transmission of a single trap or inform PDU to a list of
            notification destinations.

            If additional configuration changes occur within the
            throttling period, then notification-events for these
            changes should be suppressed by the agent until the current
            throttling period expires.  At the end of a throttling
            period, one notification-event should be generated if any
            configuration changes occurred since the start of the
            throttling period.  In such a case, another throttling
            period is started right away.

            An NMS should periodically check the value of
            entLastChangeTime to detect any missed entConfigChange
            notification-events, e.g., due to throttling or transmission
            loss."
    ::= { entityMIBTrapPrefix 1 }
```

Heart-beat trap definitions are in this class, and are sometimes encountered. They usually contain no data, and are sent at a rate measured in seconds or a few minutes. In many cases such traps are unnecessary—most managers contain logic to regularly poll agent platforms and to generate local (to the manager) alarms when agents fail to respond.

Trap–Single DisplayString Data Object

A MIB contains one trap definition, which includes one DisplayString data object. The DisplayString value is intended by the agent developer to convey any and all information regarding any event that might ever occur.

Enterprise trap *example*

```
vronxStatusChangeEv NOTIFICATION-TYPE
   OBJECTS
   {
      vronxStatusMessage   -- SYNTAX DisplayString
   }
   STATUS  current
   DESCRIPTION
      "Sent when product status changes.
       DisplayString text explains the change."
   ::= { vronxStatus 11 }
```

This trap definition facilitates rapid agent development. Software developers simply call one function with a pointer to a text string, and the trap is generated.

In some cases, this string may reflect the text from a *system log* file, and there may be documented information on the exact contents of the text. In other cases, the programmer simply makes up the text as needed.

If there is insufficient information about expected DisplayString values, it will be difficult for network engineers to construct filters—any filter must be based on text-matching of DisplayString values. The filter designer may need to wait long periods of time (weeks) to see what DisplayString values are being sent by the agent in order to complete filter configuration.

Trap–System Log Entries

These are traps based on system log information. System logs contain information well known to network engineers, and they appreciate traps conveying this familiar information. Sometimes the log information is sent as is, sometimes it is parsed into multiple trap data objects, and sometimes trap objects will contain referential information back to the system log entry (e.g., to the log entry index value).

MIBs often define additional traps along with system-log-based traps.

Example from RFC-3805 Printer MIB v2—this is the only trap defined in the standard Printer MIB, and has some interesting features; discussions follow. This is a thoughtfully designed trap.

```
printerV2Alert NOTIFICATION-TYPE
    OBJECTS {   prtAlertIndex,
                prtAlertSeverityLevel,
                prtAlertGroup,
                prtAlertGroupIndex,
                prtAlertLocation,
                prtAlertCode }
    STATUS  current
    DESCRIPTION
        "This trap is sent whenever a critical event is
         added to the prtAlertTable.

        NOTE: The prtAlertIndex object was redundantly included in the
        bindings of the 'printerV2Alert' notification in RFC-1759, even
        though the value exists in the instance qualifier of all the
        other bindings.  This object has been retained to provide
        compatibility with existing RFC-1759 implementations."

    ::= { printerV2AlertPrefix 1 }
```

The NOTE in the DESCRIPTION field relates to the issue of sending INDEX values in traps, and whether INDEX objects should be not-accessible. This important topic is discussed in Chapters 13 and 19.

prtAlertIndex references the corresponding log entry in the prtAlertTable. You can view this trap model strategy as either:

> *all logged entries are sent as traps*

> *all traps are also logged*

In either case, if a manager receives a trap containing a non-contiguous prtAlertIndex value, it can (if properly configured) perform *get* operations to retrieve data from the prtAlertTable, which has one indexed row per sent trap. This design feature addresses the UDP connection-less protocol issue (trap delivery not guaranteed).

prtAlertSeverityLevel is an enumerated:

> INTEGER { other(1), critical(2), warning(4), warningBinaryChangeEvent(5) }

and is sent to indicate the agent's intended severity for this event.

prtAlertGroup is an enumerated INTEGER indicating the printer subunit generating this trap. Example (subset of) enumerations:

    cover(6),
    localization(7),
    input(8),
    output(9),
    marker(10),
    markerSupplies(11),
    markerColorant(12),
    mediaPath(13),
    channel(14)

prtAlertGroupIndex is an Integer32 that indicates a particular instance within the prtAlert-Group for this event. For example marker, #3 is identified as:

    prtAlertGroup = marker(10)
    prtAlertGroupIndex = 3

prtAlertLocation is an Integer32, and further refines the origin of the event, along with prtAlertGroup and prtAlertGroupIndex. For example, there is an alert from input #2 at location #7.

    prtAlertGroup = input(8)
    prtAlertGroupIndex = 2
    prtAlertLocation = 7

prtAlertCode defines the actual event, and is a very long list of enumerated INTEGER values, a few of which are listed here:

    coverOpen(3),
    coverClosed(4),
    subunitEmpty(13),
    subunitAlmostFull(14),
    subunitFull(15),
    subunitTurnedOn(20),
    subunitTurnedOff(21),
    subunitOffline(22)

Notice that not all prtAlertCode's apply to all prtAlertGroup's. For example:

    prtAlertCode = coverOpen(3)

will be associated only with a prtAlertGroup = cover(6)

General Trap Definition–Many Data Objects

Some MIBs define a single, cleverly designed, comprehensive trap to support a very complex product or multiple products. This general trap contains a significant number of data OBJECTS that assume values describing a multitude of event situations.

This approach may be appropriate or not, depending on how it is designed—the Printer MIB trap just discussed is a an example of a good design that includes elements of this model.

This section provides an enterprise MIB example of such a trap, and discusses pros along with some possible cons.

> **SNMP Jargon.** *General trap* definitions are sometimes named as *generic traps* in enterprise MIBs, not to be confused with standard MIB generic traps (such as coldStart or authenticationFailure).

Example SMIv2 general trap aggregated from several enterprise MIBs

```
generalProductTrap NOTIFICATION-TYPE
        OBJECTS {
            trapSequence,
            trapSeverity,
            trapTime,
            trapType,
            trapState,
            trapResourceKey,
            trapResourceAddress,
            trapResourceType }
        STATUS current
        DESCRIPTION
            "This is a general trap that reports many events."
        ::= { vronxGenericEvent 1 }
```

trapSequence is an incrementing Unsigned32 object that (like the Printer MIB) allows managers to detect missing *traps*. If this is also an index into a *trap log table*, the manager can *get* missing (undelivered) trap information, a nice feature.

trapSeverity is an enumerated INTEGER { normal(1), warning(2), minor(3), major(4) }. MAX-ACCESS is accessible-for-notify—a good choice, since its value has no relevance outside of traps. This value facilitates sorting of events into manager logs based on event severity.

trapTime is a DisplayString, with MAX-ACCESS accessible-for-notify. This information is somewhat redundant. Trap message syntax contains a time-stamp field (related to sysUpTime of the agent), and most managers will also time-stamp logged messages with received *Date and Time of Day*.

trapType is an enumerated INTEGER defining close to 600 unique enumerations. A number of comments apply to the particular implementation of this object.

- Many of these enumerations have cryptic names that require considerable network engineer product knowledge. Full trap filter configuration will require perhaps 600 to 1,200 filters—a big job. Where to begin? Perhaps wait for actual events to occur, and create filters for those events first.

- A vendor providing a MIB with so many traps should be certain that all of this information is essential for system management. If a product is generating hundreds of traps a day, network engineers will tend to ignore all of them, even serious traps.

- Some of the enumerated value definitions are in okay/error pairs (e.g., deviceOnLine/deviceOffLine), and some appear to be error events with no corresponding okay events (e.g., chassisDoorOpen event is defined but no chassisDoorClosed event is defined). This inconsistency makes it difficult (and confusing) to configure trap filter auto-acknowledge logic.

trapState is an enumerated INTEGER { active(1), inactive(2) }, and appears to be redundant with some definitions of trapType. This further complicates trap filter auto-acknowledge logic.

For example, the sequence of expected traps for the chassis door might be:

        (chassisDoorOpen, active)
        (chassisDoorOpen, inactive)   -- will this occur?
                                             -- and is it equivalent to door closed?

For device status traps, which of these two sequences will occur? Until you observe actual traps, you cannot know.

Sequence A   **Sequence B**
(deviceOnLine, active)   (deviceOnLine,active)
                                      (deviceOffLine,inactive)
(deviceOffLine, active)   (deviceOnLine,inactive)
                                      (deviceOffLine,active)

trapResourceKey is a non-enumerated integer that uniquely defines the resource associated with this trap. This allows you to configure filters that auto-acknowledge traps for matching resource keys, a good feature. However, the DESCRIPTION clause does not describe how keys map to meaningful resource definitions, which would be nice to know.

trapResourceAddress is a DisplayString that also uniquely defines the resource generating the trap. This may be redundant with trapResourceKey (at least in terms of configuring auto-acknowledging traps). The DESCRIPTION clause does not explain the format of the data, which again would be nice to know.

trapResourceType is an enumerated INTEGER defining over 65 unique resources (e.g., powerSupply, systemTimer, temperatureSensor). This will be useful information to display in the event log. But not all trapResourceType definitions can assume all trapType values. For example, a trapResourceType = systemTimer will never have trapType = chassisDoorOpen.

The *general trap model* has its attractions. It is easy for developers to add enumerated values to data objects for new situations. Information for a wide variety of events can be conveyed to managers using this single trap. The software API to the *send-trap* code is straightforward.

But, for the example discussed, this model can present difficulties to network engineers configuring manager filters. The number of traps to be processed is quite large, understanding their significance is confusing, and sorting the ones requiring corrective action from the informational will be difficult.

Some of the OBJECTS sent with the trap have vague DESCRIPTION clauses, furthering confusion.

There appears to be overlap between definitions of:

> { trapResourceKey and trapResourceAddress } and between
> { trapType and trapState }

which further complicate the task of configuring auto-acknowledging filters.

Many Traps–Little Data

This model is the inverse of the general trap model. Each of the 600 trapType INTEGER enumerations becomes a unique trap—so the single general trap may translate into 600 traps.

For example, instead of one generalProductTrap definition, the MIB would define notification objects:

> chassisCoverOpenTrap
> chassisCoverClosedTrap
> deviceOnLineTrap
> deviceOffLineTrap
> signalT1LossTrap
> signalT1OkayTrap
> portVoltageTrap

Another example—creating unique traps for physical entities, where the physical entity data might be better sent as data with a more general trap definition.

```
vronxAlarmExtInput1
vronxAlarmExtInput2
vronxAlarmExtInput3
vronxAlarmExtInput4
vronxAlarmExtInput5
```

Many of the issues confronting a network engineer designing trap filters for this model are similar—lots of work and potentially confusing issues.

Do-it-yourself Trap Definitions

Managers are often configurable to generate *local events* based on polled data. Local events are processed (by configuring filter logic) just as if they were traps from an agent. This a powerful manager feature.

For some types of events, MIB designers may want to forgo some trap definitions and provide suitable poll-able data objects instead.

A user configures the manager for:
- Managed device of interest (IP address)
- MIB data object OID.instance of interest
- Manager polling periodicity (usually in seconds or minutes)
- Data threshold
- Data comparison operation (e.g., > , < , =)
- Action to be taken when dataValue compares favorably with dataThreshold
- Action to be taken when dataValue compares unfavorable with dataThreshold

There also exist MIB definitions that allow similar logic to be configured at the agent level. A user interfaces with a manager to *set* MIB object values to an agent on a remote platform. Manager row-create logic can be useful in implementing this design model.
- MIB data object pointer to OID.instance of interest
- Agent polling periodicity
- Data threshold
- Data comparison operation (e.g., > , < , =) (an enumerated INTEGER)
- When dataValue compares favorably/unfavorably with the data threshold, the agent will send a trap to the manager

Recognizing Equivalent Trap Models

Several trap models have been discussed. Next, a few simple examples are presented as a continuum of *equivalent* trap object definitions.

For each of these examples (A..D), *equivalent trap filter* configurations can be created.

A) Trap name defines event type and event severity. Trap data identifies the chassis of interest.

```
chassisTempCriticalTrap NOTIFICATION-TYPE
    OBJECTS
      {
          chassisName
      }
    STATUS current
    DESCRIPTION
        "Chassis temperature is critical."
    ::= { vronxEvent 1 }
```

B) Trap name defines event type. Trap data objects identify the chassis of interest and define event severity.

```
chassisTempTrap NOTIFICATION-TYPE
    OBJECTS
      {
          chassisName,
          trapSeverity      -- warning(1), critical(2)
      }
    STATUS current
    DESCRIPTION
        "Chassis temperature trap."
    ::= { vronxEvent 2 }
```

C) Trap name defines event severity. Trap data objects identify the chassis of interest and define event type.

```
chassisCriticalTrap NOTIFICATION-TYPE
    OBJECTS
      {
          chassisName,
          trapType         -- chassis(Temp(1), powerSupplyVoltage(2)
      }
    STATUS current
    DESCRIPTION
        "Critical trap."
    ::= { vronxEvent 3 }
```

D) General trap. Trap data identifies chassis of interest, event type, and event severity. As long as the list of OBJECTS is not large and does not contain confusing object definitions, this is a form preferred by many network engineers.

```
chassisGeneralTrap NOTIFICATION-TYPE
    OBJECTS
      {
          chassisName,
          trapType,        -- chassis(Temp(1), powerSupplyVoltage(2)
          trapSeverity     -- warning(1), critical(2)
      }
    STATUS current
    DESCRIPTION
        "General trap."
    ::= { vronxEvent 4 }
```

Summary of example trap model equivalences

Trap Name	Trap Data Objects
chassisTempCriticalTrap	chassisName
chassisTempTrap	chassisName trapSeverity
chassisCriticalTrap	chassisName trapType
chassisGenericTrap	chassisName trapType trapSeverity

Stateful Traps

An important function of manager trap filters is to auto-acknowledge previous traps. This depends on trap definitions that are *stateful*, having complementary states.

Bad traps ACK *good* traps, and *good* traps ACK *bad* traps. *majorIssue* will also ACK *minorIssue*. This is sometimes referred to as trap *correlation*.

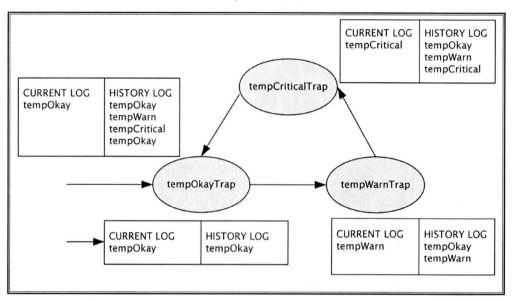

A *bad* trap will be logged as per its configured severity (such as *critical*), and the mapped device icon assumes a color reflecting its most severe unacknowledged trap (such as *red*).

Once the device problem is repaired, there are two methods to clear the *bad* trap from the manager log (and to restore icon color to something less alarming, like *green-normal*):
  • Manually by a knowing human
    ◦ A logistical nightmare, prone to confusion and error
  • Automatically by an auto-acknowledging *good* trap
    ◦ Requiring corresponding trap filter configuration

However, not all trap definitions are *stateful*.

Unary traps report events that are not state related (such as authenticationFailure).

Stateful traps include *binary traps* reporting good/bad conditions, and *multi-state* traps reporting states such as okay/warning/minor/critical.

Often event scenarios that *could be* modeled in a MIB by *stateful* trap definitions are not.

Simple Example—how would you create auto-acknowledging filters for a trap reporting these status values?

```
batteryStatusTrap NOTIFICATION-TYPE
    OBJECTS
    {
        batteryStatus  -- okay(1), degraded(2), failed(3), recharging(5)
    }
    STATUS current
    DESCRIPTION "Battery status trap."
    ::= { vronxEvent 14 }
```

Answer Matrix

Auto-ACK Matrix		then ACK logged event			
		okay	degraded	failed	recharging
If Trap =	okay		yes	yes	
	degraded	yes		yes	
	failed	yes	yes		
	recharging				

This is not an optimally designed trap object. State *recharging* is out of place, and a *notRecharging* or *fullyCharged* status would be useful.

But recovery is possible—four trap filters will be configured:

batteryOkayFilter	{ ACKs degraded and failed }
batteryDegradedFilter	{ ACKs okay and failed }
batteryFailedFilter	{ ACKs okay and degraded }
batteryRechargingFilter	-- a Unary Event

Exercises

1. Discuss good and bad points of the following trap design.

```
vronxStatusEv NOTIFICATION-TYPE
   OBJECTS
   {
      vronxEventCounter,
      vronxStatusMessage   -- SYNTAX DisplayString
   }
   STATUS  current
   DESCRIPTION
      "Sent when product status changes. DisplayString text
       explains the change."
   ::= { vronxStatusEvList 11 }
```

2. What are stateful traps? And why are these so useful?

Chapter 19

More on Trap Syntax

Potential issues regarding *trap object syntax* and *trap message syntax* are discussed in this chapter. One of the issues with message syntax can be avoided by proper MIB syntax.

Trap Syntax Issues

SMIv2-to-SMIv1 Conversion

This very important issue is repeated from Chapter 11.

NOTIFICATION-TYPE objects defined in an SMIv2 MIB may need future conversion into TRAP-TYPE objects in an equivalent SMIv1 MIB. This requires that the parent node of SMIv2 NOTIFICATION-TYPE objects have an OID that terminates in ".0". Syntax examples are shown in Chapter 11.

If this requirement is not met, the conversion to SMIv1 syntax will create a trap object with a *different* OID than defined by the SMIv2 MIB. If this SMIv1 MIB is loaded into a manager tool, the manager will not be able to correlate the OID of a trap received from an agent coded to the SMIv2 standard.

Not all MIB compilers will flag this problem.

"not-accessible" INDEX Objects

Strict checking by validation compilers requires that table INDEX objects have a MAX-ACCESS not-accessible. A brief discussion of *why* appears in Chapter 13. An expanded example is described here.

If the index object is arbitrary (no physical or logical mapping), there should not be issues. However, if the index does have physical or logical significance, a possible issue is discussed below.

Chapter 18 explained that manager trap filters normally operate on data values transported as PDU bindings with the trap.

The multi-step example below illustrates the issues.

Example shows an indexed table, vronxEntityStatusTable, with two indexes:

INDEX { entityModuleIdentity, entityPortNumber }

that have physical significance, and a trap:

vronxEntityStateChangeTrap

that sends a status value, entityStatus, defined in the indexed table:

```
vronxEntityStatusTable   OBJECT-TYPE
   SYNTAX SEQUENCE OF VronxEntityStatusEntry
   MAX-ACCESS not-accessible
   STATUS current
   DESCRIPTION "Table of slot, port status values."
   ::= ( vronxEntityStatus  1 )

vronxEntityStatusEntry OBJECT-TYPE
   SYNTAX VronxEntityStatusEntry
   MAX-ACCESS not-accessible
   STATUS current
   DESCRIPTION "Entry node"
   INDEX { entityModuleIdentity, entityPortNumber }      -- indexes
   ::= { vronxEntityStatusTable 1 }


VronxEntityStatusEntry ::= SEQUENCE {
   entityModuleIdentity    INTEGER,    -- {moduleQ (1),   -- MAX-ACCESS issue
                                       --   moduleR (4),
                                       --   moduleT (5)}
   entityPortNumber        Unsigned32,-- {1.. 32}          -- MAX-ACCESS issue
   entityStatus            INTEGER    -- {okay(1), inactive(2), test(3)}
   }
```

The MAX-ACCESS value for the two data objects specified in the INDEX clause is the issue.

A two-part example illustrates two possible traps to indicate a Vronx entity status change.

> *Example-1.* Trap definition—indexes entityModuleIdentity and entityPort-Number have MAX-ACCESS read-only, and their values are sent as notification OBJECTS. For this trap definition, manager trap filters are easily configured to inspect the values of entityModuleIdentity, entityPortNumber, and entityStatus, and to create filters based on those values.

```
NOTIFICATION-TYPE
    OBJECTS {      entityModuleIdentity,

                   entityPortNumber,

                   entityStatus }
    STATUS    current
    DESCRIPTION "Sent whenever entityStatus changes"
    ::= {vronxEventList 1 }
```

> *Example-2.* Trap definition—indexes entityModuleIdentity and entityPort-Number have MAX-ACCESS not-accessible, so the notification definition cannot include these as notification OBJECTS, and only the entityStatus value is sent. Discussion follows.

```
vronxEntityStateChangeTrap  NOTIFICATION-TYPE
    OBJECTS { entityStatus }

    STATUS    current
    DESCRIPTION "Sent whenever entityStatus changes"
    ::= { vronxEventList 1 }
```

for:

    entityModuleIdentity   = moduleR (enumerated value = 4)
    and entityPortNumber = 14

the value for entityStatus will be sent with the trap, bound with its OID and instance values:

    OID.*instance* = entityStatusOid.entityModuleIdentity.entityPortNumber
    OID.*instance* = entityStatusOid.4.14

A manager that wants to filter on values of entityModuleIdentity or entityPortNumber must have the ability to parse them out of the *instance* values of the entityStatus object.

Not all managers currently have this capability. This is an important consideration when defining table index objects and their access.

Trap and Notification Object Macros

One of a network engineer's tasks is to create manager filters for each trap object. Filters define logic to be executed when a trap is received. This was described in Chapter 17.

Some MIB vendors supply *macros* embedded in traps (as comment fields interspersed with trap syntax) that are targeted to a particular manager product. These macros facilitate automatic configuration of trap filters on that manager—when the MIB is compiled into the manager, filters for traps are automatically created.

Simple example of SMIv1 trap object with embedded macro logic

```
trapName TRAP-TYPE
    ENTERPRISE enterpriseString
    -- &ACTION  {action list}
    -- &CLEARS  {clears Trap#}
    -- &MATCH   {variable-name}
    -- &MESG    "The event log message text"
    DESCRIPTION "trap description"
::= trapNumber
```

&ACTION lists email, paging, and other activities to be performed.

&CLEARS identifies traps to be auto-acknowledged.

&MATCH defines data object value matching logic that triggers actions and trap clearing.

&MESG defines the message to be logged.

Note that all of the filter macro information is embedded in comments (following double dashes). There are no RFC-based standards for such macros, and macro definition syntax varies, depending on the targeted managers.

If macros are targeted to your manager product, this can be very helpful—if not, you *may* have a problem.

If macros are targeted to manager product A, but the MIB is loaded onto manager product B, which supports different macro conventions, the compiler may fail to load trap objects successfully. Instead of ignoring the comment lines, it recognizes the "--&" as an intended macro, assumes it is in manager product B format, attempts to parse the information in a different manner, and fails. Compiler errors will be logged.

> **MIB Diagnosis Hint.** If this problem is encountered, it will be necessary to edit all macro definition lines out of trap object syntax.

Trap Message Syntax Issues

SNMP trap message lengths greater than 484 bytes can create problems. This limit is easily exceeded if:
- DisplayString object values are sent.
  - For this reason, some MIB designers avoid including any DisplayString objects in trap definitions.
- Too many OBJECTS have been included in the trap definition.
  - Some managers will ignore more than 10 or 12 OBJECTS bindings. Manager behavior may be subtle—the manager may compile the trap object definition with no complaints, but will nevertheless ignore trap message OBJECT bindings beyond the 10th or 12th, and any filter configurations based on those bindings will not work.
- INDEX *instance* values that are lengthy can also contribute to this problem.

Message length issues need to be considered in MIB trap object design. Network engineers observing odd manager behavior in processing traps should consider this as a possible cause.

SNMP trap message syntax sometimes has problems.
- SNMP trap data object bindings are sometimes *missing data instance values.*
- Incorrect *trap message syntax* has also been observed, including malformed PDUs and incorrect trap OIDs. This is usually manifested as a mysterious (and quite ugly) manager event log entry.

> *For developers*—reasons faulty trap message syntax can occur:
>   - Agent SDK APIs can make it relatively difficult to form a correct SNMP trap message—it is easy to make a coding mistake.
>   - In testing agent code, it can be difficult to simulate or create product conditions that force an agent to send all possible traps. However, thorough testing is essential.
>   - A suitable trap capture tool should be used by developers, to ensure each trap is received, parsed, and displayed properly.

SNMP Tidbit. Some developers add a read-write MIB object that allows a manager to *set* a value for a trap number, which the agent interprets as a command to send an example of that trap. The developer may want to remove this capability from the MIB actually shipped to customers, or make it available to network engineers as a debug tool in setting up their SNMP networks.

Chapter 20

Trap Semantics for Agents

What are *agent semantics*? Semantics describe agent behavior in managing different circumstances and are particularly important in management of traps. This chapter first discusses good design practices, then provides examples of MIB data objects that are useful for controlling agent behavior.

Good MIB–Agent Design Practices

One of the easiest and most useful MIB enhancements is the crafting of excellent DESCRIPTION clauses to describe agent semantics.

Example of pretty good semantics description

```
cdChassisTempAlarmEv NOTIFICATION-TYPE
   OBJECTS
   {
      cdDynCfgUserAlias,
      cdStCfgModel,
      cdChStTemperature,
      cdEvSeverity,
      cdEvDescription
   }
   STATUS  current
   DESCRIPTION
      "Sent when cdChStTemperature > cdChassisTempAlarmThresh.
      Will not be re-sent until cdChStTemperature drops below
      cdChasisTempAlarmThresh less 10%.
      This trap can be disabled by setting
      cdChassisTempEvTrapEn = trapDisable."
   ::= { cdEventList 10 }
```

Developers do not set out to develop problem agents, but naïve agent behavior can easily creep in. Here are some typical problems (and suggested solutions).

- An agent detects an alarming condition, sends a *trap*, and keeps on sending the same *trap* until the condition clears. If sent too frequently, this is referred to as a *trap storm,* and will overwhelm managers.
  ○ *Suggestion.* Never re-send *warning* or *minor* traps. *Major* or *critical* traps may warrant re-sending, but at some controlled (and well-documented) rate that will not overwhelm managers or irritate personnel working with the manager. Always design agents to avoid trap storms.

- The trap example above illustrates *hysteresis logic.* If a temperature rises above a threshold, a *trap* is sent. If the temperature hovers around the threshold, multiple traps may be sent.
  ○ *Suggestion.* Define (and document) a hysteresis level that the temperature must drop below before the trap is rearmed to be sent again.

- *Debounce logic* filters out transient events in a subsystem undergoing a mode or status change. For example, an agent may be monitoring a signal level on a field-replaceable unit (FRU). While a FRU module is being inserted or removed from its slot, multiple transient events may occur, but which do not represent true failures.
  ○ *Suggestion.* Good agent logic will detect the first event, set up a wait timer, and recheck for the condition again. If it persists, a *trap* is sent.
  ○ *Suggestion.* Define an *informational* trap that reports FRU removals and insertions.

- *Agent disconnect logic* ensures that if the monitored entity (hardware or software) disappears, the agent behaves nicely, and sends an appropriate *trap.* Some observed cases:
  ○ Some subagents are designed to *initialize* and then check to see if the subsystem they are designed to monitor is currently on-line. If it is not, the subagent shuts down. This is reasonable logic.
  ○ A subagent was dedicated to monitoring a specific type of storage device. If the device was on-line when the agent started up, the agent remained alive to monitor it; else the agent terminated. At a point in time, the device suffered a solid failure. Rather than reporting the failure, the subagent simply shut down and reported nothing.
  ○ An agent was designed to acquire data via an API to another software application. The monitored software application terminated, and the agent went into an infinite loop waiting to reacquire API contact, using 100% of CPU cycles while waiting.

MIB Data Affecting Agent Behavior

Developers spend a lot of time designing MIBs to model, monitor, and manage their products, but often neglect to include data useful in defining agent semantics. Ideas for such MIB objects are discussed next, and may or may not apply to your particular design situation.

Agent Trap Rate Control

Agents that send too many traps can overwhelm manager tools (they may freeze up or discard traps arbitrarily while trying to keep up), as well as the personnel using the tools. One way to control this type of agent behavior is to define a MIB object to throttle down agent trap generation to an acceptable rate. Design may also require a queueing mechanism to ensure that traps are not just discarded by the agent.

This rate may apply to all traps under an agent's control (i.e., never send more than one trap every T-time period), or to individual traps (never send a single trap type more often than once every T-time period).

Chapter 18's Entity MIB entConfigChange trap syntax example includes a DESCRIPTION clause that discusses agent throttling semantics for that trap.

read-write Object Value Thresholds

Expansion of previous example. A read-write threshold value that lets users control the trappable temperature value. Note the specification of a default value used by the agent prior to any manager *set* value.

```
cdChassisTempAlarmThresh   OBJECT-TYPE
    SYNTAX        Integer32
    UNITS         "Celsius"
    MAX-ACCESS  read-write
    STATUS        current
    DESCRIPTION
        "User settable to define the Chassis Temperature
        past which a Chassis Temperature Alarm will occur.
        Agent semantics will apply hysteresis logic so
        traps do not repeat unnecessarily when
        chassis temperature is very close to this threshold.
        Persistent through system resets."
    DEFVAL { 40 }
    ::= { cdEventControl 2 }
```

The example above is typical of what can be found in MIBs. However, allowing users control over thresholds should be done with some discretion—a user may set a high value and miss traps that are indicative of failing equipment. Yet allowing the user some control over minimizing frequent, annoying, and (in the user's mind) non-urgent traps should be considered. Developers may want to specify such thresholds as an allowable range settable by users.

Agent Polling Frequency

This is commonly found in enterprise MIBs.

Example of a read-write agent polling frequency—how often the agent polls data for *alarming* values. This allows users some control over agent use of CPU cycles, and also provides a mechanism for disabling all traps (by setting the poll rate to zero).

```
cdEvCtlAgtPollFreq  OBJECT-TYPE
    SYNTAX        Unsigned32
    UNITS         "seconds"
    MAX-ACCESS  read-write
    STATUS        current
    DESCRIPTION
        "How often the Agent polls the CD Player for trap-able conditions.
        Set = 0 to disable all traps.
        Persistent through system resets."
    DEFVAL {30}
    ::= { cdEventControl 1 }
```

In some systems, allowing user control over agent polling frequency can be dangerous. For example, in television real-time production equipment, increasing the agent polling rate to be very rapid could upset overall system timing and result in ugly on-air artifacts. If such control is allowed, developers may want to allow adjustment only within a specified value range.

A *polling frequency* for traps has been confused with polling and caching data for populating MIB object values. In general, an agent that receives a *get* request from a manager should return the most current value for the object, not a cached value based on a polling frequency.

Disabling Traps (or Groups of Traps)

MIB data objects may be provided which allow the user to *set* values to enable/disable single traps or trap groups. This capability is similar to SNMPv3's ability to configure agents to control trap transmission behavior.

Enumerated integer objects for this purpose are sometimes included in MIBs, and can be expressed as enterprise-specific textual conventions.

> *Example* from RFC-3418 *Management Information Base (MIB) for the Simple Network Management Protocol (SNMP)* SNMPv2-MIB

```
snmpEnableAuthenTraps OBJECT-TYPE
    SYNTAX      INTEGER { enabled(1), disabled(2) }
    MAX-ACCESS  read-write
    STATUS      current
    DESCRIPTION
        "Indicates whether the SNMP entity is permitted to
        generate authenticationFailure traps.  The value of this
        object overrides any configuration information; as such,
        it provides a means whereby all authenticationFailure
        traps may be disabled.

        Note that it is strongly recommended that this object
        be stored in non-volatile memory so that it remains
        constant across re-initializations of the network
        management system."
    ::= { snmp 30 }
```

An extension of the trap enable/disable concept by a particular enterprise incorporated a number of interesting ideas:
- When up-stream units (outputting video signals) were shut down for maintenance, down-stream products under SNMP management would generate *critical traps*. This was undesirable behavior.
- A TruthValue (read-write) maintenanceMode object was created. When *set* to true, all traps were inhibited.
- Another Unsigned32 (read-write) maintenanceModeTimer (UNITS "hours") object was created.
  - When maintenanceMode was *set* true, maintenanceModeTimer would begin counting down. When it reached zero, maintenanceMode was set false by the agent. This ensured that traps were not disabled indefinitely (if the technician forgot to re-enable them after maintenance work was completed).

Enabling Traps Based on Severity

We previously described the explicit or implied severity of all traps.

If a MIB and an associated agent have a concept of severity, it may be expressed in the trap object name, by an enumerated INTEGER value sent with the trap, or by a DisplayString value sent with the trap, or be described in the trap object DESCRIPTION field.

MIB data objects can then be defined to enable/disable traps by specifying a severity threshold value.

Example of MIB object to control severity of traps sent to managers

```
vronxEventSeverityThreshold   OBJECT-TYPE
    SYNTAX     INTEGER
            { normal(1)
              warning(2),
              minor(3),
              major(4),
              critical(5)
            }
    MAX-ACCESS  read-write
    STATUS      current
    DESCRIPTION
        "User settable to control the severity threshold for traps to be sent.
        For example, if set = major(4),
        only major and critical traps will be sent."
    DEFVAL { normal }
    ::= { vronxEventControl 1 }
```

The severity values can be defined by a TEXTUAL-CONVENTION, which is also used to define severity values sent with traps.

Exercises

1. Give an example of poor agent trap semantics and its consequences.

2. Give an example of good agent trap semantics.

Part 6

MIB Organization

The next chapters discuss broader issues of MIB design—MIB types and functionality, organizing MIB data, and the MIB design process. *Partitioning* and *style* ideas are discussed rather than standards.

There is no one best way to organize MIBs, but it is important that MIB developers have a plan and that chosen styles be consistent throughout the enterprise.

Chapter 21, *Standard MIBS,* discusses a subset of standard MIBs that SNMP practitioners should be aware of.

Chapter 22, *Types of Enterprise MIBs,* explains common partitioning. Some enterprises have one type of MIB that is all encompassing (okay), while others design MIBs in a more modular fashion (better).

Chapter 23, *Data Organization and Uses,* offers ideas and examples. Ambitious SNMP practitioners will read a variety of additional MIBs to appreciate further possibilities.

Chapter 24 describes a *MIB Design Process* that has worked well. Developers are encouraged to adopt a similar process to ensure MIB quality and usefulness to customers.

Standard MIBs

Chapter 4 discussed main categories of standard MIBs—management MIBs under the mib-2 node, experimental MIBs, and SNMPv2 and SNMPv3 support MIBs. In addition there are a few standard MIBs under an IEEE node.

Near the end of Chapter 4, there is an *integrated OID diagram* that will be useful to review before reading this chapter.

Many of the chapters have provided examples of objects from specific standard MIBs. This chapter presents more details and expected MIB support by standard platform agents, and describes IETF MIB and IANA MIB partitioning.

The topic of standard MIBs is huge, and the goal here is familiarization, not exhaustive descriptions.

Expected Agent Support for Standard MIBs

Standard agent support for standard MIBs refers to common or normally expected agent support for MIB objects by most out-of-the-box agents, regardless of application.

For network engineers, standard support refers to what will likely be encountered on any SNMP-compliant workstation. Specialized platforms such as routers and data base servers will support these basics and much more.

For developers, these are the expectations of capabilities provided by the chosen agent SDK (probably by the master agent or an included subagent), leaving only subagent code for enterprise MIBs to be developed.

Expected support will vary by product, but in general, support will be found for:
- Under the mib-2 node
  - System table
  - Interface tables
  - IP tables
  - ICMP tables
  - TCP tables
  - UDP tables
  - SNMP tables
  - Host resources MIB tables (common, but optional support)
- Under the snmpV2 node
  - Tables related to SNMPv2c and SNMPv3 agents

As always there are exceptions. There is a very specialized enterprise agent that supports only enterprise traps—no standard MIB support, and no *get* or *set* support for enterprise data objects. But most agents will provide as a minimum something like the capabilities described in this chapter.

MIBs and Tables Under mib-2

Many IETF standard MIBs are organized under the mib-2 node defined in RFC1213-MIB. Some of these supported objects are defined within the RFC1213-MIB, but many are defined in separate MIBs which IMPORTS the mib-2 node definition. Important, commonly supported groups are diagramed below.

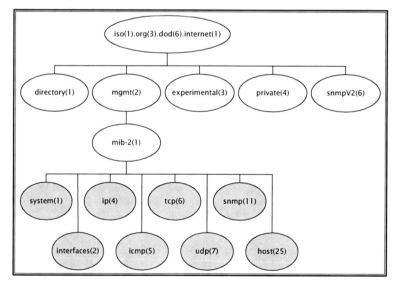

Under the mib-2(1).system(1) node there a scalar table that is very familiar to SNMP users—the mib-2 system table.

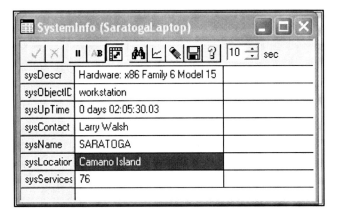

sysDescr is a read-only DisplayString providing information about the platform.

Note that sysObjectID is typed as an OBJECT IDENTIFIER, but is displayed by the manager as the equivalent textual name of an object defined in the Microsoft MSFT-MIB. sysObjectID was discussed extensively in Chapter 4.

sysUpTime is typed as TimeTicks (hundredths of a second), but is displayed by the manager in a more convenient format.

sysContact, sysName, and sysLocation are all read-write DisplayString objects that can be *set* from a manager.

Under the mib-2(1).interfaces(2) node there is the indexed ifTable describing interfaces on this system. The indexes used in this table are very commonly referenced by other, more complex standard MIB tables (for example, from RMON and RMON2 MIBs).

Example subset of data from the ifTable

ifIndex	ifDescr	ifType	ifMtu	ifSpeed	ifPhysAddress
1	MS TCP Loopback interface	softwareLoopback	1520	10000000	
2	Broadcom NetXtreme 57xx	ethernetCsmacd	1500	1000000000	00 18 8b d0 78 8f
3	Dell Wireless 1390 WLAN	ethernetCsmacd	1500	54000000	00 19 7e 7a 49 8f

The *generic traps* linkUp and linkDown are events related to the ifTable and contain data objects from the ifTable, including ifIndex.

Under nodes:

> mib-2(1).ip(4)
> mib-2(1).icmp(5)
> mib-2(1).tcp(6)
> mib-2(1).udp(7)
> mib-2(1).snmp(11)

are tables detailing statistics for each of those protocols.

When debugging SNMP networks, *snmp group* information can be valuable, providing SNMP input, output, and error statistics.

Examples of some *snmp group* data object values appear to the right.

Data includes performance statistics as well as error counters.

snmpInfo (SaratogaLaptop)	
EnableAuthenTraps	enabled
InPkts	1457
OutPkts	1460
InBadVersions	0
InBadCommunityNames	0
InBadCommunityUses	0
InASNParseErrs	0
InTooBigs	0
InNoSuchNames	0
InBadValues	0
InReadOnlys	0
InGenErrs	0
InTotalReqVars	8159
InTotalSetVars	0

Agent support for mib-2(1).host(25) node data is less common, yet is frequently available. Host data is defined in the HOST-RESOURCES-MIB, and is rich in content. It includes information on users, software processes, storage devices, memory usage, and CPU usage. Some of the raw statistics provided are amenable to manager calculations to create values in custom tables.

The major subgroups in the Host Resources MIB are

hrSystem	OBJECT IDENTIFIER ::= { host 1 }
hrStorage	OBJECT IDENTIFIER ::= { host 2 }
hrDevice	OBJECT IDENTIFIER ::= { host 3 }
hrSWRun	OBJECT IDENTIFIER ::= { host 4 }
hrSWRunPerf	OBJECT IDENTIFIER ::= { host 5 }
hrSWInstalled	OBJECT IDENTIFIER ::= { host 6 }
hrMIBAdminInfo	OBJECT IDENTIFIER ::= { host 7 }

Example SNMPc display of host resources information

hrSWRunIndex	hrSWRunName	hrSWRunID	hrSWRunPath	hr
1	System Idle Process	0.0		
4	System	0.0		
212	WLTRYSVC.EXE	0.0	C:\WINDOWS\System32\	
248	AsfIpMon.exe	0.0	C:\Program	
272	AluSchedulerSvc.exe	0.0	C:\Program	
328	BCMWLTRY.EXE	0.0	C:\WINDOWS\System32\	
384	cisvc.exe	0.0	C:\WINDOWS\system32\	
404	DataServer.exe	0.0	C:\Program Files\Wave	
532	iexplore.exe	0.0	C:\Program Files\Internet	
572	spoolsv.exe	0.0	C:\WINDOWS\system32\	
624	scardsvr.exe	0.0	C:\WINDOWS\System32\	
656	sqlservr.exe	0.0	c:\Program Files\Microsoft	
684	cbg.exe	0.0	C:\Program Files\Capture By	
716	WLTRAY.EXE	0.0	C:\WINDOWS\system32\	

Window title: HrSWRunEntry (SaratogaLaptop) — toolbar: 10 sec

This table displays information (not all shown above) about the software modules running on this device:

- Table index
- Software name
- The program path
- Run parameters
- Identifies it as a system program or as an application
- A read-write enumerated value:

{ invalid, notRunnable, runnable, running }

Another table (not shown) AUGMENTS this table and shows CPU and memory usage for each of the software modules.

SNMPv2 and SNMPv3 Support MIBs

Under the node:

> iso(1).org(.3).dod(.6).internet(.1).snmpV2(.6)

are MIB objects related to SNMPv2 definitions, and several MIBs used for SNMPv3 configuration.

The node:

snmpV2(6).snmpModules(3).snmpMIB(1).snmp-MIBObjects(1).snmpTraps(5)

organizes the SNMPv2 versions of the generic traps:

> coldStart (.1)
> warmStart (.2)
> linkDown (.3)
> linkUp (.4)
> authenticationFailure (.5)
> egpNeighborLoss (.6)

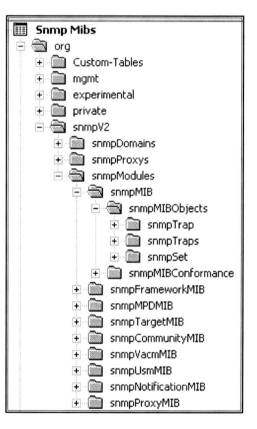

SNMPv3 configuration MIBs are organized under the node:

> snmpV2(.6).snmpModules(.3)

and include the following MIBs:

> snmpFrameworkMIB (.10)
> snmpMPDMIB (.11)
> snmpTargetMIB (.12)
> snmpCommunityMIB (.18)
> snmpVacmMIB (.16)
> snmpUsmMIB (.15)
> snmpNotificationMIB (.13)
> snmpProxyMIB (.14)

IETF and IANA MIBs

Most standard product-related or technology-related MIBs are defined under the mib-2 node and are published by the IETF in RFCs. Some of these have been discussed already, and examples of objects from IETF MIBs have been given.

Closely related to IETF MIBs are IANA (Internet Assigned Numbers Authority) MIBs. IANA MIBs are used for name space definitions that are administered by IANA. IANA MIBs include:

- TEXTUAL-CONVENTION definitions that define standard enumerated INTEGER values
- Standard textual conventions based on BITS data objects
- Administratively defined OBJECT IDENTIFIER (OID) values for globally unique enumeration definitions
- IANA is also responsible for assignment of OBJECT IDENTIFIER values for new standard MIB MODULE-IDENTITY statements, which define child nodes under the mib-2 node

Example from RFC-4181 *Guidelines for Authors and Reviewers of MIB Documents*

For example, something along the following lines would be appropriate for an Internet-Draft containing a single MIB module with MODULE-IDENTITY descriptor powerEthernetMIB that is to be assigned a value under the 'mib-2' subtree:

The MIB module in this document uses the following IANA-assigned OBJECT IDENTIFIER values recorded in the SMI Numbers registry:

```
Descriptor              OBJECT IDENTIFIER value
-------------           -----------------------------------
powerEthernetMIB        { mib-2 XXX }
```

The distinction between IETF and IANA MIBs, and the organization of these on separate web sites, is relatively recent.

Several examples of IANA MIBs are listed below. The reader may want to inspect these references to become more comfortable with the distinctions between IETF MIBs and IANA MIBs.

> RFC-3805 *Printer MIB v2* contains two MIBs (an IANA MIB and an IETF MIB):
>
> > IANA-PRINTER-MIB defines textual conventions
> >
> > Printer-MIB defines managed objects, and IMPORTS definitions from the IANA-PRINTER-MIB
>
> RFC-1573 *Evolution of the Interfaces Group of MIB-II* contains two MIB definitions:
>
> > IANAifType-MIB defines textual conventions
> >
> > IF-MIB defines managed objects, and IMPORTS definitions from the IANAifType-MIB
> >
> > However the IANA web site contains an updated version of the IANAifType-MIB:
> >
> > > www.iana.org/assignments/ianaiftype-mib
>
> RFC-2932 *IPv4 Multicast Routing MIB* contains the IPMROUTE-STD-MIB, which IMPORTS textual convention definitions from the IANA-RTPROTO-MIB. The latter can be found at:
>
> > www.iana.org/assignments/ianaiprouteprotocol-mib
>
> RFC-4836 *Definitions of Managed Objects for IEEE 802.3 Medium Attachment Units (MAUs)* contains the MAU-MIB and the IANA-MAU-MIB. The IANA-MAU-MIB can also be found on the IANA web site:
>
> > www.iana.org/assignments/ianamau-mib
>
> > The IANA-MAU-MIB is a comprehensive example of IANA types of definitions:
> > - Textual conventions based on BITS
> > - Textual conventions based on enumerated INTEGER
> > - Globally unique object identifier enumerations

Sleuthing RFCs, IETF MIBs, and IANA MIBs

Network engineer job descriptions usually include something like *detective skills desirable*, and this also holds true for their SNMP activities. They need to be good at determining which RFCs are most current, and where to find the most current IETF and IANA MIBs.

Some of the issues:

- Determining which MIB revisions are supported by delivered agents.
  - RFCs and MIBs may have been revised and updated, but your agent may not (yet) support those updates.
  - Or your agents may support updated RFCs not yet loaded into your manager. They may appear to be running well with the older MIBs, but could provide additional information with newer MIBs in the manager.
  - Contact agent suppliers to determine MIB support requirements.
- Early IETF MIBs defined in RFCs assumed names associated with the RFC number (e.g., RFC1213-MIB). Later, revised MIBs assumed names related to MIB functionality (e.g., IF-MIB)—which can create confusion.
- Early IANA MIBs were contained in RFCs. Versions of those MIBs found in RFCs may no longer be current (and were not updated in subsequent RFCs) but can now be found on the IANA web site; this can also create confusion.

Determining Interface Table MIB Updates—Example

Rather than a general discussion, an example involving the *interfaces table* follows. Refer to the IETF web site, the RFC Index and the RFC documents themselves, to facilitate understanding of the situation described.

The diagram below illustrates actual problems that may need to be solved—which MIBs are needed to support a particular agent revision.

This example is more complex than most situations normally encountered by network engineers, but the process of resolving issues is typical.

The diagram is followed by discussion.

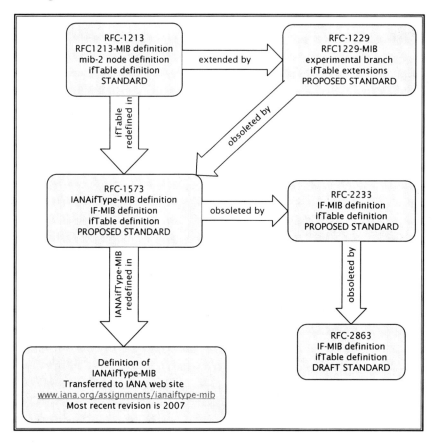

RFC-1213 contains the original ifTable definition as part of the RFC-1213 MIB (as well as other data). This is an important table, and other MIBs reference ifTable indexed objects by IMPORTS FROM RFC1213-MIB.

RFC-1229 *Extensions to the generic-interface MIB* contains a new MIB named RFC1229-MIB and is built on the experimental branch. It contains extensions to the ifTable. A particular deployed agent may require this MIB in addition to RFC1213-MIB.

RFC-1573 obsoletes RFC-1229 and contains an updated definition of ifTable. The name of this MIB is IF-MIB. At this point in the evolution of SNMP, naming of standard MIBs no longer tracked the RFC number but became more descriptive of a MIB's purpose. In addition, a new IANAifType-MIB was defined, which the IF-MIB IMPORTS information from.

RFC-2233 obsoletes RFC-1573 and also contains the updated definition of ifTable in the IF-MIB. The IANAifType-MIB is no longer defined in this RFC—its definition is now controlled on an IANA web site:

www.iana.org/assignments/ianaiftype-mib

RFC-2863 obsoletes RFC-2233 and contains yet another updated definition of the ifTable in the updated IF-MIB.

The ifTable defined in all of these RFCs contains similar objects, although some definitions have subtle changes (e.g., expanded INTEGER enumerations), and the STATUS of some objects are deprecated.

An agent in a particular unit of deployed equipment will support one of the situations described above.

Network engineers:
   a.   Must read vendor data sheets and release notices to determine which MIB revisions are needed by their managers to support vendor agents.
   b.   May need to research the IETF web site to understand RFC and MIB revision histories and support differences.
   c.   However, they should unduly not worry about loading the IF-MIB from RFC-2863 on top of the IF-MIB from RFC-2233 (and so on).

   The discussion on MIB object registration and agent and MIB revision issues in Chapter 4 clarifies this point further.

Exercises

1.   What is the relationship of IETF standard MIBs and IANA standard MIBs?

2.   Most standard MIBs defining objects are organized under the *mgmt* node. Where else are some standard MIBs located?

3.   You have just taken delivery of SNMP-compliant cable television modems. The documentation is a little vague regarding what MIBs are supported. How will you research this topic, how will you determine which standard MIBs are most current, and how will you obtain copies?

Chapter 22

Types of Enterprise MIBs

This chapter is a discussion of partitioning based on functionality. There are advantages to this modular approach vs. the all-in-one approach, just as there are in hardware and software design.

Self-Contained MIBs

Some enterprises publish only one type of MIB, all-in-one *Product Management MIBs.* Each of those MIBs repeats header information contained in all other product MIBs.

For example, the SMIv1 header for the Chateau Systems CD-Player management MIB would look like

```
IMPORTS enterprises FROM RFC1155-SMI;

chateausystems OBJECT IDENTIFIER              ::= { enterprises 10910 }
chateauRegistrations OBJECT IDENTIFIER        ::= { chateausystems  2 }
chateauProducts OBJECT IDENTIFIER             ::= { chateauRegistrations 2 }
chateauConsumerProducts OBJECT IDENTIFIER     ::= { chateauProducts 3  }
chateauCDProduct OBJECT IDENTIFIER            ::= { chateauConsumerProducts  1 }
chateauCDProductMIB OBJECT IDENTIFIER         ::= { chateauCDProduct 1  }
```

For a new MIB describing DVD players, the first five lines would be repeated, and care would be taken in defining the following two node OIDs to ensure that they do not conflict with other, previously published MIBs.

Such MIBs may also encapsulate textual convention definitions and global OID enumerations.

A better approach is to partition definitions into several separate MIBs and to IMPORTS needed definitions into the product MIBs. Enterprise partitioning can include:
- Judicious use of standard MIBs
- SMI registrations MIB
- Textual convention definitions MIB
- Subsystem MIBs
- Product MIBs
- Trap definition MIBs

For very small MIBs and very small product lines, this may not be worth the effort. But for most enterprises, elements of this chapter will be useful.

SMI Registration MIB

Enterprise SMI registration MIBs can serve a number of purposes by defining global OIDs that are IMPORTS by other MIBs authored by the same enterprise.

Management of Enterprise OID Space

In much the same way IANA issues enterprise OIDs, an enterprise will register OIDs assigning MIB nodes to departments or to development teams, which in turn become responsible for management of the OID space under their nodes.

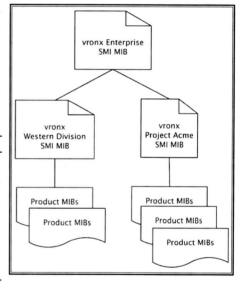

These *registered* node OIDs are defined in an enterprise SMI registration MIB which is likely (should be) a controlled document. It may require formal revision control with management approvals to change, or may be more simply controlled using a software-based revision control system.

The example above and right shows a simple corporate organization.

The Vronx corporate SMI MIB defines OID space for the Vronx Western Division, and for the Acme special-project activity. Product MIBs are organized under both of these nodes, and further organization of OID space becomes the responsibility of the Western Division management and Project Acme management. Lines connecting MIBs indicate the IMPORTS relationships.

Chateau Systems SMI MIB Registrations

CHATEAUSYSTEMS-REGISTRATIONS-MIB definitions appear in Appendix G, along with a graphical representation of the entire MIB. A subset of that diagram appears to the right.

All released MIBs are organized under a chateauProducts(.2) node.

Also defined is a chateauExperimental(.1) node that can be used to test experimental MIBs, which will be relocated under the chateauProducts node prior to release.

A chateauGlobalRegistrations(.1) node is also defined under which OID global enumerations intended for sysObjectID use (or other uses) can be organized.

In more complex environments additional nodes might be appropriate.

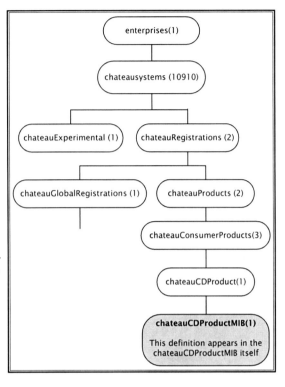

Examples:

chateauDivisions

Nodes allocated to company divisions (or departments) could be defined. Each division might then define a divisional SMI MIB to organize its own product MIB space.

chateauSubsystems

Commonly used subsystems that are components in products may have their own MIB support, rather than duplicating those object definitions in multiple product MIBs. For example, power supplies, fans, processor boards, software modules.

chateauInternal

Internal-use-only MIBs are organized under this node. A company may use SNMP to monitor a manufacturing process (or a television broadcast facility) using MIBs and agents developed in-house, and only used in-house.

chateauThirdParty

MIB support for third party products are organized here. Example: A product or subsystem with no SNMP support is purchased, and a supporting MIB and agent are developed.

In defining and organizing nodes, leave OID space for future additions, so they can be appended naturally.

For example, if you decide to obsolete the MIB for your *Super Fast Router* (SFR-MIB), and replace it with a MIB for a *Super Fast Router New Generation* (SFR-NG-MIB), there should be a place to add it that looks like you planned the OID space that way in advance.

Definition of globally unique OID enumerations. These are used to provide values to objects of type OBJECT IDENTIFIER.

For example, the CISCO-PRODUCTS-MIB defines OID enumerations used to provide product identification values for mib-2 sysObjectID objects.

Other OID enumerations can be used to define subsystem types, component types, and anything that lends itself to global uniqueness.

Textual Convention Definition MIB

Organizations will benefit from defining data subtypes that will provide a common look and feel to all of their MIBs.

Examples:

- An enumerated INTEGER object that defines
    { trapEnable(1),
      trapDisable(2) }

- Enumerated INTEGER describing trap severity
    { informational (1),
      okay(2),
      warning(3),
      major(5),
      critical (6) }

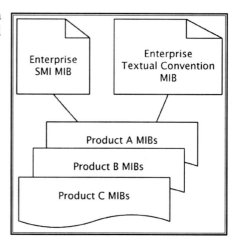

- An Unsigned32 object that defines agent trap polling frequency in seconds.

These definitions can be coded into a separate MIB that is IMPORTS by all product MIBs.

The CISCO-TC MIB provides an example of a MIB that contains only textual convention definitions—a few *examples*:

    CiscoNetworkProtocol
    CiscoNetworkAddress
    Unsigned64
    CiscoAlarmSeverity
    TimeIntervalMin
    Microseconds

Textual convention MIBs can also be found among standard MIBs.

> *Two examples:*

RFC-3977 *Alarm Management Information Base (MIB)* contains two MIBs:

    ALARM-MIB and IANA-ITU-ALARM-TC-MIB

The latter contains only textual convention definitions.

RFC-3805 *Printer MIB v2* contains two MIBs:

    IANA-PRINTER-MIB and the Printer-MIB

The first MIB contains only textual convention definitions, which are used by the second MIB.

Product Management MIBs

There are various strategies for defining product MIBs.

Developers should first review what standard MIBs are already available to manage their products. For some industries, support for specific standard MIBs is expected and may be sufficient.

Inspection of standard MIBs may also present opportunities for defining enterprise MIB tables that extend existing standard MIB tables (i.e., adding columns to those tables for enterprise-specific data objects).

After reviewing standard MIB applicability, unique enterprise MIBs are designed as needed to fully manage the product.

Comprehensive product MIBs manage all aspects of the product. This includes MIB objects for:
- Modeling the product
- Status information
- Long-term value trending
- Configuration
- Control
- Traps

Some enterprises define MIBs to manage *component* and *system* behavior separately.

> *For example*:
>
> MIBs that manage a company's power supplies, fans, processor boards, and proprietary protocols
>
> Separate MIBs to manage the behavior of integrated systems (or products), built from components

The standard Entity MIB (RFC-4133) is an interesting approach. A product's components and their relationships are modeled, and OID pointers can be used point to the MIBs that manage the components. Physical component objects are combined to create logical objects.

MIBs Dedicated to Trap Definitions

Some MIBs are designed to contain only trap definitions, using data OBJECTS that are IMPORTS from another MIB (or MIBs).

A standard MIB example is given below—enterprise MIB examples also exist.

> RFC-2455 and RFC-2456 provide an example of MIBs supporting APPN (Advanced Peer-to-Peer Network) traps.
>
> RFC-2455 *Definitions of Managed Objects for APPN* APPN-MIB, contains data definitions and one NOTIFICATION-TYPE definition.
>
> RFC-2456 *Definitions of Managed Objects for APPN MIBS* APPN-TRAP-MIB, contains mostly NOTIFICATION-TYPE definitions, and IMPORTS most data object definitions from the APPN-MIB.

Integrated Support for Products

Products usually ship with subagents that support multiple MIBs.

> *Example* of typical partitioning:
> ○ Master agent support for standard MIBs such as mib-2's system table, the interface table, possibly the host resources table, and others
> ○ Subagent support for enterprise subsystem components (one subagent per component MIB)
> ○ Separate subagent support for the system-level product

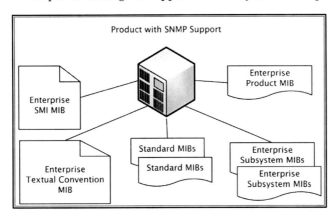

Exercises

1. Enterprises may organize their MIBs in a variety of ways. But name three common categories (or types) of MIBs.

2. What are the advantages of such organization?

Chapter 23

Data Organization and Uses

The CD player product MIB example in Appendix H illustrates many of the ideas discussed in this chapter. Please review it—much of the commentary in the MIB DESCRIPTION clauses reflects topics in this chapter (and topics throughout the book).

Node objects are used to organize data into logical categories. A few are discussed in this chapter. The goal is not an exhaustive list of categories and object examples, but to introduce useful ideas. Actual products will require MIBs with additional or refined categories.

Object Semantics

Object semantics help explain MIB objects to the MIB consumer, and can be conveyed in a number of ways. MIB designers should take full advantage of object syntax to describe semantics. Poorly written MIBs frequently ignore opportunities to document data and related agent behavior.

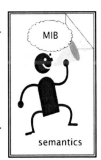

Object Naming

Object names should be descriptive and progressive and communicate the data category (e.g., status) and specific purpose (e.g. the Vronx GPS status object for position might be named vronxGpsStatPosition).

Data SYNTAX Choices

These choices should be exercised—a suitable base type, standard textual convention, or enterprise textual convention should be chosen to reflect the purpose of the data object.

There are fundamentally just two types of SNMP data, OCTET STRING and INTEGER—but choosing DisplayString, BITS, IpAddress, Unsigned32,

Counter32, etc. conveys to the end user the intended use. It also communicates to managers that data values should be displayed in specific formats.

Data Range and Size Constraints

Data ranges for integers and size constraints for octet strings should be included in the syntax. This not only communicates information to the user, but managers use this information to disallow user-initiated *set* requests with value-out-of-range (or octet string size-out-of-range) data. *For example*:

```
SYNTAX Gauge32 (0..100)
```

DEFVAL *Clause*

The DEFVAL clause for read-write data objects provides the user a recommended reasonable value, as well as defining what value the agent will use prior to any *set* operation. *For example*:

```
DEFVAL { 50 }
```

UNITS *Clause*

The UNITS clause should be used whenever this clarifies the intent of the data object. *For example:*

```
UNITS "percent"
```

DESCRIPTION *Clause*

DESCRIPTION clauses are very important in documenting agent semantics, especially for trap-type objects. A small amount of time spent editing decent descriptions will be invaluable to network engineers.

DISPLAY-HINT *Clause*

DISPLAY-HINT specifications should be provided when defining enterprise textual conventions. This will allow managers to display object data values in optimal fashion.

Example of poor trap object semantics (adapted from an actual MIB)

```
mpFSH TRAP-TYPE
    ENTERPRISE vronxTraps
    VARIABLES { }
    DESCRIPTION "MP fsh enterprise trap"
    ::= 11
```

The name of the trap provides little clue as to its purpose. There are no data objects sent with the trap. The description clause merely repeats the trap name.

Example of poor data object semantics (adapted from an actual MIB)

```
csiRuleDefn OBJECT-TYPE
    SYNTAX DisplayString
    MAX-ACCESS read-only
    STATUS current
    DESCRIPTION "Definition of the rule."
    ::= { csiRuleEntry 9 }
```

This data object defines some sort of rule to be followed, but the name of the object does not convey any more information. The rule is a DisplayString which is very free-form, so there is no information about the format or content of this rule string. The description clause is trivial and provides no rule documentation. Even a single rule example would be helpful.

Product MIB Organization

There are many ways to organize product MIBs. One suggestion is diagrammed here—only nodes are shown, along with suggested OID suffixes (.n).

This diagram assumes that there is an enterprise SMI registration MIB that defines a superstructure not shown here. Discussion continues on the next page.

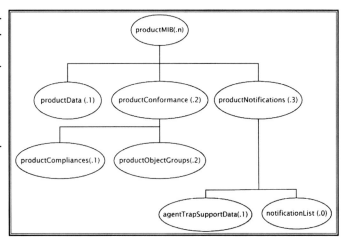

productData(.1)

Child nodes and data object definitions appear under this node.

productConformance (.2)

This node has two subnodes, one defining a place for data and trap object group definitions and another for compliance objects.

productNotifications (.3)

This node has two sub-nodes:
- The first is for organizing any trap-related data that is not product specific. For example:
  ○ accessible-for-notify data such as trap severity
  ○ agent polling frequency
  ○ trap enable/disable objects
- Trap objects themselves are organized under the notificationList(.0) node (for SMIv2 syntax).

Data Organization

Data should be organized under nodes as per intended purpose. There are no formal or strict rules regarding organization—suggestions appear below. Note that an alternate location for agent configuration data is shown.

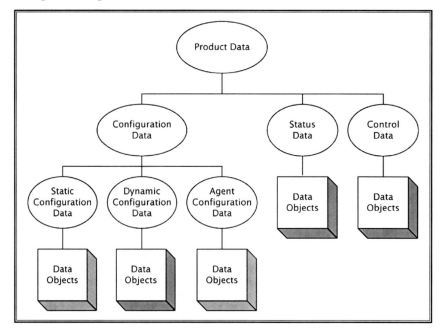

Configuration Data Examples

Many other examples and ideas can be discovered by reading existing MIBs.

Static Configuration Data (read-only)

Revision levels for various system elements can be useful for the end user and for the vendor customer service organization.

> *Examples*:
> - Hardware revision
> - Firmware revision
> - Operating system revision
> - Software application revision
> - SNMP agent software revision
> - Versions of protocols in use

Unit descriptive data may be useful to the vendor and the customer.

> *Examples*:
> - Model (could be an integer, display string, OID identifier)
> - Serial number
> - Manufacturer's description

Sizes of indexed tables are often provided in a data object parallel to the table object definition, as shown to the right.
- Maximum possible table size
- Actual current table size (agent creates rows based on actual product configuration—the number of rows may vary over time).

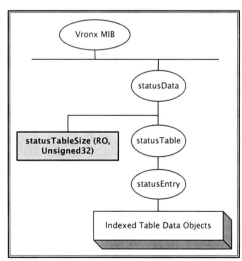

Dynamic Configuration Data (read-write)

Dynamic configuration data allows users to assign meaningful management information to a device. Normally such information is preserved through system resets, and this semantic issue should be discussed in the DESCRIPTION clause.

Alias names that describe user-assigned functionality
- ○ Chassis name (e.g., "videoFarmRouter")
- ○ Signal names for ports (e.g., "satelliteA-downlink")

Cross-referential information
- ○ Provisioning or inventory information
- ○ Bar-code data

Functional configuration
- ○ The user may be able to specify aspects of device functionality

For example:

enableConsolePasswordProtection

Agent Configuration Data

Users may be able to configure aspects of agent behavior. Some argue that this should never be done, and that the developer is responsible for hard-coding all aspects of agent logic—arguments center around specific design issues, and every design situation is unique.

This discussion is related to Chapter 20's discussion of *MIB Data Affecting Agent Behavior*.

Guidelines:
- • Allow reasonable user control from the manager, but do not over-burden your MIB with too much agent-specific data. Some agent control data may be better configured using non-SNMP methods. Examples are discussed below.

Agent configuration methods include:
- • Editing a text file that is read by the agent when starting
- • Telnet dialog to configure the agent
- • GUI menu selection
- • Defining read-write objects in the MIB itself

- Some combination of the above
  - ◦ A standard MIB example is the configuration to *enable agent authentication error traps.*
  - ◦ A manager can *set* a value to MIB object snmpEnableAuthenTraps.
  - ◦ Some agents can be configured by editing a value into a text file read by the agent at startup.
  - ◦ The Windows agent configures this value in a GUI associated with master agent service properties.
  - ◦ Other agents configure this value via Telnet.

Examples of agent configuration data—often defined by MIB objects:
- Agent polling frequency defines (in seconds) how often the agent inspects product data to determine if a *trap* should be sent.
- Trap-target IP addresses (and trap community strings) can sometimes be *set* from a manager into the agent MIB data store. row-create logic applies here.
- Trap INTEGER { enable(1), disable(2) } objects.
- Trap severity threshold values.

Examples of agent configuration data—suggestions for non-MIB data:
- Wait 'S' seconds after startup before sampling monitored system status. This allows the system to fully initialize and settle down prior to checking for alarming conditions, and avoids unnecessary traps.
- Enable/disable (status = good) trap reporting on agent startup (especially if the number of such traps is large). If disabled, send only traps reporting problems.
- Trap re-send periodicity. If a major or critical condition persists, should traps be re-sent, how frequently, and how many times?

Status Data (read-only)

Stateful Data

Often status data also provides state information, which is useful in defining traps that allow auto-acknowledging trap filters to be configured for managers.

Examples:
- Input signal status (present, notPresent)
- Chassis cover (closed, open)
- Fan status (running, notRunning)
- Operational status (online, offline)
- Monitored software link (okay, broken)
  - ◦ If an agent monitors another piece of software to acquire MIB-related data, it should also monitor the status of the link to the API. Failure to incorporate such logic is a common cause of poor agent behavior.

Status Counters and Trending Data

Counters are useful for many purposes.

Examples:
- Software process restart counter
- Video monitor power (on/off) cycle counter
- Parity error counters (Remember that if counter types are trended, the trended values will be normalized to, for example, parity-errors-per-second)

The instantaneous values of some data objects may not be interesting, but long-term trends may be. Managers can be configured to periodically poll for such values, to compare values with configured thresholds, and to generate local *events*.

Examples:
- Fan speed in RPMs can be used to predict failures
- Accumulated laser operational time might be used to predict failures
- Microwave radio received signal levels
- Chassis temperatures

Control Data (read-write)

Control data can be risky. How much control do you want to provide, especially when using SNMPv1 or SNMPv2c community string security?

Examples:
- *set* a device to main(1) or backup(2) state
- Data processing rate control
- Invoke encryption or plain transmission
- *set* an address
- *reboot* the product
  - This sounds dangerous (and usually is), but it may be a convenient alternative to sending a technician to reboot a microwave radio on an Alaskan mountain top in winter.
  - There are products that do include this feature.
  - Safeguards can be designed into the MIB to ensure this is not done inadvertently. For example, a quasi-secret value (code) not listed in an enumeration must be *set*. Or two related object values must be simultaneously *set* in a single SNMP message.

SNMPv3 VACM Considerations

SNMPv3 implements a number of security enhancements. A full explanation of SNMPv3 is beyond the scope of this book, but two features relate to MIB structure.

SNMPv3 introduces the concept of defined *users* that must be known (via configuration) to managers and to managed agents for SNMP communications to be successful. Another configuration step configures *users* into *groups*.

SNMPv3 also introduces the ability to configure agents to control which MIB objects *groups* are allowed to access. This is called the *View-Based Access Control Model* (VACM). VACM privileges must be configured at each agent platform, and each *group* has unique VACM privileges.

Example:
- A system administrator group has privileged access to all MIB data.
- IT operations personnel responsible for responding to problems have more limited privileges.
- Engineering managers can view only summary read-only data.

VACM privileges to particular MIB data are specified by configuring OID masks that specify objects to be included or excluded from a group's view.

MIBs which are organized with VACM in mind will make the agent configuration process simpler. For example, dynamic configuration data might appear under two nodes:
- Privileged data, and
- Common data

Exercises

1. Describe how intelligent use of object syntax elements enhances data object, trap object, and agent semantics.

2. What is the difference between static configuration data and dynamic configuration data? Are these formal SNMP categories defined by IETF standards?

Chapter 24

MIB Design Process

This chapter serves as a checklist to be used as developers move through the MIB design process. Appendixes G and H contain MIB diagrams that illustrate recommended concepts.

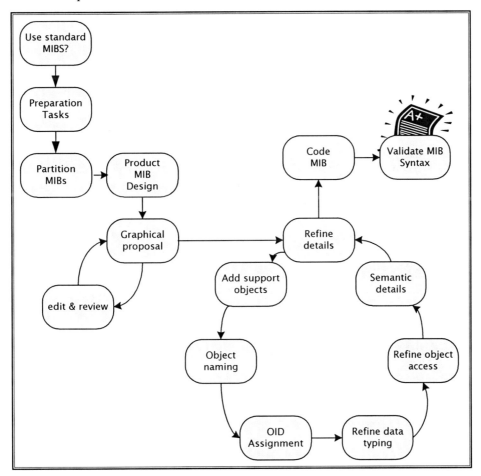

Research Standard MIBs

Your industry may expect compliance with particular standard MIBs in addition to your enterprise-specific MIBs.

Examples:

Standard Printer MIB
MIBs for monitoring protocols
Cable TV Modem MIB

Standard MIBs may contain indexed tables which you need to support, but with enterprise MIB extensions that describe your product's unique features.

Examples:

RFC-1695 *Definitions of Managed Objects for ATM Management Version 8.0 using SMIv2* contains the ATM-MIB.

Cisco's CISCO-ATM-IF-MIB defines a table that uses the AUGMENTS clause—

    AUGMENTS { atmInterfaceConfEntry }

from the ATM-MIB.

MIBs that apply to your product may be available from the IETF as well as other standards bodies (e.g., IEEE). Even peer product vendors may have non-copyrighted MIBs that can be used.

Standard MIBs may also offer monitoring capabilities you were planning to embed into your MIB. The entire standard MIB may not apply, but particular objects may.

For example, a vendor proprietary application was responsible for controlling a critical data crunching application, which logged critical events to a disk file. Their MIB was designed to monitor the application and to *trap* on the same critical events.

They also wanted to monitor the size of the log file and to *trap* if it became too large for its partition. This latter capability was relegated to the SNMP manager which polled the master agent for relevant data already included in the Host Resources MIB.

Preparation

Read other vendors' MIBs. Read the MIBs of competitors. Review some well-written MIBs (such as from Cisco). Have in mind a sense of MIB *style* you want to pursue. Don't just lay down data and traps as they come to mind. Think through MIB organization as well as content. Be creative.

Have a good grasp of MIB syntax, and of typical uses of data, all which is discussed in this book.

Review Chapter 3, *Getting the Most Out of SNMP*. Seasoned SNMP practitioners quickly distinguish between well-written MIBs and beginner MIBs. Don't embarrass yourself or your company.

Very often SNMP implementation closely tracks primary product development efforts, and the data to be monitored and events to be sent are well understood and documented. But if they are not, create a working document (white paper) that describes SNMP goals, data, and traps prior to MIB design efforts.

MIB organization does not have to mimic the product's user interface.

Model your product's *generic functionality* as much as possible so that the MIB can be reused among different products. Making use of conformance statements also supports generic MIB goals.

MIB Partitioning

Chapter 22 discussed MIB partitioning strategies—define your strategy and specify your partitions.

First MIBs take longer to develop than subsequent designs. The decisions you make will be reflected in your SNMP products for years to come. If this is your organization's first MIB, putting some thought into your *enterprise SMI registration MIB* will set precedents regarding where future MIBs will be organized in your enterprise's managed OID space.

Is defining an OID enumeration to supply a value for mib-2's sysObjectId appropriate? Probably *yes*, and if so, where will it be defined? It can be defined in the enterprise SMI MIB, in a separate MIB dedicated to this purpose, or within the product MIB itself.

Will there be separate textual convention definition MIBs?

Will you have subsystem (or component) MIBs that supplement primary product MIBs?

Product MIB Design

The multi-step process described below works well. The multi-pass graphical MIB definition tasks may take weeks. Most of that time involves repeated cycles of:

> *proposal* → *review* → *edit*

But if done well, the final two steps, *coding* and *testing* the MIB, should take no more than a day or so.

Graphical Organization

When you first start visualizing and organizing MIBs, working in a graphical format helps a lot. *Graphical* can be done manually (template and pencil)—this is also quite efficient for network engineers trying to understand the scope of an existing MIB.

Software tools can also be used and are more applicable to the development environment, where the graphical design will be passed around a lot prior to agreement.

The goal is a first-pass graphical organization of MIB objects using data names familiar to the enterprise. Rough data typing should be noted (e.g., *integer*), along with proposed access (e.g., *read-only*).

Think in terms of *usefulness*. Just because you *can* provide data does not mean it will be useful. Development engineers have a tendency to code everything they know about a product (which is usually a lot) into their MIB. Network engineers' eyes glaze over when trying to understand the usefulness of many of these objects.

Identify the content of all indexed tables, including indexing objects and their data types. Will indexes be accessible or not?

Define all trap objects and note any data that must be sent with traps. All such data needs definition in a MIB. Are there standard MIB data objects whose values will be useful in enterprise traps? *For example,* sysDescr or sysLocation from mib-2's system table. If so, these objects can be IMPORTS and values used.

Document where the agent will find values for all of the data objects.

> *For example,* in a hardware register, from a system call, from an API to another software application.

Iterate within the development team until there is consensus.

Graphical Details

Add Supporting Objects

Remember that any data sent with a trap must have existence as a MIB object (e.g., *trapSeverity*).

Other objects may be defined which affect agent behavior (e.g., *polling frequency*).

Object Naming

Move from familiar names to syntactically correct and progressive naming style, described in Chapter 4. For example, the product *Firmware Revision* object might be renamed vronxFrsStaticCfgFwRev.

Include appropriate suffixes (e.g., plural indications, Ev or Trap for traps).

Names should be descriptive, progressive, and unique within the MIB. Ideally they should be unique throughout all of this enterprise's MIBs.

Object Identifier Assignments for All Objects

Sometimes OID assignments may have cross-referential usefulness to other enterprise documentation.

Remember that OID assignments also define lexicographical ordering, and managers will return values for *getnext* requests in OID.instance order. It may be useful to leave *holes* in an OID numbering strategy to leave space for future similar data that will be nicely ordered.

For example, FRS MIB Revision 1.0 may contain static configuration data (where "(.n)" indicates the OID's last decimal digit):

```
vronxFrsStaticCfgFwRev  (.1)
vronxFrsStaticCfgHwRev (.2)
vronxFrsStaticCfgHwModel (.10)
vronxFrsStaticCfgNbrChannels(.11)
```

In a later release, if an object describing a *protocol revision* must be added, an orderly (and planned) place for it is

```
vronxFrsStaticCfgFwRev  (.1)
vronxFrsStaticCfgHwRev (.2)
vronxFrsStaticProtocolRev (.3)     -- new MIB object
vronxFrsStaticCfgHwModel (.10)
vronxFrsStaticCfgNbrChannels(.11)
```

Refine Data Typing

For example, change rough typing of *integer* to Integer32, Unsigned32, Counter32, or enumerated INTEGER (along with appropriately named enumerated values).

Define enterprise textual convention definitions to facilitate cross-product commonality and to clarify object purposes (semantics).

Specify data value ranges and data size limits as appropriate.

Refine Data Access

to read-only, read-write, accessible-for-notify, not-accessible.

Add Detailed Semantics

MIB syntax supplies semantic information (e.g., use of a Gauge32 type vs. an Integer32 type), but still leaves a lot unsaid about the management plan for an object. Most of this information should be edited into DESCRIPTION clauses, and is useful to end users as well as to software developers responsible for coding agent logic.

Coding the MIB

This should be a straightforward manual translation from the MIB diagram to a MIB text file. If you have an existing standards-compliant MIB file, cut-and-paste is an easy way to avoid syntax errors. The Chateau Systems MIBs printed in the appendixes are examples of SMIv2-compliant MIBs; they are available from the MIB Depot web site and from this publisher's web site www.wyndhampress.com.

SMIv2 syntax is strongly recommended, with an eye to ensuring conversion to SMIv1.

Be sure all semantic issues are conveyed in the MODULE-IDENTITY object, DESCRIPTION clauses, and other syntax clauses. These are very important to network engineers, and may be the only documentation they have to understand and appreciate agent behavior.

Add *conformance objects*. It's easy to do and will ensure validation compliance at the highest checking level. If agent implementation of portions of the MIB is conditional, then it is imperative that conformance objects describe those conditions.

Testing the MIB

Chapter 5 discusses some of the compilers available to validate your MIB. It takes little extra time to run it through multiple compilers.

If you have access to a manager tool (and developers should), load your MIBs and browse them to ensure they *look* and *feel* as intended. This review may reveal organizational flaws as well as unintended OID assignments.

RFCs and Other References

Much of this reference information appears elsewhere in the book, but has been collected in this appendix for convenience.

Request for Comments—RFCs

RFCs define many networking standards, including SNMP, and can be found on the IETF (Internet Engineering Task Force) web page. SNMP definitions include MIB syntax, SNMP messages, and standard MIBS.

The RFC Index can be used to determine the most current version of any standard MIB, and needed MIBs can be stripped out of RFCs.

www.ietf.org

Enterprise Identifier Assignments

The IANA (Internet Assigned Numbers Authority) is responsible for assigning SNMP Enterprise OIDs to organizations that plan to design their own MIBs and supporting agents.

www.iana.org

SMIv1 MIB Syntax

RFC-1155
Structure and Identification of Management Information for TCP/IP-based Internets

RFC-1212
Concise MIB Definitions

RFC-1215
A Convention for Defining Traps for use with the SNMP

SMIv2 MIB Syntax

RFC-2578
Structure of Management Information Version 2 (SMIv2)

RFC-2579
Textual Conventions for SMIv2

RFC-2580
Conformance Statements for SMIv2

Additional MIB-Related RFCs of Interest

RFC-3584
Coexistence between Version 1, Version 2, and Version 3 of the Internet-standard Network Management Framework
Explains some subtle differences between SMIv1 and SMIv2 syntax

RFC-4181
Guidelines for Authors and Reviewers of MIB Documents
Primarily intended for developers of standard MIBs, but recommended reading for any MIB developer

Common textual convention definitions from standard MIBs:

www.ops.ietf.org/mib-common-tcs.html

SMIv2 Syntax Errata List:

www.ibr.cs.tu-bs.de/ietf/smi-errata

RMON and RMON2 MIBs References

Remote Monitoring MIBs are an example of complex MIBs, but they are extremely useful in monitoring networks at all OSI levels.

> RFC-2819
> *Remote Network Monitoring Management Information Base*
> Contains the RMON MIB

> RFC-2021
> *Remote Network Monitoring Management Information Base Version 2*
> *using SMIv2*
> Contains the RMON2 MIB

> RFC-3577
> *Introduction to the Remote Monitoring (RMON) Family of MIB Modules*
> A very good review of the RMON and RMON2 MIBS, and extension MIBs

> *RMON: Remote Monitoring of SNMP-Managed LANs*, David T. Perkins,
> Prentice hall PTR

Entity MIB References

The Entity MIB is another advanced MIB example that is used to model product assemblies. It is often of interest to developers for possible use, or as a source of modeling ideas.

Network engineers will encounter agent implementations of this MIB by Cisco and others.

Extensions of the Entity MIB have been defined in recent years, and also appear in this reference list.

> RFC-4133
> *Entity MIB (Version 3)*
> Contains the ENTITY-MIB

> RFC-3433
> *Entity Sensor MIB,* contains the ENTITY-SENSOR-MIB
> Extends the Entity MIB to provide generalized support for access to physical sensor data. Sparsely augments the entPhysicalTable for entries with entPhysicalClass equal to sensor(8)

RFC-4268
Entity State MIB
Contains the ENTITY-STATE-TC-MIB and the ENTITY-STATE-MIB, and provides information about the state of physical entities

Cisco MIBs—References

Links to Cisco SNMP references:
- Cisco sets a high standard for SNMP support that other developers might want to emulate.
- Network engineers frequently encounter Cisco MIBs.

SNMP Introduction and Cisco specifics:

www.cisco.com/univercd/cc/td/doc/product/webscale/css/css_740/admgd/snmp.htm

Select products of interest, and supported MIBs will be listed:

http://www.cisco.com/public/sw-center/netmgmt/cmtk/mibs.shtml

Cisco SNMP Object Navigator. Enter OID or object name, and details will be revealed. (You can also navigate to this tool by going to Cisco's home page, and searching for *navigator*.):

http://tools.cisco.com/Support/SNMP/do/BrowseOID.do?local=en

Finding Needed Enterprise MIBs

The MIB Depot web site allows you to browse MIBs from vendors of interest, and to search for object names and OIDs.

www.mibdepot.com

Validation Compilers

Simple Web Validation Compiler

http://wwwsnmp.cs.utwente.nl/ietf/mibs/validate

Agent++ Validation Compiler

www.agentpp.com/mibtools/mibtools.html

libsmi Validation Compiler

www.ibr.cs.tu-bs.de/projects/libsmi/tools/

SNMPv1 Standards

RFC-1157
Simple Network Management Protocol (SNMP)
Classified as HISTORIC, but SNMPv1 agents will be found running in managed products for a long time to come

SNMPv2 Standards

RFC-3416
Protocol Operations for SNMPv2

RFC-3417
Transport Mappings for SNMPv2

RFC-3418
Management Information Base (MIB) for the Simple Network Management Protocol (SNMP)

RFC-1901
Introduction to Community-based SNMPv2
Discusses using SNMPv2 PDUs within a community string message wrapper

SNMPv3 Standards

Many of the SNMPv3 RFCs contain MIB definitions used for manager and agent configuration.

RFC-3410
Intro and Applicability Statements for Internet Std Mgmt Framework

RFC-3411
An Architecture for Describing SNMP Mgmt Frameworks

RFC-3412
Message Processing and Dispatching for SNMP

RFC-3413
SNMP Applications

RFC-3414
User-based Security Model for Version 3 of the SNMP

RFC-3415
View-based Access Control Model for the SNMP

RFC-3416
Version 2 of the Protocol Operations for the SNMP

RFC-3417
Transport Mappings for the SNMP

RFC-3418
Management Information Base (MIB) for the SNMP

RFC-3584
Coexistence between V1, V2, and V3 of the Internet-standard Network Management Framework

Glossary of Terms

"1" and "2"

Overloaded definitions. Version numbers that describe revisions of separate parts of SNMP technology. Not all 1's and 2's are equivalent, and can create confusion. Examples { SNMPv1, SNMPv2c, SNMPv3 }, { SMIv1, SMIv2 }, { RMON-1, RMON-2 }, { MIB-1, MIB-2 }.

AgentX Protocol

Effort to standardize the protocol between master agents and subagents. Defined by:
- RFC-2741 *Agent Extensibility (AgentX) Protocol version 1*
- RFC-2742 *Definitions of Managed Objects for extensible SNMP Agents.* Contains a MIB for management of AgentX configuration and operation.

Aggregate Node

A MIB node that has children.

ASN.1

Abstract Syntax Notation *dot* 1. See Appendix D.

BER

Basic Encoding Rules—BER for encoding data into transmission bit patterns. An ISO standard associated with ASN.1.

Binding

Combining an object identifier (OID) with its instance value in an SNMP message. For example:

{ OID.instance, value } Also see **PDU**.

Community Name

A text string included in SNMPv1 and SNMPv2c messages. Can be viewed as a *password* used to authenticate messages. It is also used sometimes to specify *context*.

Compiler (MIB)

The term *MIB compiler* describes software programs that process MIB text files for various purposes. For example, loading MIBs into managers, generating code stubs for agent development. Validating compilers process a MIB file and report on its syntactic correctness.

Context

SNMPv1/SNMPv2c community strings are sometimes also used to specify *context* to an agent that manages multiple logical instances of objects (e.g. multiple routers). SNMPv3 messages contain a dedicated context object in the header.

Enterprise

Multiple uses in SNMP, which are explained in Appendix E.

Extensible

Agents which are extensible can be easily programmed to manage additional MIBs. Monolithic agents may be extensible, and the master agent–subagent paradigm implies extensibility.

Extension Agents

Another term for subagents.

Fully Instanced Object

A data object OID extended by its instance value.

Generic Traps

The set of six standard traps that apply to all agents. SNMPv1 encodes these in the message layer. SNMPv2c re-defined these traps into a MIB as NOTIFICATION-TYPE objects with OID definitions.

coldStart, warmStart, linkDown, linkUp, authenticationFailure, egpNeighborLoss

IANA—Internet Assigned Numbers Authority

Responsible for assigning SNMP enterprise IDs (and much more for the Internet community). IANA also defines MIBs with globally unique numeric definitions.

IETF—Internet Engineering Task Force

Responsible for defining SNMP standards (and much more). Standards are defined in RFCs, which may also contain standard MIB files.

Instance

SNMP data object OIDs are appended with instance values to specify the instance of interest. For indexed tables *instance = index*. For scalars, *instance = 0*. Integer indexes appended one dotted integer per instance value. Non-integer index types (such as DisplayString) append multiple dotted integers per instance value.

Lexicographical Ordering

The logical ordering of OID.instance values for data objects. Agents return object values for *getnext* requests in lexicographical order.

MIB browsers display MIB structure, ordering objects in lexicographical OID order.

Managed Devices

Physical devices containing an SNMP agent that manages data defined in MIBs.

Managed Objects

MIB data and trap objects.

Master Agent

Agent software organization, where the master agent is responsible for SNMP message formatting and communicating with managers. A master agent is also connected to one or more subagents that manage actual MIB data values, and communicate that information to the master agent (using a proprietary protocol or the AgentX protocol).

MIB—Management Information Base

A file defining managed SNMP objects, along with supporting information.

MIB-2

A well-known MIB originally defined by RFC-1158 that superseded MIB-1 definitions, and contained a number of tables (e.g. system table, interface table, IP table). RFC-1213 superseded this definition, and some of the original tables have new or extended definitions in yet newer RFCs. All IETF non-experimental standard MIBs are organized under the mib-2 node defined in RFC-1213.

Monolithic Agent

A single executable that encompasses all agent functionality vs. the master agent–subagent architecture. Commonly found in embedded systems.

MOSY Compiler

An open source MIB compiler that is also found in some commercial products, often with enhancements.

Nodes

Often used to refer to a managed device (*managed node*) in a network.

An OID definition that is used to build organizational trees for MIB data and traps. Terminology used in this book to facilitate discussion of MIB structure.

Notification

SMIv2 and SNMPv2c term for traps.

NMS

Common abbreviation for Network Management System.

Object Identifier (OID)

A dot-separated list of integers that uniquely identifies MIB objects.

PDU

Protocol Data Unit. SNMP messages contain MIB-defined data object values encoded into PDUs. General form of a PDU:

{ operation, errorFlags, listOf [OID.instance, value] }

Also see **Binding**

Proxy Agent

There are a variety of SNMP definitions, but in general this is an agent acting on behalf of another agent or a different IP address. A proxy agent can also be responsible for protocol translation.

Registration

Refers to enterprise registration with IANA, and assignment of an ID to that organization. Also refers to the act of publishing a MIB, at which time the OIDs that are defined become *registered*.

RFC—Request for Comments

Standards documents administered by the IETF.

RMON2

A standard MIB used for monitoring remote networks (vs. just devices). Used along with the RMON-1 MIB (also called the RMON MIB).

Scalar Data Object

Any MIB data object defined outside of an indexed table.

SMI—Structure of Management Information

Two MIB syntax specifications exist: SMIv1 and SMIv2.

SMICng Validation Compiler

SMI Compiler new generation. A validating compiler distributed with the book *Understanding SNMP MIBs*, by David Perkins and Evan McGinnis.

Standard MIBs

MIBs defined within IETF RFCs, as differentiated from enterprise MIBs.

Subagent

See **Master Agent**.

Textual Convention (TC)

A formal mechanism included in SMIv2 syntax for subtyping SNMP base types of data. Subtyping can also be accomplished using SMIv1 syntax, but in a slightly different way.

Trap Message

Originally an SMIv1 and SNMPv1 term, but is also commonly used to refer to SMIv2 and SNMPv2c notifications. Also called events or alarms (alarms are serious events).

Trivial Authentication

SNMPv1 and SNMPv2c community string security.

MIB Diagnosis Checklist

A network engineer is tasked with bringing up new SNMP-compliant equipment. The new MIBs are compiled into the manager, and errors are logged. The engineer cannot proceed until the MIBs are diagnosed and repaired.

Possible problems have been described in the chapters—this appendix provides a more easily accessible list. Not everything that can go wrong is listed here. After network engineers have been at this a while, they can probably create their own list and perhaps even write their own book.

Many problems can be repaired by editing the MIB—but be sure to back up the original for reference and for possible repair restart, and be sure to use a text editor.

Compiler Passes Issue

A MIB was validated with a two-pass compiler but is being loaded with a one-pass compiler. Definitions used in the earlier part of the MIB are not defined until later in the MIB. For example, traps are defined early in the MIB and referenced data objects defined later. The one-pass compiler reports errors *undefined objects.*

This is a compiler capabilities issue, not a MIB problem, but is fixable by editing and revising MIB object order.

Missing Dependent MIB

A MIB is compiled with IMPORTS definitions from another MIB, which has not yet been loaded.

The solution is to find the missing MIB and compile it.

Some compilers recompile all MIBs whenever a new one is loaded, and require that the list of MIBs be in IMPORTS order. Others make two passes through the list, and ordering in the list does not matter.

There are well-known IMPORTS'ed objects that are frequently imported. For example, SMIv1 keywords or data types, SMIv2 keywords or data types, or standard textual conventions. Many compilers have inherent knowledge about these definitions (they are pre-loaded), but some may require you to explicitly load required standard MIBs.

Missing IMPORTS Declarations

There are well-known definitions that should be included in a MIB's IMPORTS statement, but the MIB author has not done so. For example, the SMIv2 textual convention for DisplayString. A permissive compiler won't complain, because it knows what a DisplayString is and overlooks the issue. The same MIB loaded into a validating (or less permissive) compiler will generate errors.

This is easily repaired by editing the needed IMPORTS information.

IMPORTS of Definitions Not Required

It is not necessary to IMPORTS definitions for these data types:

> BITS, INTEGER, OCTET STRING, OBJECT IDENTIFIER

If they do appear in an IMPORTS statement and a compiler complains, this is easy to fix—delete these IMPORTS.

Comment Field Problems

MIB comment fields begin with double dashes.

> -- This is a comment

Comment fields can be terminated by double dashes or by an end-of-line.

Embedded dashes within a comment can cause problems.

Some compilers do not handle terminating double dashes well, especially if MIB syntax follows.

Simple MIB edits will repair this problem.

Date and Time Formats

SMIv2 LAST-UPDATED and REVISION clauses (in the MODULE-IDENTITY statement) include date and time information.

Older compilers may not handle the newer (since year 2000) YYYYMMDDHHMMZ format well.

Newer compilers may not handle the older YYMMDDHHMMZ format well. Or they may handle it just fine, but may stumble if YY appears to have a value in the early 1900s (e.g., YY = 07).

Some compilers will not flag invalid date or time values (e.g., MM (month) = 14, or HH (hour) = 25), and others will.

In the MODULE-IDENTITY statement, at least one REVISION statement is required, and successive REVISION statements must be in reverse chronological order. Some compilers will catch these problems; others will not.

Compilers typically issue only *warnings* for these problems.

Object Names

Duplicate object names within a single MIB are not permitted. Most compilers will catch this.

Duplicate object names within an enterprise's entire OID space may cause subtle problems with some compilers.

Names should begin with a lower-case alphabetic character, and may not contain underscores.

Names should not contain hyphens. This is legal in SMIv1, but not in SMIv2. Some compilers may ignore the rule, and others do not.

MODULE-IDENTITY Statement Ordering

An SMIv2 MODULE-IDENTITY statement must always follow the IMPORTS statement. Some compilers will not flag this, and others will.

If an error is reported, whatever appears following the IMPORTS can be cut and pasted to come after the MODULE-IDENTITY statement.

INTEGER Enumerated Value Names

Enumerated value name rule violations may be encountered.

Example of correct naming:

```
SYNTAX INTEGER {
    upState(1),
    downState(2),
    disabledState(3) }
```

Examples of incorrect naming:

```
SYNTAX INTEGER {         SYNTAX INTEGER {         SYNTAX INTEGER {
    up-state (1),            UPSTATE (1),             UpState (1),
    down-state(2),          DOWNSTATE (2),           DownState(2),
    disabled-state (3) }    DISABLEDSTATE (4) }      DisabledState(4)}
```

Trap Syntax Macros

SMIv1 TRAP-TYPE or SMIv2 NOTIFICATION-TYPE object syntax may contain macro declarations encoded within double-dashed comments. These macros will automatically configure trap filters when loaded into targeted manager-Alpha. If you attempt to load this MIB into a manager-Gama that also supports macros but of a different format, manager-Gama may report compile errors.

You can safely edit out troublesome macros.

Invalid Enumeration Values

Negative INTEGER enumerated values are illegal in SMIv1, but will be accepted by some compilers. Although they are not reported by a manager compiler, later problems may be manifested. For example, enumerated values arriving in *traps* may be logged as very large positive integers, and filters that attempt to match values will not work.

SMIv2 allows enumerated values < 0, while SMIv1 does not. Some compilers will accept them for SMIv1 also. Others will complain.

All of these are impossible for a network engineer to repair. The MIB could be edited, but the agent will still send the problem enumerated values.

TC Definition Based on Another TC

This is generally considered illegal—some compilers let it go by, and others flag it.

If you encounter this error, you can edit the textual convention definition to be dependent on a base type. The DisplayString subtyping example in Chapter 10 shows a solution.

Conflicting OID Definitions

Within a single MIB this problem is rare (but has been seen). A more likely situation is that a vendor exercises poor OID management control—a first MIB is built on a branch, and sometime in the future another product group reuses the same branch in a second MIB definition. If both MIBs are loaded on the same manager, the problem is revealed.

Another problem is modification of an OID definition in a subsequent MIB revision. For example, the data type of an object has changed. Managers may load this new definition, but if the previously defined object has been used to define a trap filter or used to generate trend reports or custom tables, subtle but ugly problems may surface.

Subtle Mixing of SMIv1 and SMIv2 Syntax

SMIv1 and SMIv2 syntax are quite similar, and there are a lot of small things that can go wrong. Many manager compilers will overlook small problems, but their checking algorithms will differ. The chapters on syntax are your complete reference—a shorter list is presented here.

Fortunately, most of these are easily repaired with a little editing. *Examples*:

> Using the ACCESS clause for an SMIv2 object vs. MAX-ACCESS (and vice versa for SMIv1)

> Omitting the DESCRIPTION clause from an SMIv2 object

> Confusing SMIv1 and SMIv2 data types (e.g., Counter vs. Counter32)

> Using a UNITS clause in SMIv1 object

> SMIv1 data object ACCESS clause with a value of not-accessible or accessible-for-notify

> Incorrect values for SMIv1 and SMIv2 STATUS clauses (mandatory vs. current)

Gross Mixing of SMIv1 and SMIv2 Syntax

You may encounter a MIB that has severely mixed SMIv1 and SMIv2 syntax.

Example combined from several actual MIBs

```
VRONX-ALARM-MIB-V2 DEFINITIONS:= BEGIN

IMPORTS
    enterprises              FROM RFC1155-SMI
    sysDescr                 FROM RFC1213-MIB
    vronxErrorType, vronxAction
                             FROM VRONX-BASE-MIB
    NOTIFICATION-TYPE, OBJECT-TYPE, IpAddress
                             FROM SNMPv2-SMI
    DisplayString            FROM RFC1213-MIB
    MacAddress ,TimeStamp
                             FROM SNMPv2-TC;

    vronx                OBJECT IDENTIFIER
    ::= { enterprises 99999 }


    vronxV2Traps         OBJECT IDENTIFIER
    ::= { vronx 10 }


    vronxTrapPrefix      OBJECT IDENTIFIER
    ::= { vronxV2Traps 0 }


    vronxCheckFailed     NOTIFICATION-TYPE
        OBJECTS { sysDescr, vronxErrorType, vronxAction }
        STATUS current
        DESCRIPTION  "vronx check has failed."
        ::= { vronxTrapPrefix 1 }

END
```

The MIB name indicates that this is intended as an SMIv2 MIB.

IMPORTS enterprises FROM RFC1155-SMI is appropriate for an SMIv1 MIB.

In an SMIv2 MIB enterprises should be imported from SNMPv2-SMI, not from RFC1155-SMI.

DisplayString is imported from RFC1213-MIB. While RFC1213-MIB contains an SMIv1 equivalent definition of DisplayString, it should more properly be imported from SNMPv2-TC, as are MacAddress and TimeStamp just below. This has the advantage of including DISPLAY-HINT clause information, as well as being more correct.

The required SMIv2 MODULE-IDENTITY statement is missing.

Nodes are defined using OBJECT IDENTIFIER keywords, which is valid for SMIv1 and SMIv2 MIBs. It's a matter of style but SMIv2 OBJECT-IDENTITY would look better and offer the benefits of a STATUS clause and a DESCRIPTION clause.

It is hard to say what types of errors a particular compiler might generate for this MIB. Compilers look at the first few lines of a MIB to decide if it is parsing an SMIv1 or SMIv2 MIB. The IMPORTS FROM RFC1155-SMI may signal an SMIv1 MIB, or a compiler might look further and decide this is an SMIv2 MIB. Generated errors will vary based on that decision.

Abstract Syntax Notation—ASN.1

ASN.1 References

Introduction to ASN.1—link:

http://asn1.elibel.tm.fr/introduction/index.htm

ASN.1 Complete—by Professor John Larmouth. A comprehensive language reference. Available from on-line book stores, or you can download a copy from:

http://www.oss.com/asn1/larmouth.html

ASN.1—Communication Between Heterogeneous Systems—by Olivier Dubuisson. A practical programming tutorial that complements Larmouth's book. Available from on-line book stores, or you can download a copy from:

http://www.oss.com/asn1/dubuisson.html

Understanding SNMP MIBs—by David Perkins and Evan McGinnis, Prentice Hall 1997. A good summary of SNMP vs. ASN.1 keywords, and of Basic Encoding Rules (BER) for SNMP messages.

ASN.1 Overview

ASN.1 is a formal data description language that dates from 1984. Data objects defined in ASN.1 can be mapped into equivalent structures for C, C++, or Java for use in applications. It has been used to define the SNMP protocol, as well as Voice Over IP, cellular phone protocols, and many other messaging systems.

ASN.1 includes basic data types such as INTEGER and BOOLEAN, and other keywords such as SEQUENCE.

It is also closely associated with standard Basic Encoding Rules that translate data objects into message structures.

ASN.1 Uses in SNMP

A subset of ASN.1 is used to define two aspects of SNMP:

1. *MIB syntax* is defined as an adapted subset of ASN.1—similar syntax but not a true subset of ASN.1 syntax. Some data types are the same; SNMP lacks some ASN.1 types, and in some cases substitutes an SNMP type for an ASN.1 type.

2. *SNMP messages* are defined by a pure subset of ASN.1. ASN.1 is useful in understanding SNMP's Basic Encoding Rules —mapping data objects into message formats.

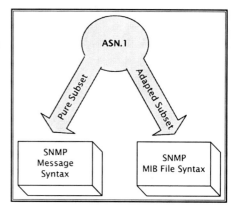

ASN.1 looks very similar to MIB syntax, and you
will encounter ASN.1 in some of the SNMP definitional RFCs. This can be mildly confusing—reading a syntax being used to define another similar syntax.

For most SNMP practitioners the topic of ASN.1 can be safely ignored. Only if you need to manually parse SNMP messages (SNMPv1, SNMPv2c, or SNMPv3), or if you are a member of a standards committee, might ASN.1 knowledge be important.

Enterprise Definitions

The SNMP term *enterprise* is used in several different (but related) ways. It shows up in SNMP-related configuration GUIs, and aspects can be confusing (in particular for enterprise trap definitions).

Enterprise Organizations

An *enterprise organization* is any group that has been assigned a unique identifier by the IANA (Internet Assigned Numbers Authority). All MIBs developed by that organization will be organized under the node defined by the IANA assignment.

Example of IANA enterprise OID assignments

Enterprise Name	Enterprise OID Prefix For All MIBs
Cisco	1.3.6.1.4.1.9
Hewlett Packard	1.3.6.1.4.1.11
Chateau Systems	1.3.6.1.4.1.10910
Compu-Share	1.3.6.1.4.1.26885

Enterprise MIBs

An *enterprise MIB* is any MIB developed by an enterprise, as contrasted with *standard MIBs* defined within RFCs created and controlled by the IETF or IANA.

The Chateau Systems MIB examples in Appendixes G and H are examples of enterprise MIBs.

Enterprise Traps

An *enterprise trap* is any trap that is not one of the six *generic traps* listed below:

coldStart	egpNeighborLoss
warmStart	linkDown
authenticationFailure	linkUp

Enterprise traps can be defined in enterprise MIBs (*of course!*).

Enterprise traps also appear in standard MIBs (*surprise!*).

To understand *why*, SMIv1 TRAP-TYPE syntax and SNMPv1 message structure will be described. Also discussed are SMIv2 NOTIFICATION-TYPE syntax and SNMPv2c message structure.

Trap message syntax is abbreviated to show only details relevant to this discussion.

SMIv1 and SNMPv1 Traps

Within an SMIv1 MIB the keyword ENTERPRISE is used within TRAP-TYPE syntax to specify the *enterprise node* of the trap. In some MIB designs the name of the object following the ENTERPRISE keyword is the IANA-assigned enterprise OID, but in most cases it will be a different node defined within a MIB.

Example of SMIv1 trap definition (and *enterprise node* definition)

```
chateauCDProdEvents  OBJECT IDENTIFIER ::= { chateauCDProductMIB 10 }

cdPowerSupplyEv TRAP-TYPE
    ENTERPRISE chateauCDProdEvents     -- refers to a previously defined node
    VARIABLES
    {
       cdDynCfgUserAlias,
       cdStCfgModel,
       cdChStPowerSupply,
       cdEvSeverity,
       cdEvDescription
    }
    DESCRIPTION
       "Sent when cdChStPowerSupply changes from okay to voltageError,
       or from voltageError to okay.
       This trap can be disabled by setting cdPowerSupplyEvTrapEn = trapDisable."
    REFERENCE "Optional Reference Clause"
    ::= 20
```

The OID of this trap definition is:

chateauCDProdEvents.0.20

The *enterprise* of this trap definition is chateauCDProdEvents

The *trap number* relative to this *enterprise* is 20

An SNMPv1 message (with abbreviated encodings) to transport an SMIv1 trap is shown below. Note how generic traps are encoded in the message layer vs. being defined by an OID. If the *generic trap number* field contains a value = 6, then an enterprise trap is indicated, and the *enterprise OID* and *enterprise trap number* fields are used.

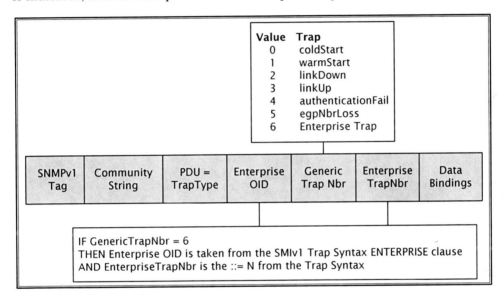

For the specific enterprise trap example on the previous page

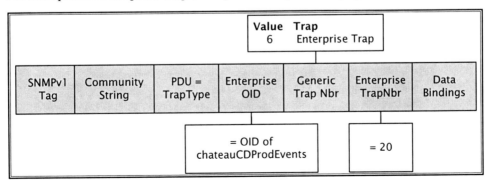

SMIv2 and SNMPv2 Traps

SMIv2 MIB NOTIFICATION-TYPE syntax does not contain the ENTERPRISE keyword, but managers and other tools still refer to the *enterprise of the trap.*

A correctly designed SMIv2 notification's parent node is a node (that does not appear in an equivalent SMIv1 MIB) with OID extension = '.0'. The parent node of the '.0' node is the *enterprise* of the notification object.

Example of equivalent SMIv2 syntax (with preceding node definitions)

```
chateauCDProdEvents  OBJECT-IDENTITY  -- the ENTERPRISE OID for this Trap
   STATUS current
   DESCRIPTION
      "CD Player Event Data
       and Trap Definitions are
       organized under this node."
   ::= { chateauCDProductMIB 10 }


cdEventList  OBJECT-IDENTITY  -- SMIv2 node, does not exist in SMIv1  MIB
   STATUS current
   DESCRIPTION
      "Notification Objects are
       organized under this node."
   ::= { chateauCDProdEvents 0 }   -- .0 is required


cdPowerSupplyEv NOTIFICATION-TYPE
   OBJECTS
   {
       cdDynCfgUserAlias,
       cdStCfgModel,
       cdChStPowerSupply,
       cdEvSeverity,
       cdEvDescription
   }
   STATUS  current
   DESCRIPTION
      "Sent when cdChStPowerSupply changes from okay to voltageError,
       or from voltageError to okay.
       This trap can be disabled by setting cdPowerSupplyEvTrapEn = trapDisable."
   REFERENCE "Optional Reference Clause"
   ::= { cdEventList 20 }
```

The OID of this trap definition is the same as for the SMIv1 definition:

chateauCDProdEvents.0.20

The *enterprise* of this trap definition is chateauCDProdEvents

The *trap number* relative to this *enterprise* is 20

SMIv2 and SNMPv2 redefined generic traps with the syntax shown above, and with specific OIDs. These are defined in RFC-3418 *Management Information Base (MIB) for the Simple Network Management Protocol (SNMP)* SNMPv2-MIB.

Generic Trap SNMPv1 Encoding	Equivalent Trap OID SNMPv2c
Cold Start (0)	1.3.6.1.6.3.1.1.5.1
Warm Start (1)	1.3.6.1.6.3.1.1.5.2
Link Down (2)	1.3.6.1.6.3.1.1.5.3
Link Up (3)	1.3.6.1.6.3.1.1.5.4
Authentication Failure (4)	1.3.6.1.6.3.1.1.5.5
EGP Neighbor Loss (5)	1.3.6.1.6.3.1.1.5.6

SNMPv2 message syntax for traps is new and no longer uniquely encodes generic traps in the message layer—they are transported just like enterprise traps using the new OID definitions. Abbreviated encoding of an SNMPv2 trap is shown below.

SNMPv2 Tag	Community String	PDU = v2Trap Type	sysUpTime Binding	Trap OID Binding	OBJECT Data Bindings

SNMP Tidbit. A few more details regarding the message encoding of the data bindings. The first binding is the sysUpTime value for the agent at the time the trap is sent. The seconding binding contains the trap OID. The following bindings are as defined in an SMIv2 Notification OBJECTS clause or in an SMIv1 Trap VARIABLES clause.

SNMPv1/2 Transport of SMIv2/1 NOTIFICATIONs

This presents no problem. Since SMIv1 and SMIv2 trap syntax are interchangeable, the agent software calls the appropriate SNMPv1 or SNMPv2 API to format and send traps.

SMIv1 TRAP-TYPE objects can be transported in SNMPv2 messages.

SMIv2 NOTIFICATION-TYPE objects can be transported in SNMPv1 messages.

Trap Information Display Examples

Example manager display of trap properties as object names

Trap Properties

General

Enterprise:	chateauCDProdEvents
Trap Name:	cdPowerSupplyEv
Trap Number:	20

Example manager display of trap properties as object identifiers

Trap Properties

General

Enterprise:	1.3.6.1.4.1.10910.2.2.3.1.1.10
Trap Name:	1.3.6.1.4.1.10910.2.2.3.1.1.10.0.20
Trap Number:	20

Exercise Responses

Answers to quiz-type exercises are given below. Some exercises are hand-on exercises, and no response is necessary.

Chapter 2. SNMP Tutorial

1.   What are the three major elements of SNMP architecture?

   Managers, Agents, MIBs

2.   Name the three SNMP message protocol standards.

   SNMPv1, SNMPv2c, SNMPv3

3.   Name the two SNMP MIB syntax standards.

   SMIv1, SMIv2

      a.   And list some of the improvements of the most recent standard.

         SMIv2 improvements include: MODULE-IDENTITY *statement*, NOTIFICA-TION-TYPE *replaced* TRAP-TYPE *syntax, more objects with* DESCRIPTION *fields, some new data types, formalized textual convention (derived types) syntax, conformance statements.*

      b.   Does the newer standard obsolete the first?

         No, although SMIv2 is preferred and is required for IETF standard MIBs, a large number of SMIv1 MIBs continue to be in service.

4.   What is the most commonly used message transport protocol used for SNMP?

UDP, *using ports 161 and 162. Support for other connection-less protocols exists but is encountered less frequently.*

5. MIB syntax defines a variety of objects. Information associated with two types of objects is transported by SNMP messages. What are those object types?

   Data Objects and Trap Objects.

6. Can data and trap objects defined in SMIv2 MIBs be transported in:

   a. SNMPv1 messages? *Yes, with the exception of Counter64 data objects*
   b. SNMPv2c messages? *Yes*
   c. SNMPv3 messages? *Yes*

7. Managers and agents communicate using data and trap *handles.* What is the SNMP terminology for these *handles?*

   Object identifiers (OIDs). An OID of a data object often needs to also be append-ed with the object's instance value.

8. How do standard MIBs and enterprise MIBs differ? Which MIB syntax (SMIv1 or SMIv2) can be used for each type?

   Standard MIBs are issued by the IETF (and some by IANA). Enterprise MIBs are issued by other organizations, often by manufacturing companies to man-age proprietary products. Older standard MIBs are written in SMIv1, all newer ones must be coded in SMIv2. Enterprise MIBs can be coded in either SMIv1 or SMIv2. Some vendors (e.g., Cisco) ship their MIBs in both formats.

Chapter 4. MIB Object Identifiers and Names

1. Identify the following OID prefixes (i.e., what type of MIBs are they prefixing).

   a. 1.3.6.1.2.1   IETF Standard MIBs
   b. 1.3.6.1.3   Experimental Standard MIBs
   c. 1.3.6.1.6   SNMPv2 and SNMPv3 Support standard MIBs
   d. 1.3.6.1.4.1   Enterprise MIBs

2. Browse the IANA web site to see if your organization has an enterprise identi-fier.

   www.iana.org

3. What problems do you see with the following MIB object name (hint, there are 3 problems)?

    Csi_CdPlayerStatus.1

    Should being with lower case letter, underscores not allowed, embedded dot not allowed.

4. What is an object *instance* value and how is it related to the object's OID?

    Instance value for an object contained in an indexed table is the same as the index value. For scalars (objects not in indexed tables), the instance value is always zero. Instance values are appended to an OID as additional dotted decimal values.

5. Research the name of the enterprise that is responsible for the MIB defining the data object with the following OID:

    1.3.6.1.4.1.148.1.1.2.1.1.2

    Bellcore

6. Name the six *generic traps*.

    Cold start, warm start, link down, link up, authentication failure, EGP neighbor loss.

7. Your manager is reporting multiple *authentication failure traps* for a device on the network. What is happening?

    Some other SNMP entity on the network is attempting to communicate (get or set) with that agent with an incorrect SNMPv1 or SNMPv2c community string.

8. You are using your manager's MIB browser to *get* sysDescr from the MIB-2 system table. This is a well-known textual object with OID = 1.3.6.1.2.1.1

    The agent returns an error message *Unknown Object Identifier*. You double check the OID you are sending the agent, and it is definitely correct.

    What is going wrong?

    get operations must specify an object instance value appended to its OID.

Chapter 5. Managing MIBs – Tools and Hints

1. Name some common MIB file suffixes.

    *.my
    *.mib

2. MIB syntax allows for importing definitions from other MIBS using the IM-PORTS (*definition*) FROM (*something*). What is *something*?

    It is the MIB name being IMPORTS *from. MIB name is specified in the first line of a MIB file, and is usually not the same as the MIB file name.*

4. Your MIB browser has determined that the sysObjectID value for a device on the network is (1.3.6.1.4.1.9.1.520). Determine what type of equipment this is.

    A quick inspection indicates that this is a Cisco (= '9') product. Using MIB Depot or the Cisco Navigator Tool, we can "search" for this OID to determine that the equipment type is a Cisco MWR1941DC.

Chapter 6. MIB Structure

1. Your need to extract (*strip*) a needed standard MIB from an RFC. You retrieve the RFC from the IETF website. It is usually wise to first check for multiple embedded MIBs within the RFC. What is a quick way to do this?

    Repeatedly search for MIB keyword BEGIN *until all embedded MIBs have been found.*

2. What is one large, general improvement of SMIv2 over SMIv1?

    Better documentation opportunities, which supports better descriptions of objects and agent semantics.

3. Details of example MIB problems.

    -   IMPORTS of Counter32, TimeTicks, and Unsigned32 is unnecessary since none of these data types are used in the MIB.
    -   IMPORTS of node object mib-2 is not used, and is not necessary.
    -   IMPORTS of conformance objects from SNMPv2-CONF are not used.
    -   MODULE-IDENTITY statement lacks a REVISION clause. At least one is expected, even for first publication.

- MODULE-IDENTITY object OID definition has one style issue and one error:
  - It is good style to import the definition of the enterprises node rather than specifying the entire OID progression.
  - The OID for node csiMib will be identical to the OID for chateausystems. This was probably not intended. The OID progression lacks a trailing ".n" final integer that should follow the node definition for chateausystems.
- OBJECT IDENTIFIER for SMIv2 node definitions is fine, but OBJECT-IDENTITY would be preferable (allows for STATUS and DESCRIPTION clauses).
- The trapDescription OBJECT-TYPE uses the SMIv1 ACCESS clause instead of the required SMIv2 MAX-ACCESS clause.
- The generalTrap and trapDescription object names would be better named something like csiGeneralTrap and csiTrapDescription to avoid possible name duplications in other vendor MIBs.
- This MIB is very simplistic and not very useful. It defines one trap and one data object. The only purpose of the data object is to include text information in the trap. Network engineers will not be able to configure manager trap filters—at least not until they have a great deal more information about what actual textual strings will be sent.
- The trapDescription object SYNTAX SnmpAdminString allows for a string size of zero—there is no purpose in sending this trap with zero textual information.
- The trapDescription object ACCESS read-write is silly. There is no reason a manager would want to *set* values into this object.
- The trap definition should follow a node with a final ".0" OID element to enable this trap to be converted to SMIv1 syntax if necessary (with no OID differences).
- Normally SMIv1 data objects and trap objects should be included in at least one conformance group.

Chapter 7. MIB Header, IMPORTS, Comments

1. How are MIBs mapped to files?

   A file can contain one or more MIBs. Concatenating multiple dependent MIBs into one file for submission to validating compilers is common.

2. What is wrong with the following syntax?

   IMPORTS vronx FROM vronxSmi.mib;

   It is attempting to IMPORTS *from a MIB file name rather than the MIB name.*

3. Name some of the types of definitions imported by MIB IMPORTS syntax.

   Syntax keywords, base data type keywords, node definitions, indexed table entry object definitions, textual convention definitions, OIDs of objects defined in other MIBs.

Chapter 8. Node Definitions

1. What are MIB Node definition objects used for?

   Organizing data, traps, and conformance statements into logical categories.

2. Name the SMIv1 node objects.

   Table definition objects
   Table Entry definition objects
   OBJECT IDENTIFIER

3. Name the SMIv2 node objects.

   MODULE-IDENTITY
   Table definition objects
   Table Entry definition objects
   OBJECT IDENTIFIER
   OBJECT-IDENTITY

Chapter 9. Data Object—Base Types

1. Name a common cause of MIB compiler complaints.

   SMIv1, SMIv2 mixed syntax

2. MIB data object syntax includes a SYNTAX clause. What information follows the keyword SYNTAX?

   The data type (base type or derived type)

3. Explain how the MAX-ACCESS accessible-for-notify value is used, and how it differs from other possible values.

   The value for such an object can be included in trap object syntax, and sent with traps, but cannot be read or written directly by any manager

4. What are the two very general types of data that all MIB formal data types can be reduced to?

   Integers and strings of hex octets (which can represent text, IP addresses, and other types of values).

5. MIB syntax allows restriction of data base type *sizes* and *values*. Explain the difference between the two.

   Value limits can be specified for integer-types, and size limits can be specified for octet-string-types.

6. What SMIv2 base type cannot be transported in SNMPv1 messages?

   Counter64

7. Are there any SMIv1 or SMIv2 base types that cannot be transported in SN-MPv3 messages?

   No

8. The DEFVAL clause is not appropriate for which base data types?

   Counter, Counter32, Counter64

9. The MIB-2 system table includes the data object sysObjectId. What is its data type, and what is this object used for (by managers)?

   Type is OBJECT IDENTIFIER.

   It is a globally unique OID that is used as a globally unique enumeration defining what type of device is being managed. A properly configured manager can match this value with an appropriate device icon to populate its network device map.

10. Neither SMIv1 nor SMIv2 syntax defines a floating point number base type. What options does a MIB developer have to represent FPNs?

    Represent as an integer and use the UNITS *clause to specify decimal point information.*

    Encode FPN bits as an SNMP Opaque *type.*

    Represent as a DisplayString.

Chapter 10. Data Object—Derived Types

1. What is a textual convention?

    An SNMP derived type based on a base type, with descriptive naming, and usually with value or size limits specified, often with unique semantics.

2. How are textual conventions defined in SMIv2 MIBs?

    Using the TEXTUAL-CONVENTION *syntax.*

3. Is there any way to define textual conventions in SMIv1 MIBs?

    Yes, using a simple notation equating (::=) the name of the derived type with a base type name.

4. What values can the TruthValue textual convention assume?

    true = 1
    false = 2

5. The textual convention TestAndIncr is intended for use in a manner similar to what common software mechanism?

    semaphore

6. What is wrong with the following SMIv2 textual convention definition?

    ```
    UserAlias := TEXTUAL-CONVENTION
        STATUS        current
        DESCRIPTION
        "User assigned name for the entity"
        SYNTAX DisplayString (SIZE(6..24))
    ```

    It is based on an existing textual convention instead of a base type.

Chapter 11. Trap Objects

1. What is the minimum number of VARIABLES clause data objects that must be defined in SMIv1 TRAP-TYPE syntax, and sent with SNMPv1 Traps?

    Zero—traps can be defined containing no data objects.

2. When designing an SMIv2 NOTIFICATION-TYPE, what important issue must be addressed to ensure it can be re-coded as an equivalent SMIv1 TRAP-TYPE?

    The parent node OID for SMIv2 notification objects must end in ".0"

Chapter 12. Conformance Objects (SMIv2)

1. Conformance objects were introduced in SMIv2 MIB syntax. What corresponding SNMPv2 message types were added to allow managers to obtain conformance object information from agents?

    None, managers cannot get or set conformance object information.

Chapter 13. Indexed Tables

1. In SNMP indexed tables, what do the columns represent? What do the rows represent?

    Columns are the object names
    Rows are the index values

2. Explain the relationship of table index values to data object OID instance values.

    There are a few subtleties, but in general, the instance value = the index value.

3. Name the three syntactic elements needed to define an SNMP indexed table.

    Table object (also defines a node)
    Entry object (also defines a node)
    SEQUENCE *statement*

4. Which of the three elements contains the INDEX object declarations?

    The entry object using the INDEX *or* AUGMENTS *clause.*

5. What is lexicographical ordering? How does the selection of the INDEX object (by the MIB developer) affect this ordering?

    Lexicographical is the logical ordering of OID.instance values, and is the order in which object values are returned by agents in response to getnext requests,

    The INDEX *object value is the instance value, and the type of this object will thus affect ordering.*

6. What is the preferred ACCESS (SMIv1) or MAX-ACCESS (SMIv2) value for INDEX data objects?

    not-accessible

7. You want to define a table with two indexes. How do you code this syntax?

    INDEX { object-name-index1, object-name-index2 }

8. Extensions of existing tables can be coded using:

    INDEX { name-of-index-object-from-base-table }, or

    AUGMENTS { name-of-something }

    What is the name-of-something?

    Name of the table entry object, for the table being augmented.

    How do these two methods differ?

    Using AUGMENTS *adds column values for all table object indexes.*

    Using INDEX *allows for sparse table extensions.*

Chapter 14. Index Data Types

1. Index types include integers. How do integer index values map to data object instance values?

    Directly. An instance value is exactly the integer index value.

2. Index types also include several based on OCTET STRING. How do such index values map to data object values?

    Octet string based objects contain multiple hex values, and are translated into similar, multiple dotted integer instance values. In some cases these multiple dotted values are preceded by their count.

Chapter 15. Row-Create Tables

1. Explain agent row-creation vs. manager row-create logic.

    Agent row-creation occurs when an agent observes a managed resource that has appeared, and the agent adds a row to a table to describe object values for that new resource.

    Manager row-creation occurs when a user wants to add information to a remote table using the manager. The manager communicates this request to the agent, and the row is added, along with values provided by the manager.

5. Name some IETF standard MIBs that are dependent on manager row-create logic.

    Standard PING MIB, SNMPv3 Configuration MIBs, RMON and RMON2 MIBs.

Chapter 16. Elements of Advanced MIB Complexity

1. Modify the Linked List example to include an object that allows managers to direct agents to return list data in either lexicographical order or in linked list order.

    ```
    transponderLinkedListReturnOrder   OBJECT-TYPE
        SYNTAX      INTEGER { lexicographical(1), linked (2) }
        MAX-ACCESS  read-write
        STATUS      current
        DESCRIPTION
            "Controls order in which list order is returned
            by the agent for getnext requests."
        ::= { transponderObjects 3 }
    ```

Chapter 17. Trap Filter Configuration

1. Trap filters, configured in a manager, filters on what types of information?

    Agent address, platform category, trap OID, values of data sent with traps.

2. Trap filters allow managers to respond to specific trap conditions with specific

actions. Name some of those actions.

Format log message and record in specified log file, send page, send email, send cellular phone call, forward information to another application, execute custom script, clear previous active log events.

Chapter 18. Trap Models

1. Discuss good and bad points of the following Trap Design.

```
vronxStatusEv NOTIFICATION-TYPE
  OBJECTS
  {
     vronxEventCounter
     vronxStatusMessage   -- SYNTAX DisplayString
  }
  STATUS  current
  DESCRIPTION
     "Sent when product status changes. DisplayString text
     explains the change."
  ::= { vronxStatusEvList 11 }
```

Good point – event counter allows manager to detect lost or un-delivered events.

Bad point – it will be difficult to create trap filters for values received in this single DisplayString.

2. What are stateful traps? And why are these so useful?

Stateful traps are those that are in pairs or sometimes tuples, which are mutually negating. Manager filters can be configured such that when "B" occurs, "A" is automatically ACK'ed (or removed) from the active log.

Chapter 20. Agent Trap Semantics

1. Give an example of poor agent trap semantics and its consequences.

One example—a redundant power supply fails, and the agent repeatedly sends traps to the manager. The network engineer monitoring such traps may create filter that ignores this trap permanently.

2. Give an example of good agent trap semantics.

A redundant power supply fails, and the agent sends a single trap. If the power supply is still problematic an hour later, the agent sends a reminder trap.

Chapter 21. Standard MIBs

1. What is the relationship of IETF standard MIBs and IANA standard MIBs?

    IETF standard MIBs contain definitions of nodes and managed data objects and trap objects. IETF MIBs often IMPORTS *definitions from IANA MIBs.*

    IANA MIBs contain definitions involving numbers—textual conventions defining enumerated INTEGER *objects and those based on* BITS, *as well as globally unique OID enumeration definitions.*

2. Most standard MIBs defining objects are organized under the *mgmt* node. Where else are some standard MIBs located?

    Under the experimental *node, and the* snmpv2 *node.*

3. You have just taken delivery of SNMP-compliant Cable Television Modems. The documentation is a little vague regarding what MIBs are supported. How will you research this topic, how will you determine which standard MIBs are most current, and how will you obtain copies?

    Go to the IETF web page, view the RFC Index, and search for terms such as modem *and* catv *to find relevant RFCs. View these RFCs to see if they contain MIBs—if they do, you will also need any MIBs* IMPORTS'ed *by them. Once you have a good list of MIBs, use the RFC Index to find which are the most current.*

    Simply using a web search engine to search for "SNMP Cable TV Modem MIB" may turn up additional information.

Chapter 22. Types of Enterprise MIBs

1. Enterprises may organize their MIBs in a variety of ways. But name three common categories (or types) of MIBs.

    SMI Registrations MIB
    Textual Convention Definitions MIB
    Product Management MIBs

2. What are the advantages of such organization?

Secure control of enterprise OID space
Common textual convention definitions used throughout the enterprise

Chapter 23. Data Organization and Uses

1. Describe how the intelligent use of object syntax elements enhances data object, trap object, and agent semantics.

    The following syntactic elements all convey information to the MIB-reader regarding object use and agent implementation:

    Data SYNTAX choices
    Data range and size specifications
    Object names
    DEFVAL clause
    UNITS clause
    DESCRIPTION clause
    DISPLAY-HINT clause in textual convention definitions

2. What is the difference between static configuration data and dynamic configuration data? Are these formal SNMP categories defined by IETF standards?

    Static configuration objects are read-only.

    Dynamic configuration objects are read-write.

    These categories are suggestions, not IETF standards.

SMI Registrations MIB Example

The following pages provide an example of an Enterprise SMI Registration MIB. A diagram of the MIB is first shown, followed by the MIB itself. It is imported by the CD player MIB example in Appendix H.

This MIB conforms to SMIv2 syntax and will pass validation compiler testing with no problems. It is given as a simple example of a decent MIB—elements may be suitable for enterprise developers.

Note that header information (comments) is fairly extensive. In particular, all object names are listed along with their OIDs. Documentation for MIBs should be contained within the MIBs themselves, and serves several purposes:

1. It is a quick reference for network engineers inspecting a MIB to understand its scope, or looking for a particular object. However it might be easier to load the MIB into a MIB browser tool, and inspect it that way.

2. Creating this list of object names and associated OIDs can be edited quite quickly by the developer. Doing this first provides the developer with a complete outline of intended objects and OIDs, which can be used as a reference as each object is edited into the MIB. This minimizes possibilities for object name error and OID errors.

3. And it looks good—it sets this MIB apart from many others. This attention to detail is no different than designing the best graphics possible on a control panel.

This MIB is available as a text file from www.wyndhampress.com, and from the MIB Depot web site.

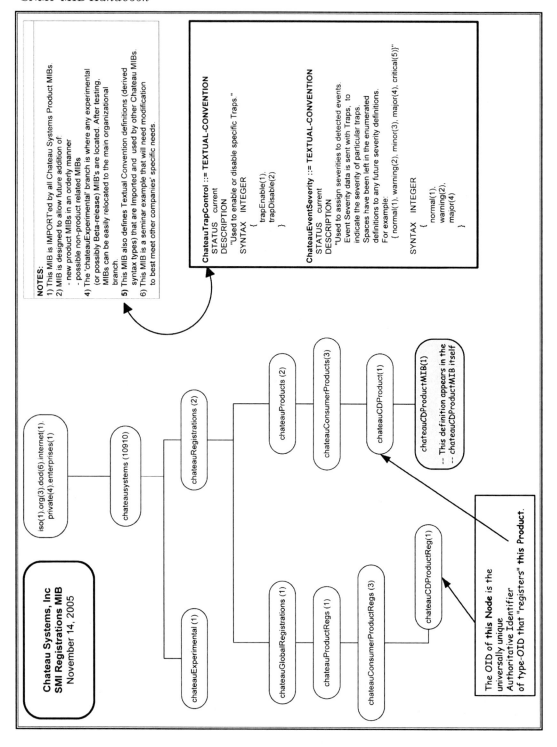

```
CHATEAUSYSTEMS-REGISTRATIONS-MIB DEFINITIONS ::= BEGIN


--
--              Chateau Systems, Inc
--           SMI Registrations MIB
--                  SMIv2
--             November 14, 2005
--
--
-- This MIB registers certain high level node definitions,
-- under which all Chateau Systems MIBs are organized.
--
--
-- The objects defined in this MIB are located under the
-- private.enterprises subtree as shown below:
--
--
--
--   iso(1).org(3).dod(6).internet(1)
--                    |
--               private(4)
--                 |
--             enterprises(1)
--                  |
--           chateausystems(10910)
--                  |
--         _____|_____
--         |                       |
--   chateauExperimental(1)  chateauRegistrations(2)
--                                  |
--                                  |
--           _____|_____
--           |                              |
--           |                              |
--   chateauGlobalRegistrations(1)    chateauProducts(2)
--           |                              |
--           |                              |
--           |                   chateauConsumerProducts(3)
--      chateauProductRegs(1)             |
--           |                              |
--   chateauConsumerProductRegs(3)   chateauCDProduct(1)
--           |
--      (OID Registrations)
--
```

-- OBJECT SUMMARY:
--
-- All objects within this MIB are prefixed with the OBJECT IDENTIFIER "cs"
-- where "cs" is defined by:
--
--   iso(1).org(3).dod(6).internet(1).private(4).enterprises(1).
--   chateausystems(10910)
--
-- OBJECT NAME   OBJECT OID
-- -------------------------------------   --------------------
--
-- chateauExperimental   cs.1
-- chateauRegistrations   cs.2
--   chateauGlobalRegistrations   cs.2.1
--   chateauProductRegs   cs.2.1.1
--   chateauConsumerProductRegs   cs.2.1.1.3
--   chateauCDProductReg   cs.2.1.1.3.1
--   chateauProducts   cs.2.2
--   chateauConsumerProducts   cs.2.2.3
--   chateauCDProduct   cs.2.2.3.1
--
--

        IMPORTS
            MODULE-IDENTITY, OBJECT-IDENTITY, enterprises
                FROM SNMPv2-SMI
            TEXTUAL-CONVENTION
                FROM SNMPv2-TC;

        chateausystems MODULE-IDENTITY
        LAST-UPDATED "200511090000Z"
        ORGANIZATION "Chateau Systems, Inc."
        CONTACT-INFO
        "www.chateausystems.com"

        DESCRIPTION
         "This MIB defines high level nodes that are used to
          organize Chateau Systems Registrations and
          MIBs into ordered groups.

          This MIB also contains Chateau Systems Enterprise-specific
          Textual Convention definitions.

          This MIB is intended to be IMPORT'ed by all other

Chateau Systems MIBs.

This MIB has been distributed as part of the handout
materials from the SNMP Technology Seminar presented
by Chateau Systems.

Any person or organization making use of this example MIB is
responsible for ensuring its complete suitability for their
own purposes. This includes the text of the legal disclaimers
below, as well as all other aspects.

Chateau Systems reserves the right to make changes in
specifications and other information contained
in this document without prior notice.
The reader should contact Chateau Systems to determine
whether or not such changes have been made.

In no event shall Chateau Systems be liable for any
incidental, indirect, special, or consequential damages
whatsoever (including but not limited to lost profits)
arising out of or related to this document or the
information contained in it, even if Chateau Systems has
been advised of, known, or should have known, the
possibility of such damages.

Chateau Systems grants vendors, end-users, and other interested
parties a non-exclusive license to use this specification
in connection with the management of Chateau Systems products.

Copyright November 2005 Chateau Systems, Inc."

REVISION   "200511090000Z"
DESCRIPTION
"Added Consumer CD Product Nodes."

REVISION   "200202200000Z"
DESCRIPTION
"First Release."

    ::= { enterprises 10910}

--
-- Chateau Systems Experimental Registrations
--

chateauExperimental OBJECT-IDENTITY
    STATUS current
    DESCRIPTION
      "All experimental MIBs are organized under
      this node. When those MIBs have been fully developed and tested,
      they will be moved under the chateauRegistrations Node.
      MIBs which are in Beta-test status may also appear
      under this experimental node."
    ::= { chateausystems 1 }

--
-- Chateau Systems Registrations for Released MIBs and Global Registrations
--

chateauRegistrations OBJECT-IDENTITY
    STATUS current
    DESCRIPTION
      "All MIBs (that have completed testing),
      along with associated registration data, are
      organized under this node. This includes Global
      Registrations, Product MIBs, and registration of
      MIBs in other categories."
    ::= { chateausystems 2 }

--
-- Chateau Systems Global Registrations
--

chateauGlobalRegistrations OBJECT-IDENTITY
    STATUS current
    DESCRIPTION
      "This node is intended for global registration information
      only. EG, OID definitions that register products."
    ::= { chateauRegistrations 1 }

chateauProductRegs OBJECT-IDENTITY
    STATUS current
    DESCRIPTION
      "Specific Product Registrations are under this node."
    ::= { chateauGlobalRegistrations 1 }

```
chateauConsumerProductRegs OBJECT-IDENTITY
    STATUS current
    DESCRIPTION
      "Consumer Product Registrations are under this node."
    ::= { chateauProductRegs 3 }

chateauCDProductReg OBJECT-IDENTITY
    STATUS current
    DESCRIPTION
      "The OID of this node is the definition of the authoritative
      registration for the Chateau Systems CD Product."
    ::= { chateauConsumerProductRegs 1 }


--
-- Chateau Systems Product MIB Registrations
--


chateauProducts OBJECT-IDENTITY
    STATUS current
    DESCRIPTION
      "All Chateau Systems Product MIBs are organized
      under this node."
    ::= { chateauRegistrations 2 }

chateauConsumerProducts OBJECT-IDENTITY
    STATUS current
    DESCRIPTION
      "All Chateau Systems Consumer Product MIBs are
      organized under this node"
    ::= { chateauProducts 3 }

chateauCDProduct OBJECT-IDENTITY
    STATUS current
    DESCRIPTION
      "Chateau CD Product MIBs are organized under this node."
    ::= { chateauConsumerProducts 1 }


--
-- Chateau Systems Corporation unique TEXTUAL-CONVENTION definitions
--


ChateauTrapControl ::= TEXTUAL-CONVENTION
    STATUS   current
    DESCRIPTION
```

"Used to enable or disable specific Traps."
SYNTAX   INTEGER
            {
              trapEnable(1),
              trapDisable(2)
            }

ChateauEventSeverity ::= TEXTUAL-CONVENTION
    STATUS   current
    DESCRIPTION
        "Used to assign severities to detected events.
        Event Severity data is sent with Traps, to
        indicate the severity of particular Traps.
        Spaces have been left in the enumerated
        definitions to any future severity definitions.
        For example:
        { normal(1), warning(2), minor(3), major(4), critical(5)}"

    SYNTAX   INTEGER
            {
              normal(1),
              warning(2),
              major(4)
            }

END

CD Player MIB Example

The following pages provide an example of an enterprise CD player product MIB. A diagram of the MIB is first shown, followed by the MIB itself. It is IMPORTS information from the SMI Registrations MIB example in Appendix G.

This MIB conforms to SMIv2 syntax and will pass validation compiler testing with no problems.

It is given as a simple example of a decent MIB—elements may be suitable for enterprise developers.

Note that header information (comments) is fairly extensive. In particular, all object names are listed along with their OIDs. This information was taken directly from the diagram and edited into the MIB. This information serves several purposes:

1. It is a quick reference for network engineers inspecting a MIB to understand its scope, or looking for a particular object. However it might be easier to load the MIB into a MIB browser tool, and inspect it that way.

2. Creating this list of object names and associated OIDs can be edited quite quickly by the developer. Doing this first provides the developer with a complete outline of intended objects and OIDs, which can be used as a reference as each object is edited into the MIB. This minimizes possibilities for object name error and OID errors.

3. And it looks good—it sets this MIB apart from many others. This attention to detail is no different than designing the best graphics possible on a control panel.

This MIB is available as a text file from www.wyndhampress.com, and from the MIB Depot web site.

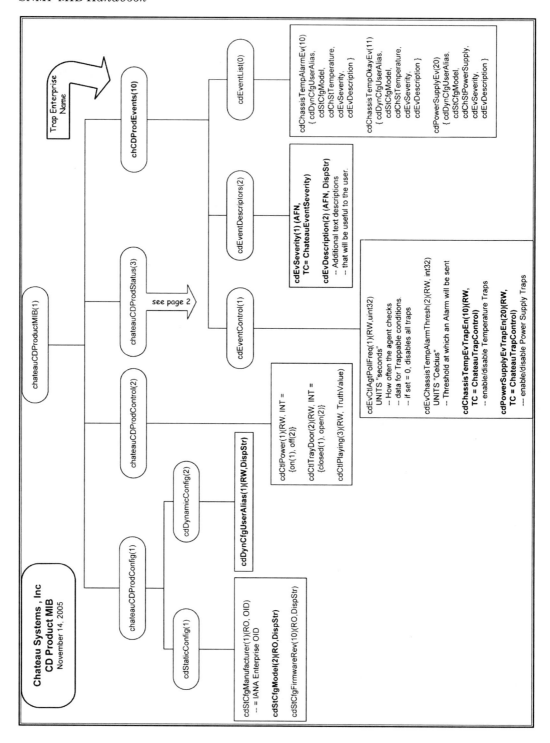

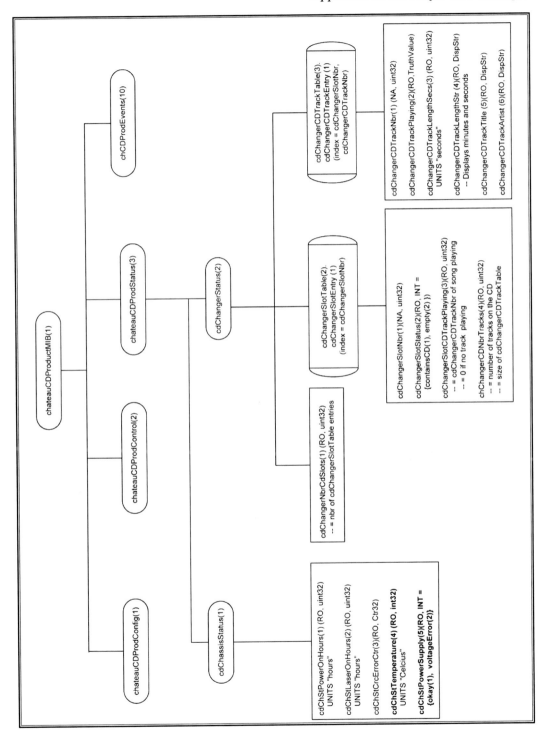

CHATEAU-CD-PRODUCT-MIB DEFINITIONS ::= BEGIN

```
--
--              Chateau Systems, Inc
--                 CD Product MIB
--                    SMIv2
--               November 14, 2005
--
--
-- The objects defined in this MIB are located under the
-- private.enterprises subtree as shown below:
--
--
--
--   iso(1).org(3).dod(6).internet(1)
--                  |
--              private(4)
--                  |
--             enterprises(1)
--                  |
--            chateausystems(10910)
--                     |
--        --------------|---------------
--        |                            |
--   chateauExperimental(1)  chateauRegistrations(2)
--                                     |
--                                     |
--        ----------------------------|-----------
--        |                                      |
--   chateauGlobalRegistrations(1)        chateauProducts(2)
--        |                                      |
--        |                                      |
--        |                            chateauConsumerProducts(3)
--   chateauProductRegs(1)                       |
--        |                                      |
--   chateauConsumerProductRegs(3)      chateauCDProduct(1)
--        |                                      |
--   (OID Registrations)              chateauCDProductMIB(1)
--
--
--
--
--
```

```
-- OBJECT SUMMARY:
--
-- All objects within this MIB are prefixed with the OBJECT IDENTIFIER "ccdp"
-- where "ccdp" is defined by:
--
--      iso(1).org(3).dod(6).internet(1).private(4).enterprises(1).
--      chateausystems(10910).chateauRegistrations(2).chateauProducts(2).
--      chateauConsumerProducts(3).chateauCDProduct(1)
--
-- OBJECT NAME                                OBJECT OID
-- ----------------------------------         ----------------
--
-- chateauCDProductMIB                        ccdp.1
--   chateauCDProdConfig                      ccdp.1.1
--     cdStaticConfig                         ccdp.1.1.1
--       cdStCfgManufacturer                  ccdp.1.1.1.1
--       cdStCfgModel                         ccdp.1.1.1.2
--       cdStCfgFirmwareRev                   ccdp.1.1.1.10
--     cdDynamicConfig                        ccdp.1.1.2
--       cdDynCfgUserAlias                    ccdp.1.1.2.1
--   chateauCDProdControl                     ccdp.1.2
--     cdCtlPower                             ccdp.1.2.1
--     cdCtlTrayDoor                          ccdp.1.2.2
--     cdCtlPlaying                           ccdp.1.2.3
--   chateauCDProdStatus                      ccdp.1.3
--     cdChassisStatus                        ccdp.1.3.1
--       cdChStPowerOnHours                   ccdp.1.3.1.1
--       cdChStLaserOnHours                   ccdp.1.3.1.2
--       cdChStCrcErrorCtr                    ccdp.1.3.1.3
--       cdChStTemperature                    ccdp.1.3.1.4
--       cdChStPowerSupply                    ccdp.1.3.1.5
--     cdChangerStatus                        ccdp.1.3.2
--       cdChangerNbrCdSlots                  ccdp.1.3.2.1
--       cdChangerSlotTable                   ccdp.1.3.2.2
--         cdChangerSlotEntry                 ccdp.1.3.2.2.1
--           cdChangerSlotNbr                 ccdp.1.3.2.2.1.1
--           cdChangerSlotStatus              ccdp.1.3.2.2.1.2
--           cdChangerSlotCDTrackPlaying      ccdp.1.3.2.2.1.3
--           cdChangerCDNbrTracks             ccdp.1.3.2.2.1.4
--         cdChangerCDTrackTable              cdp.1.3.2.3
--           cdChangerCDTrackEntry            ccdp.1.3.2.3.1
--             cdChangerCDTrackNbr            ccdp.1.3.2.3.1.1
--             cdChangerCDTrackPlaying        ccdp.1.3.2.3.1.2
--             cdChangerCDTrackLengthSecs     ccdp.1.3.2.3.1.3
```

```
--          cdChangerCDTrackLengthStr      ccdp.1.3.2.3.1.4
--          cdChangerCDTrackTitle          ccdp.1.3.2.3.1.5
--          cdChangerCDTrackArtist         ccdp.1.3.2.3.1.6
--      chateauCDProdEvents                ccdp.1.10
--       cdEventControl                    ccdp.1.10.1
--        cdEvCtlAgtPollFreq               ccdp.1.10.1.1
--        cdChassisTempAlarmThresh         ccdp.1.10.1.2
--        cdChassisTempEvTrapEn            ccdp.1.10.1.10
--        cdPowerSupplyEvTrapEn            ccdp.1.10.1.20
--       cdEventDescriptors                ccdp.1.10.2
--        cdEvSeverity                     ccdp.1.10.2.1
--        cdEvDescription                  ccdp.1.10.2.2
--       cdEventList                       ccdp.1.10.0
--        cdChassisTempAlarmEv             ccdp.1.10.0.10
--        cdChassisTempOkayEv              ccdp.1.10.0.11
--        cdPowerSupplyEv                  ccdp.1.10.0.20
--
--
--      chateauCDProdConformance           ccdp.1.20
--       cdConformanceGroups               ccdp.1.20.1
--        cdProdConfigGroup                ccdp.1.20.1.1
--        cdProdControlGroup               ccdp.1.20.1.2
--        cdProdStatusGroup                ccdp.1.20.1.3
--        cdProdEventGroup                 ccdp.1.20.1.4
--        cdProdNotificationsGroup         ccdp.1.20.1.5
--       cdCompliance                      ccdp.1.20.2
--
--


    IMPORTS
        MODULE-IDENTITY, OBJECT-IDENTITY, NOTIFICATION-TYPE,
        OBJECT-TYPE, Unsigned32, Integer32, Counter32
            FROM SNMPv2-SMI

        OBJECT-GROUP, NOTIFICATION-GROUP, MODULE-COMPLIANCE
            FROM SNMPv2-CONF

        DisplayString, TruthValue
            FROM SNMPv2-TC

        chateauCDProduct, ChateauTrapControl, ChateauEventSeverity
            FROM CHATEAUSYSTEMS-REGISTRATIONS-MIB;

    chateauCDProductMIB  MODULE-IDENTITY
        LAST-UPDATED "200511090000Z"
```

ORGANIZATION "Chateau Systems, Inc."
CONTACT-INFO
"www.chateausystems.com"

DESCRIPTION
"This MIB defines Nodes and Data Objects to support
Chateau Systems CD Players.

This MIB has been distributed as part of the handout
materials from the SNMP Technology Seminar presented
by Chateau Systems.

Any person or organization making use of this example MIB is
responsible for ensuring its complete suitability for their
own purposes. This includes the text of the legal disclaimers
below, as well as all other aspects.

Chateau Systems reserves the right to make changes in
specifications and other information contained
in this document without prior notice.
The reader should contact Chateau Systems to determine
whether or not such changes have been made.

In no event shall Chateau Systems be liable for any
incidental, indirect, special, or consequential damages
whatsoever (including but not limited to lost profits)
arising out of or related to this document or the
information contained in it, even if Chateau Systems has
been advised of, known, or should have known, the
possibility of such damages.

Chateau Systems grants vendors, end-users, and other interested
parties a non-exclusive license to use this specification
in connection with the management of Chateau Systems products.

Copyright November 2005 Chateau Systems, Inc."

REVISION   "200511090000Z"
DESCRIPTION
"First Release."

::= { chateauCDProduct 1 }

```
--
--    chateauCDProdConfig                    ccdp.1.1
--


chateauCDProdConfig OBJECT-IDENTITY
   STATUS current
   DESCRIPTION
     "CD Configuration Organizational node"
   ::= { chateauCDProductMIB 1 }


--
--    cdStaticConfig                     ccdp.1.1.1
--


cdStaticConfig OBJECT-IDENTITY
   STATUS current
   DESCRIPTION
     "CD Static Configuration Node"
   ::= { chateauCDProdConfig 1 }



--        cdStCfgManufacturer              ccdp.1.1.1.1


cdStCfgManufacturer   OBJECT-TYPE
   SYNTAX      OBJECT IDENTIFIER
   MAX-ACCESS  read-only
   STATUS      current
   DESCRIPTION
     "The IANA issued Enterprise OID for this Product's Manufacturer."
   ::= { cdStaticConfig 1 }



--        cdStCfgModel                     ccdp.1.1.1.2


cdStCfgModel   OBJECT-TYPE
   SYNTAX      DisplayString (SIZE(4..16))
   MAX-ACCESS  read-only
   STATUS      current
   DESCRIPTION
     "Manufacturer's Model Designation"
   ::= { cdStaticConfig 2 }
```

```
--        cdStCfgFirmwareRev                ccdp.1.1.1.10

cdStCfgFirmwareRev   OBJECT-TYPE
   SYNTAX      DisplayString
   MAX-ACCESS  read-only
   STATUS      current
   DESCRIPTION
      "The Firmware Revision for currently loaded firmware"
   ::= { cdStaticConfig 10 }



--
--        cdDynamicConfig                   ccdp.1.1.2
--


cdDynamicConfig OBJECT-IDENTITY
   STATUS current
   DESCRIPTION
      "CD Dynamic Configuration Node"
   ::= { chateauCDProdConfig 2 }


--        cdDynCfgUserAlias                 ccdp.1.1.2.1

 cdDynCfgUserAlias   OBJECT-TYPE
   SYNTAX      DisplayString (SIZE(0..16))
   MAX-ACCESS  read-write
   STATUS      current
   DESCRIPTION
      "Any user assigned name for this CD player"
   ::= { cdDynamicConfig 1 }



--
--    chateauCDProdControl                  ccdp.1.2
--


chateauCDProdControl OBJECT-IDENTITY
   STATUS current
   DESCRIPTION
      "CD Control Organizational node"
   ::= { chateauCDProductMIB 2 }
```

```
--     cdCtlPower                          ccdp.1.2.1


cdCtlPower   OBJECT-TYPE
    SYNTAX     INTEGER
            { on(1),
              off(2)
              }
    MAX-ACCESS  read-write
    STATUS     current
    DESCRIPTION
        "Indicated CD Player Power status.
        Can be modified by the user."
    ::= { chateauCDProdControl 1 }




--     cdCtlTrayDoor                       ccdp.1.2.2


cdCtlTrayDoor   OBJECT-TYPE
    SYNTAX     INTEGER
            { closed(1),
              open(2)
              }
    MAX-ACCESS  read-write
    STATUS      current
    DESCRIPTION
        "CD Player tray door status.
        Can be modified by the user.
        If cdCtlPower = off,
        then the user cannot modify this value."
    ::= { chateauCDProdControl 2 }




--     cdCtlPlaying                        ccdp.1.2.3


cdCtlPlaying   OBJECT-TYPE
    SYNTAX     TruthValue
    MAX-ACCESS  read-write
    STATUS      current
    DESCRIPTION
        "CD Player 'play' status.
        Can be modified by the user.
        If cdCtlPower = off
        OR cdCtlTrayDoor = open,
        then the user cannot modify this value."
    ::= { chateauCDProdControl 3 }
```

```
--
--    chateauCDProdStatus                    ccdp.1.3
--

chateauCDProdStatus  OBJECT-IDENTITY
    STATUS current
    DESCRIPTION
      "CD Player Status organizational node"
    ::= { chateauCDProductMIB 3 }



--
--      cdChassisStatus                      ccdp.1.3.1
--

cdChassisStatus  OBJECT-IDENTITY
    STATUS current
    DESCRIPTION
      "CD Player Chassis status node"
    ::= { chateauCDProdStatus 1 }



--        cdChStPowerOnHours                 ccdp.1.3.1.1

cdChStPowerOnHours   OBJECT-TYPE
    SYNTAX     Unsigned32
    MAX-ACCESS  read-only
    STATUS     current
    DESCRIPTION
      "The total number of hours that this CD Player
       has been powered on in its lifetime."
    ::= { cdChassisStatus 1 }



--        cdChStLaserOnHours                 ccdp.1.3.1.2

cdChStLaserOnHours   OBJECT-TYPE
    SYNTAX     Unsigned32
    MAX-ACCESS  read-only
    STATUS     current
    DESCRIPTION
      "The total number of hours that this CD Player's
```

Laser has been powered on in its lifetime.
Trending this value may predict Laser failures."
::= { cdChassisStatus 2 }

--   cdChStCrcErrorCtr   ccdp.1.3.1.3

cdChStCrcErrorCtr   OBJECT-TYPE
    SYNTAX   Counter32
    MAX-ACCESS read-only
    STATUS   current
    DESCRIPTION
        "Counter for CRC errors encountered reading CDs.
        This Counter is initialized whenever the CD Player
        is powered on."
    ::= { cdChassisStatus 3 }

--   cdChStTemperature   ccdp.1.3.1.4

cdChStTemperature   OBJECT-TYPE
    SYNTAX   Integer32
    UNITS   "Celcius"
    MAX-ACCESS read-only
    STATUS   current
    DESCRIPTION
        "CD Player internal chassis temperature."
    ::= { cdChassisStatus 4 }

--   cdChStPowerSupply   ccdp.1.3.1.5

cdChStPowerSupply   OBJECT-TYPE
    SYNTAX   INTEGER
            { okay(1),
              voltageError(2)
            }
    MAX-ACCESS read-only
    STATUS   current
    DESCRIPTION
        "CD Player Power Supply status."
    ::= { cdChassisStatus 5 }

```
--
--      cdChangerStatus                    ccdp.1.3.2
--


cdChangerStatus  OBJECT-IDENTITY
   STATUS current
   DESCRIPTION
     "CD Player Changer status node"
   ::= { chateauCDProdStatus 2 }



--        cdChangerNbrCdSlots              ccdp.1.3.2.1

cdChangerNbrCdSlots   OBJECT-TYPE
   SYNTAX     Unsigned32 (1..8)
   MAX-ACCESS  read-only
   STATUS     current
   DESCRIPTION
     "The maximum number of CDs that can be loaded into
      this CD player.
      The size of (number of indexed entries in) the cdChangerSlotTable."
   ::= { cdChangerStatus 1 }




--
--        cdChangerSlotTable             ccdp.1.3.2.2
--          cdChangerSlotEntry           ccdp.1.3.2.2.1
--


cdChangerSlotTable OBJECT-TYPE
   SYNTAX     SEQUENCE OF CdChangerSlotEntry
   MAX-ACCESS  not-accessible
   STATUS     current
   DESCRIPTION
     "CD Changer Slot Table."
   ::= { cdChangerStatus 2 }


cdChangerSlotEntry  OBJECT-TYPE
   SYNTAX     CdChangerSlotEntry
   MAX-ACCESS  not-accessible
   STATUS     current
   DESCRIPTION
```

"An entry in cdChangerSlotTable."
INDEX   { cdChangerSlotNbr }
::= { cdChangerSlotTable 1 }

CdChangerSlotEntry ::=
  SEQUENCE {
        cdChangerSlotNbr   Unsigned32,
        cdChangerSlotStatus   INTEGER,
        cdChangerSlotCDTrackPlaying   Unsigned32,
        cdChangerCDNbrTracks   Unsigned32
        }

--   cdChangerSlotNbr   ccdp.1.3.2.2.1.1

cdChangerSlotNbr   OBJECT-TYPE
  SYNTAX   Unsigned32 (1..8)
  MAX-ACCESS not-accessible
  STATUS   current
  DESCRIPTION
     "Slot number and table index."
  ::= { cdChangerSlotEntry 1 }

--   cdChangerSlotStatus   ccdp.1.3.2.2.1.2

cdChangerSlotStatus   OBJECT-TYPE
  SYNTAX   INTEGER
           { containsCD(1),
             empty(2)
             }
  MAX-ACCESS read-only
  STATUS   current
  DESCRIPTION
     "CD Changer Slot Status."
  ::= { cdChangerSlotEntry 2 }

--   cdChangerSlotCDTrackPlaying   ccdp.1.3.2.2.1.3

cdChangerSlotCDTrackPlaying   OBJECT-TYPE
  SYNTAX   Unsigned32
  MAX-ACCESS read-only

STATUS   current
DESCRIPTION
   "If a CD is currently playing, this is the Track Number.
   This is also the value of cdChangerCDTrackNbr for the CD that is playing.
   = 0 if no CD is currently playing."
::= { cdChangerSlotEntry 3 }

--   cdChangerCDNbrTracks   ccdp.1.3.2.2.1.4

cdChangerCDNbrTracks   OBJECT-TYPE
   SYNTAX   Unsigned32
   MAX-ACCESS read-only
   STATUS   current
   DESCRIPTION
      "The number of Tracks on this CD.
      This is also the size the sub-table cdChangerCDTrackTable
      for this CD - ie, the maximum value of cdChangerCDTrackNbr."
   ::= { cdChangerSlotEntry 4 }

--
--   cdChangerCDTrackTable   ccdp.1.3.2.3
--   cdChangerCDTrackEntry   ccdp.1.3.2.3.1
--

cdChangerCDTrackTable OBJECT-TYPE
   SYNTAX   SEQUENCE OF CdChangerCDTrackEntry
   MAX-ACCESS not-accessible
   STATUS   current
   DESCRIPTION
      "Changer Track Table for a single CD."
   ::= { cdChangerStatus 3 }

cdChangerCDTrackEntry OBJECT-TYPE
   SYNTAX   CdChangerCDTrackEntry
   MAX-ACCESS not-accessible
   STATUS   current
   DESCRIPTION
      "An entry in cdChangerCDTrackTable."
   INDEX { cdChangerSlotNbr, cdChangerCDTrackNbr }
   ::= { cdChangerCDTrackTable 1 }

```
CdChangerCDTrackEntry ::=
    SEQUENCE {
        cdChangerCDTrackNbr        Unsigned32,
        cdChangerCDTrackPlaying    TruthValue,
        cdChangerCDTrackLengthSecs Unsigned32,
        cdChangerCDTrackLengthStr  DisplayString,
        cdChangerCDTrackTitle      DisplayString,
        cdChangerCDTrackArtist     DisplayString
        }
```

--   cdChangerCDTrackNbr   ccdp.1.3.2.3.1.1

```
cdChangerCDTrackNbr  OBJECT-TYPE
    SYNTAX    Unsigned32
    MAX-ACCESS  not-accessible
    STATUS    current
    DESCRIPTION
        "CD Track Number and Table Index"
    ::= { cdChangerCDTrackEntry 1 }
```

--   cdChangerCDTrackPlaying   ccdp.1.3.2.3.1.2

```
cdChangerCDTrackPlaying   OBJECT-TYPE
    SYNTAX    TruthValue
    MAX-ACCESS  read-only
    STATUS    current
    DESCRIPTION
        "= true if this Track is currently playing.
        Only one Track can be true at a time."
    ::= { cdChangerCDTrackEntry 2 }
```

--   cdChangerCDTrackLengthSecs   ccdp.1.3.2.3.1.3

```
cdChangerCDTrackLengthSecs  OBJECT-TYPE
    SYNTAX    Unsigned32
    MAX-ACCESS  read-only
    STATUS    current
    DESCRIPTION
        "Track time in seconds."
    ::= { cdChangerCDTrackEntry 3 }
```

```
--          cdChangerCDTrackLengthStr        ccdp.1.3.2.3.1.4

cdChangerCDTrackLengthStr   OBJECT-TYPE
  SYNTAX     DisplayString
  MAX-ACCESS  read-only
  STATUS     current
  DESCRIPTION
    "Track time in minutes and seconds displayed as text."
  ::= { cdChangerCDTrackEntry 4 }


--          cdChangerCDTrackTitle        ccdp.1.3.2.3.1.5

cdChangerCDTrackTitle   OBJECT-TYPE
  SYNTAX     DisplayString (SIZE(0..64))
  MAX-ACCESS  read-only
  STATUS     current
  DESCRIPTION
    "CD Track Title.
     NULL string if information is not available."
  ::= { cdChangerCDTrackEntry 5 }


--          cdChangerCDTrackArtist        ccdp.1.3.2.3.1.6

cdChangerCDTrackArtist   OBJECT-TYPE
  SYNTAX     DisplayString (SIZE(0..64))
  MAX-ACCESS  read-only
  STATUS     current
  DESCRIPTION
    "CD Track Artist.
     NULL string if information is not available."
  ::= { cdChangerCDTrackEntry 6 }


--
--   chateauCDProdEvents              ccdp.1.10
--

chateauCDProdEvents OBJECT-IDENTITY
  STATUS current
  DESCRIPTION
    "CD Player Event Data and Trap Definitions
```

389

are organized under this node."
::= { chateauCDProductMIB 10 }

```
--
--      cdEventControl                    ccdp.1.10.1
--
```

cdEventControl OBJECT-IDENTITY
  STATUS current
  DESCRIPTION
    "Node for data affecting Agent Trap Management Semantics"
  ::= { chateauCDProdEvents 1 }

```
--      cdEvCtlAgtPollFreq                ccdp.1.10.1.1
```

cdEvCtlAgtPollFreq   OBJECT-TYPE
  SYNTAX   Unsigned32
  UNITS   "seconds"
  MAX-ACCESS read-write
  STATUS   current
  DESCRIPTION
    "How often the Agent polls the CD Player for trappable conditions.
    Set = 0 to disable all traps.
    Persistent through system resets."
  DEFVAL {30}
  ::= { cdEventControl 1 }

```
--      cdChassisTempAlarmThresh          ccdp.1.10.1.2
```

cdChassisTempAlarmThresh   OBJECT-TYPE
  SYNTAX   Integer32
  UNITS   "Celcius"
  MAX-ACCESS read-write
  STATUS   current
  DESCRIPTION
    "User settable to define the Chassis Temperature
    past which a Chassis Temperature Alarm will occur.
    Agent semantics will apply hysterisis logic so
    that traps to not repeat unecessarily when the
    chassis temperature is very close to this threshold.
    Persistent through system resets."

```
        DEFVAL { 40 }
        ::= { cdEventControl 2 }


--        cdChassisTempEvTrapEn                 ccdp.1.10.1.10

cdChassisTempEvTrapEn   OBJECT-TYPE
    SYNTAX      ChateauTrapControl
    MAX-ACCESS  read-write
    STATUS      current
    DESCRIPTION
        "User settable to disable/enable Chassis Temperature alarms
        and okay events.
        Persistent through system resets."
    DEFVAL { trapEnable }
    ::= { cdEventControl 10 }

--        cdPowerSupplyEvTrapEn                  ccdp.1.10.1.20

cdPowerSupplyEvTrapEn   OBJECT-TYPE
    SYNTAX      ChateauTrapControl
    MAX-ACCESS  read-write
    STATUS      current
    DESCRIPTION
        "User settable to disable/enable Power Supply alarms
        and okay events.
        Persistent through system resets."
    DEFVAL { trapEnable }
    ::= { cdEventControl 20 }


--
--        cdEventDescriptors                    ccdp.1.10.2
--

cdEventDescriptors  OBJECT-IDENTITY
    STATUS current
    DESCRIPTION
        "Event Descriptor Node"
    ::= { chateauCDProdEvents 2 }


--        cdEvSeverity                          ccdp.1.10.2.1
```

cdEvSeverity   OBJECT-TYPE
    SYNTAX   ChateauEventSeverity
    MAX-ACCESS accessible-for-notify
    STATUS   current
    DESCRIPTION
        "This value is sent with each trap as an
        indication of the intended severity of the event."
    ::= { cdEventDescriptors 1 }

--   cdEvDescription   ccdp.1.10.2.2

cdEvDescription   OBJECT-TYPE
    SYNTAX   DisplayString (SIZE(0..64))
    MAX-ACCESS accessible-for-notify
    STATUS   current
    DESCRIPTION
        "Text which may provide the user with further diagnostic information."
    ::= { cdEventDescriptors 2 }

--
--   cdEventList   ccdp.1.10.0
--

cdEventList OBJECT-IDENTITY
    STATUS current
    DESCRIPTION
        "Notification Objects are organized under this node."
    ::= { chateauCDProdEvents 0 }

--   cdChassisTempAlarmEv   ccdp.1.10.0.10

cdChassisTempAlarmEv NOTIFICATION-TYPE
    OBJECTS
    {
        cdDynCfgUserAlias,
        cdStCfgModel,
        cdChStTemperature,
        cdEvSeverity,
        cdEvDescription
    }
    STATUS current
    DESCRIPTION

```
        "Sent when cdChStTemperature > cdChassisTempAlarmThresh.
        Will not be resent until cdChStTemperature drops below
        cdChasisTempAlarmThresh less 10%.
        This trap can be disabled by setting cdChassisTempEvTrapEn = trapDisable."
    ::= { cdEventList 10 }


--      cdChassisTempOkayEv              ccdp.1.10.0.11

cdChassisTempOkayEv NOTIFICATION-TYPE
    OBJECTS
    {
        cdDynCfgUserAlias,
        cdStCfgModel,
        cdChStTemperature,
        cdEvSeverity,
        cdEvDescription
    }
    STATUS  current
    DESCRIPTION
        "Sent when cdChStTemperature drops below cdChassisTempAlarmThresh.
        This trap can be disabled by setting cdChassisTempEvTrapEn = trapDisable."
    ::= { cdEventList 11 }


--      cdPowerSupplyEv                  ccdp.1.10.0.20

cdPowerSupplyEv NOTIFICATION-TYPE
    OBJECTS
    {
        cdDynCfgUserAlias,
        cdStCfgModel,
        cdChStPowerSupply,
        cdEvSeverity,
        cdEvDescription
    }
    STATUS  current
    DESCRIPTION
        "Sent when cdChStPowerSupply changes from okay to voltageError,
        or from voltageError to okay.
        This trap can be disabled by setting cdPowerSupplyEvTrapEn = trapDisable."
    ::= { cdEventList 20 }
```

```
-- ------------------------------------------------------------
--
-- Chateau CD Product Conformance Objects
--
-- ------------------------------------------------------------


--
--    chateauCDProdConformance                 ccdp.1.20
--

chateauCDProdConformance OBJECT-IDENTITY
    STATUS current
    DESCRIPTION
      "Organizational node for Conformance Objects."
    ::= { chateauCDProductMIB 20 }


--
--      cdConformanceGroups                    ccdp.1.20.1
--

cdConformanceGroups  OBJECT-IDENTITY
    STATUS current
    DESCRIPTION
      "Organizational node for Conformance Groups."
    ::= { chateauCDProdConformance 1 }


--        cdProdConfigGroup              ccdp.1.20.1.1

cdProdConfigGroup OBJECT-GROUP
    OBJECTS
    {
--   chateauCDProdConfig
--     cdStaticConfig
         cdStCfgManufacturer,
         cdStCfgModel,
         cdStCfgFirmwareRev,
--     cdDynamicConfig
         cdDynCfgUserAlias
    }
```

```
    STATUS current
    DESCRIPTION
    "cdProdConfigGroup"
    ::= { cdConformanceGroups  1 }



--       cdProdControlGroup              ccdp.1.20.1.2

cdProdControlGroup OBJECT-GROUP
    OBJECTS
    {
--   chateauCDProdControl
        cdCtlPower,
        cdCtlTrayDoor,
        cdCtlPlaying
    }
    STATUS current
    DESCRIPTION
    "cdProdControlGroup"
    ::= { cdConformanceGroups 2 }



--       cdProdStatusGroup               ccdp.1.20.1.3

cdProdStatusGroup OBJECT-GROUP
    OBJECTS
    {
--   chateauCDProdStatus
--      cdChassisStatus
        cdChStPowerOnHours,
        cdChStLaserOnHours,
        cdChStCrcErrorCtr,
        cdChStTemperature,
        cdChStPowerSupply,
--      cdChangerStatus
        cdChangerNbrCdSlots,
--      cdChangerSlotTable
--        cdChangerSlotEntry
--          cdChangerSlotNbr
        cdChangerSlotStatus,
        cdChangerSlotCDTrackPlaying,
        cdChangerCDNbrTracks,
--      cdChangerCDTrackTable
--        cdChangerCDTrackEntry
```

```
--              cdChangerCDTrackNbr
                cdChangerCDTrackPlaying,
                cdChangerCDTrackLengthSecs,
                cdChangerCDTrackLengthStr,
                cdChangerCDTrackTitle,
                cdChangerCDTrackArtist
        }
        STATUS current
        DESCRIPTION
        "cdProdStatusGroup"
        ::= { cdConformanceGroups 3 }



--          cdProdEventGroup                    ccdp.1.20.1.4

cdProdEventGroup OBJECT-GROUP
    OBJECTS
    {
--    chateauCDProdEvents
--       cdEventControl
            cdEvCtlAgtPollFreq,
            cdChassisTempAlarmThresh,
            cdChassisTempEvTrapEn,
            cdPowerSupplyEvTrapEn,
--       cdEventDescriptors
            cdEvSeverity,
            cdEvDescription
    }
    STATUS current
    DESCRIPTION
    "cdProdEventGroup"
    ::= { cdConformanceGroups 4 }



--          cdProdNotificationsGroup            ccdp.1.20.1.5

cdProdNotificationsGroup  NOTIFICATION-GROUP
    NOTIFICATIONS
    {
--    chateauCDProdEvents
--       cdEventList
            cdChassisTempAlarmEv,
            cdChassisTempOkayEv,
            cdPowerSupplyEv
```

```
        }
    STATUS current
    DESCRIPTION
    "cdProdNotificationsGroup"
    ::= { cdConformanceGroups 5 }


--
--      cdCompliance                      ccdp.1.20.2
--


cdCompliance MODULE-COMPLIANCE
    STATUS current
    DESCRIPTION
        "Specification of mandatory and non-mandatory
        MIB objects."
    MODULE -- This Module
    MANDATORY-GROUPS
        {
        cdProdConfigGroup,
        cdProdStatusGroup,
        cdProdEventGroup,
        cdProdNotificationsGroup
        }

    GROUP  cdProdControlGroup
    DESCRIPTION "A non-mandatory group."

    ::= { chateauCDProdConformance 2 }


END
```

About the Author

Larry Walsh is a long-time SNMP practitioner. Before SNMP his career focus was developing embedded real-time software for the television industry. An opportunity was presented to be involved in setting up a new satellite broadcast facility that used SNMP for system management and monitoring.

In this role, he developed SNMP MIBs and was involved in setting MIB standards for subsystem providers to the facility. He also developed a number of SNMP agents for Unix and Windows platforms.

This led to a new career developing MIBs and agents for a variety of clients. One thing that became clear was the need for formal client SNMP training.

In 2003 he began to edit a series of SNMP training seminars. These grew from a one day presentation to enough material to fill five days. SNMP training modules include SNMP Foundations, Understanding MIBs, SNMP Network Management Principles, SNMPv3 (the secure version), SNMP Agent Development, and Entity MIB Overview. All were crafted to be of interest to both developers and end users. This book includes material from the *Foundations, Network Management, Understanding MIBs,* and *Agent Development* modules.

Larry's client list has included some great companies (SNMP developers and SNMP end users) in the following industries: television broadcaster, television equipment manufacturers, space agency mission control engineers, automated toll collection system provider, military aircraft manufacturer, utility companies, telephone companies, government agencies, university IT department.

Your comments and suggestions regarding this book are welcome. Despite many reviews, somehow there are always residual errors. If you find one, please let us know. We would also like to hear any suggestions for future book topics.

You can reach the author at mibs@chateausystems.com. He welcomes comments, but cannot promise replies. Unfortunately he does not have the time to respond to individual design questions.

INDEX

H

I

L

T

U

V

W

Printed in the United States
118001LV00002B/16/P